THE INTERNATIONAL MARKETING OF TRAVEL AND TOURISM

THE INTERNATIONAL MARKETING OF TRAVEL AND TOURISM

A STRATEGIC APPROACH

Edited by

François Vellas and Lionel Bécherel

First published 1999 by
MACMILLAN PRESS LTD
Houndmills, Basingstoke, Hampshire RG21 6XS
and London
Companies and representatives
throughout the world

ISBN 0–333–71758–9 hardcover
ISBN 0–333–71759–7 paperback

A catalogue record for this book is available
from the British Library.

This book is printed on paper suitable for recycling and
made from fully managed and sustained forest sources.

10   9   8   7   6   5   4   3   2   1
08 07 06 05 04 03 02 01 00 99

Editing and origination by
Aardvark Editorial, Mendham, Suffolk

Printed and bound in Great Britain by
Antony Rowe Ltd, Chippenham, Wiltshire

CONTENTS

CONTENTS

LIST OF FIGURES

LIST OF FIGURES

LIST OF TABLES

LIST OF BOXES

LIST OF BOXES

NOTES ON THE CONTRIBUTORS

Professor François Vellas (co-editor, author of Chapter 9 and co-author of Chapters 1 and 12)
Professor of International Tourism Economics,
Institute of International Development Studies, University of Toulouse,
1 Science Sociales, Place Anatole, France 31042, Toulouse, CEDEX, France
Tel: +33 561 63 36 37
Fax: +33 561 21 50 27
Email: 106551.2750@compuserve.com

Lionel Bécherel (co-editor, author of Chapter 2, co-author of
Chapters 1 and 12)
Director of the International Tourism Consultancy,
14 Latchmere Road, London SW11 2DX
Tel: +44 (0) 171 223 9370
Fax: +44 (0) 171 207 0154
Email: lionel@ndirect.co.uk
http://www.ndirect.co.uk/~lionel

Philip Alford (Chapter 3)
Senior Lecturer in Tourism,
Department of Toursim and Leisure, Luton Business School, University of Luton, Park Square, Luton, Bedfordshire, LU1 3JU
Tel: +44 (0) 1582 734111
Fax: +44 (0) 1582 743143
Email: Philip.Alford@luton.ac.uk

Dr Dimitrios Diamantis and **Dr Adele Ladkin** (Chapter 4)
International Centre for Tourism and Hospitality Research,
University of Bournemouth, PO Box 2816, Poole, BH12 5YT
Tel: +44 (0) 1202 595 158
Fax: +44 (0) 1202 595 228
Email: d_diamantis@hotmail.com
Email: aladkin@bournemouth.ac.uk

Dr Edith Szivas (Chapter 5)
Lecturer in Tourism,
University of Surrey School of Management Studies for the Service Sector, Guildford, Surrey, GU2 5XH
Tel: +44 (0) 1463 300 800
Fax: +44 (0) 1483 259 387
Email: e.szivas@surrey.ac.uk

Gemma McGrath (Chapter 6)
Lecturer in Tourism,
Westminster College, Vincent Square, London, SW1P 2PD
Tel: +44 (0) 171 828 1222
Fax: +44 (0) 171 931 0347
Email: gemma_mcgrath@westminster-cfe.ac.uk

Richard Batchelor (Chapter 7)
Tourism Marketing Consultant,
68 Canonbury Park South, London, N1 2JG
Tel/Fax: +44 (0) 171 226 8982
Email: batchelor@easynet.co.uk

Dr Tim Knowles (Chapter 8 and co-author of Chapter 10)
Senior Lecturer in Hospitality Management,
Department of Tourism and Leisure, Luton Business School,
University of Luton
Tel/Fax: +44 (0) 1204 708421
Email: timknowles@email.msn.com

Peter Grabowski (co-author of Chapter 10)
Principal Lecturer in Tourism,
Department of Tourism and Leisure, Luton Business School, University of Luton,
Park Square, Luton, Bedfordshire LU1 3JU
Tel: +44 (0) 1582 743189
Fax: +44 (0) 1582 743143
Email: Peter.Grabowski@luton.ac.uk
Email: petergrabo@aol.com

Professor J. Enrique Bigné (co-author of Chapter 11)
Professor of Marketing,
Catedrático de Comercialización e Investigación de Mercados, Universitat Jaume 1,
Campus Riu Sec, 12080 Castellón, Spain
Tel: +34–964–345716
Fax: +34–964–345717
Email: bigne@emp.uji.es
http://www1.uji.es/wwwemp/

Luisa Andreu (co-author of Chapter 11)
Lecturer in Marketing,
Professor Ayudante de Comercialización e Investigación de Mercados Universitat
Jaume 1, Campus Riu Sec, 12080 Castellón, Spain
Tel: +34–964–345716
Fax: +34–964–645717
Email: andreus@emp.uji.es
http://www1.uji.es.wwwemp/

FOREWORD

This book is essential reading for tourism professionals and students. Globalisation in tourism markets and changes in supply, demand and the applicable technologies inherent to the 'New Age of Tourism' are substantially modifying the rules of the game of the business paradigm and, consequently, what it is necessary to know and how to act from an international marketing viewpoint. Vellas and Bécherel, who frequently collaborate with the World Tourism Organisation as instructors and consultants, are extraordinarily well qualified to present this detailed new perspective on tourism marketing.

The three parts of the book, which address international tourism marketing principles, issues and trends in contemporary tourism marketing and strategic marketing in the tourism sector, give a clear and well focused look at this subject and will undoubtedly be of interest to all of us who share the vision of greater professionalism in tourism.

DR EDUARDO FAYOS-SOLÁ
Director, Human Resource Development
World Tourism Organisation

ACKNOWLEDGEMENTS

The author and publishers wish to thank the following for permission to use copyright material: World Tourism Organisation, Madrid, Spain; Andrew Campbell from Ashridge Consulting, UK; and Dr Colin Hales from Surrey University.

Every effort has been made to contact all copyright holders but if any have been inadvertently omitted the publishers will be pleased to make the necessary arrangement at the earliest opportunity.

INTRODUCTION

Tourism marketing has long been considered as a branch of traditional marketing. Traditionally, it focused on designing products and identifying target markets that would be attracted to these products. The marketing effort concentrated on promotion and was limited to advertising and presenting products in a brochure where the destination was represented by photographs of hotels or tourists on the beach with a bargain price printed on the cover. The National Tourism Organisation (NTO) merely produced brochures listing the attractions and the service providers at the destination.

Middleton (1988) comments: 'Historically, the principal marketing role of NTOs has been seen in fairly narrow promotional terms of creating overall appealing destination images and messages to prospective visitors, as a necessary basis for product specific marketing activities of operators.'

For many years, this was how tourism was marketed with developments mostly involving greater segmentation of the market by product and by customer. Indeed, according to Fayos-Solá (1994) and Poon (1993), the New Age of Tourism is characterised by segmentation.

However, in recent years tourism marketing has gone through fundamental changes with the pursuit of global strategies based on strategic alliances, the breakdown of commercial borders and advances in new technologies, particularly communication and distribution technologies. These factors have greatly facilitated the commercialisation of tourism products. Global distribution systems (GDS) and the Internet are today key tools in tourism marketing for both industrialised and developing countries.

This book examines the changes shaping the international marketing of tourism and travel in three parts.

Part 1 comprises two chapters. Chapter 1 focuses on definitions and the role of international marketing in tourism. Chapter 2 describes the strategic marketing process, from analysis and strategy formulation to implementation of strategies and techniques to bring products to the market. It provides the marketing theory that the rest of the book is based on.

Part 2 focuses on specific issues that are influencing tourism marketing today. It explains how technology is affecting the way tourism firms operate and communicate with their customers and discusses the influence of environmental awareness, human resources strategy and service quality on tourism marketing.

Part 3 presents the strategic responses of each of the sub-sectors – hospitality, air transport, tour operation, travel agency and the tourism destination – to the pressures that are changing the tourism industry.

REFERENCES AND FURTHER READING

Fayo-Solá, E. (1994) Quality and Competitiveness in the New Age of Tourism in Proceedings of the European Conference on Quality in Tourism, AGTE: Athens 1–7.

Middleton V.T.C. (1988) *Marketing in Travel and Tourism*, Heinemann: Oxford.

Poon, A (1993) *Tourism, Technology and Competitive Strategies*, CAB: Oxford.

PLAN OF THE BOOK

PART 1

Overview of international tourism marketing principles

CHAPTER

1   The Marketing Concept and International Tourism Marketing

2   Strategic Analysis and Strategy Formulation

PART 2

Issues and trends in contemporary tourism marketing

CHAPTER

3   The Impact of Technology on Tourism and Marketing, E-commerce and Database Marketing

4   'Green' Strategies in the Tourism and Hospitality Industries

5   The Influence of Human Resources on Tourism Marketing

6   Managing the Service Encounter: Consistent High Quality Delivery Through 'Internal Marketing'

PART 3

Strategic marketing in the tourism sectors

CHAPTER

7   Strategic Marketing of Tourism Destinations

8   Strategic Marketing in the Hospitality Sector

9   Strategic Marketing in the Air Transport Sector

10   Strategic Marketing in the Tour Operator Sector

11   Strategic Marketing in the Travel Agency Sector

12   Future Trends in the Travel and Tourism Industry

PART 1

OVERVIEW OF INTERNATIONAL TOURISM MARKETING PRINCIPLES

Chapters 1 and 2 present marketing theory from a strategic perspective. Although operational marketing is referred to in both chapters, the focus is firmly on the identification of strategic choices made by management and on describing the range of techniques available to them to help them make these choices.

CHAPTER 1

The marketing concept and international tourism marketing

CONTENTS

THE MARKETING CONCEPT AND INTERNATIONAL TOURISM MARKETING

LIONEL BÉCHEREL AND FRANÇOIS VELLAS

DEFINITIONS OF MARKETING

Definitions of marketing and tourism marketing have been well documented and are generally described in most textbooks (see Lumsdon, 1997). For the purpose of this book, we adopt the UK Chartered Institute of Marketing's definition of marketing, which is:

> The management process responsible for identifying, anticipating and satisfying customer requirements profitably.

The American Marketing Association is even more succinct and defines marketing simply as 'finding a customer need and filling it'.

The Specificity of the Tourism Product

It is generally accepted that the tourism product is on the whole a service product with distinctive features:

Intangibility: As physical entities, goods are tangible. They can be touched, seen, examined before they are bought; they sometimes have a unique and identifiable odour. Once bought they belong to the purchaser. In contrast, services cannot be owned. They are performed and evaluated in terms of expected results and experiences enjoyed or suffered. Most tourism products have tangible elements such as the hotel and the aircraft, but the tourism offer is a service and therefore has the characteristics of services.

Perishability: In contrast to tangible goods, hotel nights and airline seats cannot be stocked or stored for future use. If they are not used they are lost forever. Service products are said to be perishable.

Inelasticity of supply: Tourism products are inelastic because they do not adapt well to changes in short- and long-term demand. Short-term increases and falls in demand for a product will have little influence on its price. It is the long-term fluctuations that determine the composition of the product and its selling price. Tourism products are dependent on existing superstructures at destinations such as hospitality facilities, transport and accommodation.

Elasticity of demand for tourism products: On the other hand, demand for tourism products reacts very quickly to events and changes in the environment such as security threats (wars, crime, terrorism and so on), economic changes (exchange rates, recessions and so on) and changing fashion.

Complementarity: The tourism product is not just one single service. It is composed of several complementary sub-products. Production of the overall service and its quality depend on the components complementing each other. A shortcoming in one of the sub-products will undermine the final product. This remains one of the greatest difficulties for tourism marketers to contend with.

Inseparability: Production and consumption take place at the same time, there is no transfer of ownership. The consumer – the tourist – has to be present when the service is performed to consume it. In fact, tourists are often involved in the production process. Their participation in the holiday (the activities and entertainment they enjoy) is often a vital component of its success. Therefore production and consumption are said to be inseparable.

Heterogeneity: The tourism product is said to be heterogeneous because it is virtually impossible to produce two identical tourism services. There will always be a difference in quality even if the nature of the proposed service remains constant. This heterogeneity allows the possibility of a certain amount of substitution within the different sub-products. However, the resulting product will never be exactly the same. Substituting one hotel for another, even if they are in the same category, will create a different experience and produce a different final product. The experience can also vary within the same hotel. Rooms sizes are rarely the same, they have different window views and different situations within the hotel (for example near noisy stairs or lifts).

High fixed costs: The initial cost of providing the basic elements of the tourism product such as transport (aircraft, train, coach and so on) and accommodation (hotels and so on) is very high. Heavy investment is made without guarantee that the investment will be recouped and profits made in the future.

Labour intensity: Tourism is a 'people industry'. Part of the travel experience is the quality of the services that the visitor receives and the skills of staff in tourism firms and at tourism destinations. Therefore, the tourism product is characterised by a high staff to client ratio, particularly customer contact staff.

The Definition of Tourism Marketing

Several authors have defined tourism marketing, and recently a societal and environmental aspect has been introduced to the definition. In 1997, Lumsdon defined tourism marketing as:

> The managerial process of anticipating and satisfying existing and potential visitor wants more effectively that competitive suppliers or destinations. The management of exchange is driven by profit, community gain, or both; either way long-term success depends on an interaction between customer and supplier. It

also means securing environmental and societal needs as well as core consumer satisfaction. They can no longer be regarded as mutually exclusive.

Seaton and Bennett (1996) identified five essential features of tourism marketing:

- a philosophy of consumer orientation
- analytical procedures and concepts
- data-gathering techniques
- organisational structure
- strategic decision areas and planning functions.

It is this last feature that we concentrate on in this book. Successful tourism organisations think about their future and act accordingly. This means using strategy to achieve their goals. Technology is a vital component in today's tourism strategies and an essential tool in an organisation's quest to compete and to surpass competitors.

We also consider tourism as an international activity requiring specialised marketing skills.

Walsh (1993) defined international marketing as:

The marketing of goods and services and ideas across national boundaries; and the marketing operations of an organisation that sells or produces within a given country when:

(a) the organisation is part of, or associated with, an enterprise which also operates in other countries; and
(b) there is some degree of control of, or influence on, the organisation's marketing activities from outside the country in which it sells and/or produces.

In this chapter we argue that the international aspect of tourism cannot be ignored as most firms in the tourism industry have contact with clients and/or suppliers from other countries, even if in some cases this is limited.

The Importance of Marketing Focus

Marketing plays a crucial role in tourism because it is rare that the customer sees, feels or tests the product he/she is going to buy. To be in a position to evaluate the product, he/she must travel to the destination. Therefore, tourism marketing must focus on communicating and highlighting product value. The total tourism product consists of both natural features and amenities such as transport and access, infrastructure (sanitation, water, electricity and so on) and public and private services (banks, telecommunication, health services and so on). Tourism marketing must also emphasise these amenities, as they are key factors influencing consumer decisions.

Therefore, tourism marketing is different from other forms of marketing because it must present an overall vision of the complete tourism product, including peripheral services from other sectors.

The Marketing Function in an Organisation

In most organisations, marketing is a separate function with the marketing department as the centre of the business, even when the organisation professes to be marketing led. Figure 1.1 shows an organisational structure with the marketing department as a central but separate function.

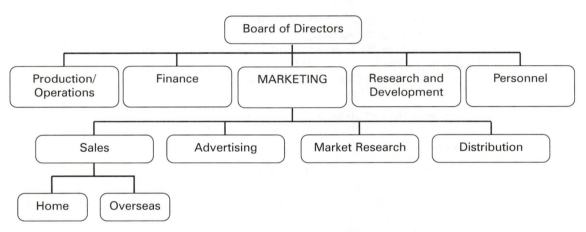

Figure 1.1   The marketing department at the centre of the organisation

However, it difficult for other functions to become directly involved in creating product value in organisations which have adopted this structural model. Porter (1985) puts forward the concept of the value chain and advocated the involvement of all functions of the firm in the competitive struggle by adding value to the product at each stage: conception, production, commercialisation, distribution and after sales service.

Peter Drucker (1968) asserts that 'marketing is so basic that it cannot be considered a separate function. It is the whole business seen… from the customer's point of view.' Therefore, marketing should permeate the whole organisation with all functions involved in and feeding the marketing department as illustrated in Figure 1.2.

All the functions of successful tourism organisations follow and contribute to a common strategic vision and are involved in the marketing of the organisation's products as well as the organisation itself.

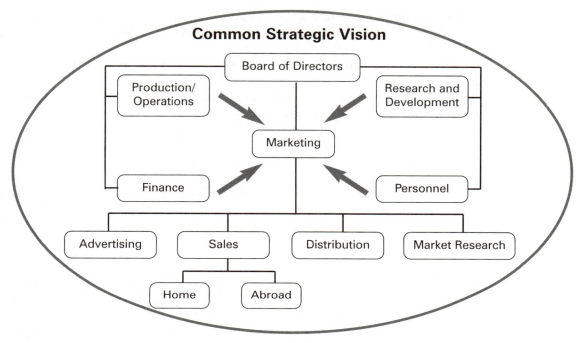

Figure 1.2   All business functions involved in marketing

Marketing in this type of organisation is more efficient, particularly for firms operating in the international arena.

TOURISM AND INTERNATIONAL MARKETING

International tourism accounts for 612 million tourist arrivals a year world-wide (WTO, 1998). Virtually all destinations and many tourism firms operating within these destinations trade with organisations or people from other countries. They are therefore involved in international marketing. Holloway and Robinson explain that there is a distinction between marketing products in the domestic market and export marketing:

> Export marketing, or international marketing, is a specialised field of marketing which will have to take into account different legal systems and business climates, different cultures affecting buyer behaviour, and the problems associated with transporting products abroad. Tourism again, is substantially concerned with export marketing. (Holloway and Robinson, 1995)

Tourism activity involving exchanges of capital between one economic system and another from a different country fall into the export marketing category.

The conditions associated with international trading affect different types of tourism organisations in different ways. These can be classified as:

- outbound tourism firms such as tour operators and transport carriers
- inbound operators who market abroad
- firms serving foreign tourists at the destination such as hotels, attractions and entertainment, restaurants, retail outlets and incoming operators
- multinational firms operating internationally such as hotel chains, large tour operators and transport carriers
- destinations positioning themselves in the global market.

Figure 1.3 shows the international relationships of different types of tourism firms servicing a destination.

Outbound Tourism Firms

Outbound tourism firms must negotiate with local firms at the destinations their customers want to visit. For tour operators, this involves designing itineraries and activities within the legal framework of the host country, selecting local suppliers within the confines of local trading conditions and business culture, and contending with foreign currency fluctuations. For transport operators such as airlines this involves negotiating arrival and departure slots, contracting ground support and building partnerships with firms established locally to provide customers with extra services. The main trading risk is the obligation to commit large amounts of resources before the tourist season starts to ensure availability and to obtain competitive prices. This translates into a level of uncertainty about return-on-investment and requires short-term tactical skills by firms to respond to unexpected changes in demand or trading conditions.

For these firms, the competitive arena is their home market and, in some cases, neighbouring markets where the services/products they provide are unavailable. They compete with local firms offering similar products as well as with other foreign firms that have become established in their home markets and market directly to their customers.

Foreign firms may also provide outbound services. Fifth freedom rights for air transport agreed at the Chicago Convention in 1944 (see Chapter 9) allow airlines to embark passengers in a country other than their own and fly them to another country.

The Swiss tour operator Kuoni has operated very successfully in other European markets, in the UK and France for instance, and has been voted 'best outbound tour operator' by UK consumer groups on several occasions.

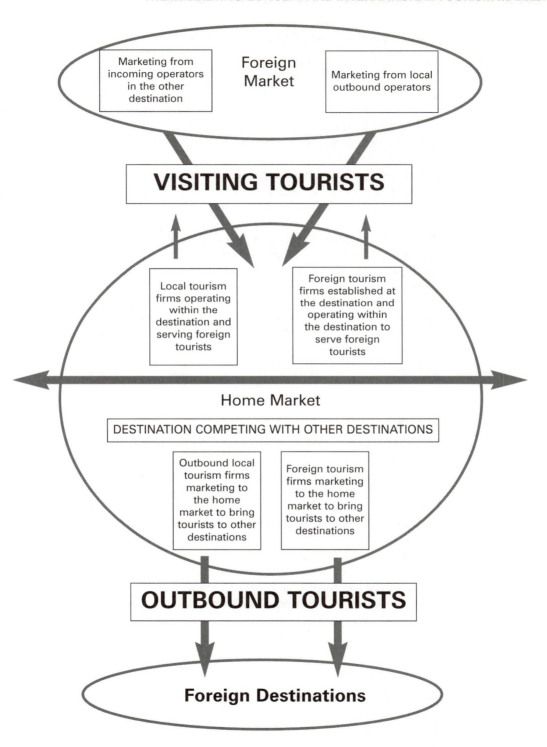

Figure 1.3   The tourism destination and international tourism

Local Firms Serving Foreign Tourists

These service providers include:

- local shops, bars and restaurants catering primarily to the local market but, because they are situated in a tourist area, also serving both foreign and domestic tourists
- tourist firms concentrating on providing for domestic tourists but may also be serving foreign tourists
- tourism firms that have identified a particular international market segment which it chooses to target, for instance a Belgian bar on the Spanish Costa Brava serving Belgian beer and food to Belgian tourists.

The most successful tourism businesses understand the needs of their foreign customers and provide facilities that will convince them to choose to use their services or buy their products, that is, providing menus in different languages, stocking foreign newspapers and brands that tourists are familiar with and so on.

Of course, this will depend on the number of foreign tourists visiting the destination. In destinations providing mainly for the domestic market, local firms may opt to ignore the few foreign tourists. However, even in these cases there are regional differences which may be emphasised by the service provider (that is, culinary specialities).

Foreign Firms Serving Foreign Tourists

Foreign firms may enter a market where local firms are not providing a service or where they are in a better position to provide the service. For instance, in many Chinese cities, Japanese hotel chains have built hotels specifically designed and operated to cater for the Japanese tourist. They are able to market these in Japan and tourists feel reassured that the services they receive are those that they are familiar with and that they expect.

On the island of Koh Samui in Thailand, entrepreneurial Europeans have set up bars offering a range of different cheese. Because cheese is not part of the local diet it is not available on the island; it must be imported from Malaysia. This concept has become so popular with western tourists that a new market has become established and new bars have now opened on the island, several of them operated by local businessmen.

Foreign Market Entry Strategies

Firms entering foreign markets are concerned with a variety of issues such as:

- which markets to enter, the sequence and timing of entry
- how to enter these markets

- which competitive marketing strategies are to be adopted for success in the market. (Bradley, 1991)

Economic and socio-cultural factors must be taken into consideration before a firm decides on a foreign market strategy. It must understand the barriers to free trade that may impede it from entering certain markets.

According to the WTO (1998), 'Forty years ago international tourism was effectively free of taxation, but taxes in the tourism industry are now increasing in number and impact.' Nowadays, taxes on tourism are seen as an easy source of income for governments. But this can seriously damage the competitive positioning of a destination and affect a foreign firm's decision to invest.

Other factors known as non-tariff barriers are also taken into account. These include:

- barriers to entry such as visa restrictions; document charges; ease of access
- exchange controls; differential exchange rates
- international regulations; technical standards (that is, EU package holiday directives); health and safety regulation
- government subsidies for local or competing firms.

In many regions of the world economic associations between countries are established to encourage free trade. The European Union, the North American Free Trade Area (NAFTA), the Association of South East Asian Nations (ASEAN) and the Economic Community of West African States (ECOWAS) are examples of regional economic agreements.

International agreements such as the General Agreement on Trade and Services (GATS) are aimed at liberalising the international exchange of services and reducing trade barriers which restrict the freedom of service providers to operate in foreign markets and which restrict market access. GATS also facilitates the movement of people supplying services who require temporary entry to work in the tourist industry of another country.

There are also a number of social and cultural difficulties facing firms entering the foreign market. Obviously an understanding of the language and of the culture is essential as well as knowledge of local conditions. One way around this is by employing local staff, but the skills needed to understand and operate the firm's business are not always available locally. Then there is the problem of adverse discrimination in situations where customers, suppliers and/or the authorities favour local firms over foreign firms.

There are several ways for firms to enter a foreign market:

- Direct investment; acquisitions
- Licensing
- Joint venture
- Strategic alliances
- Exporting.

Direct Investment and Acquisitions

The advantage of direct investment over other methods of entry is that competitive advantage achieved by the firm in other markets such as the technological leads its has over competitors are not shared with local firms and can therefore be kept away from the competition for as long as possible. Furthermore, the foreign firm does not have to share profits with local firms, as it is obliged to when it grants licences to operate under its name.

On the other hand, it the riskiest method of entering foreign markets and it is costly in terms of capital and management resources. A foreign firm may also be at the mercy of the host government which can erect hurdles in the form of supplementary taxation, the obligation of partnerships with local players and the compulsory hiring of local labour even if the necessary expertise is not available locally. Furthermore, a foreign firm will generally not have the local knowledge and contacts of a local firm.

One way of overcoming these obstacles is by taking over local firms already established in the domestic market. The international firm obtains 100 per cent ownership as well as a presence in the market, contacts in industry and with the authorities and benefits from the local expertise offered by the staff already employed by the acquired firm.

Therefore, the decision to pursue a full-ownership strategy in a foreign market will hinge on whether the firm's priority is on the ability to determine strategy without having to rely on the approval of partners or on the security of sharing risks. The UK tour operator Airtours is expanding in the international market by acquiring firms or merging with foreign firms. Its recent international ventures in European and North American markets are listed in Box 1.1.

BOX 1.1

AIRTOURS, THE UK TOUR OPERATOR: EXPANSION INTO FOREIGN MARKETS ACQUISITIONS AND JOINT VENTURES IN EUROPE AND THE UNITED STATES

News announcements from UK Business Park
- *Europe*

16 Feb 96 – Airtours is buying Simon Spies Holding, the Danish tour operator, as well as aviation assets from Conair for £10m and £50m respectively.

02 Oct 97 – Airtours is acquiring Sun International, the Belgian package holiday company which owns the Cresta Travel and Bridge Travel brands in the UK, for £70m.

15 Oct 97 – Airtours has acquired a resort in the Canary Islands for £11m, which it will convert into150 timeshare apartments.

29 Oct 97 – Airtours is to set up a package holiday business in Poland next year, under the name Ving.

BOX 1.1 (cont'd)

27 Nov 97 – Airtours has completed the acquisition of 80 per cent of Sun International, the Belgian tour operator, for £56m and it expects to acquire the remaining 20 per cent soon.

27 Jan 98 – Airtours is said to be interested in acquiring a 34 per cent stake in LTU, the German tour operator, from Westdeutsche Landesbank.

14 May 98 – Airtours has acquired a 29 per cent stake in Frosche Touristik, the German tour operator, for an initial £17m and has an option to buy the rest of the group in 2002.

■ *United States*

12 Oct 96 – Airtours, the UK tour operator, has set up Sunquest Holdings in Los Angeles, in order to sell budget package holidays to Californians.

13 Nov 96 – Airtours is setting up a 50:50 joint venture with Emerson Holdings to build a timeshare resort in Orlando.

28 May 98 – Airtours is looking to acquire holiday operators in the North-Eastern US and Eastern Canada, although no deal is imminent.

01 Oct 98 – Airtours is acquiring Vacation Express, the US tour operator, for £14m.

12 Nov 98 – Airtours is to set up a new telephone enquiry centre in Accrington, creating up to 230 jobs.

Source: UK Business Park, 1998.

Licensing

Licensing is a contractual agreement whereby a firm allows another to sell and use its products for a fee. According to Terpstra and Sarathy (1991):

> A licensing agreement is an arrangement wherein the licensor gives something of value to the licensee in exchange for certain performance and payments from the licensee. The licensor (the international company) may give the licensee (the national firm) one or more of the following things: (1) patent rights, (2) trademark rights, (3) copyrights, (4) know-how on products or processes. In return for the use of the know-how or rights received, the licensee usually promises (1) to produce the licensor's products covered by the rights, (2) to market these products in an assigned territory, and (3) to pay the licensor some amount related to the sales volume of such products.

Licensing presents a number of advantages over direct investment. Products are introduced to a new market with little risk to the licensor. The licensee has the advantage of being able to sell a proven product already endowed with a reputation, which has been established abroad.

This method of market entry is favoured by some of the international hotel corporations. Their international reputation guarantees licensees a ready-made market. Often, the licensor will also sell a management contract to provide the expertise to run the hotel. Holiday Inn has succeeded in positioning itself in the Romanian market by licensing its Crowne Plaza brand to Romania entrepreneurs and managing a new hotel in Bucharest as illustrated in Box 1.2.

BOX 1.2

THE BUCHAREST FLORA: OPERATING UNDER THE HOLIDAY INN, CROWNE PLAZA BRAND NAME IN ROMANIA

In April 1998, the first hotel in Eastern Europe under the Holiday Inn Crowne Plaza brand name was opened in Bucharest. Two years before, the Romanian ANA Investment Group had bought the ageing two-star Flora Hotel, which was conveniently located in its own park next to the exhibition centre, Romexpo, and to the World Trade Centre, close to the airport and ten minutes from the city centre. The group formed a consortium to invest US$10 million in converting the hotel to Holiday Inn standards.

The 164-room hotel targets mainly business guests and provides business facilities such as meeting rooms, conference halls, technical equipment and internet connection as well as a number of leisure facilities and special arrangements for the expatriate community.

Holiday Inn manages the hotel under a management contract and provides the marketing umbrella of the brand. Holiday Inn Hospitality is the world's largest single hotel brand with over 2,600 hotels in prime locations throughout more than 60 countries. The brand operates Holiday Inn Express, Holiday Inn Resorts – which has a hotel in Romania in the resort of Sinaia – and Crowne Plaza.

Several new hotels are planned in Romania: two four-star hotels in Bucharest as well as in Timisora, Constanta, Brasov and Sibiu.

The main disadvantage of licensing is that the licensor has less control over how the product is produced and delivered.

Joint Ventures

The difference between a joint-venture arrangement and licensing is that the international firm takes an equity stake in the local firm. As a partner, it also has a say in how the business is run. Because of the capital investment and its management involvement the international firm's risk increases so it has a greater commitment to the business. The firm's foothold in the country is stronger because it is linked with a local firm. Furthermore, if the local firm has a strong interest in the partnership the threat of expropriation from the authorities because of changes of circumstances decreases. Terpstra and Sarathy (1991) note that for this reason Club Méditerranée takes minority ownership in the villages that it operates abroad. 'They always make sure that local interests are big enough so that if Club Med is thrown out, those interests will suffer first.'

The rules governing the structure of joint ventures vary from country to country. Some countries will not allow international firms to have wholly owned operations on their territory and insist that local firms own over 50 per cent of shares in joint-venture operations.

The international firm brings capital, technology, management and marketing expertise, training and consulting and often a finished product which can be introduced immediately to the market.

National firms bring local market knowledge such as language, culture and local business conditions, local marketing skills and local contacts. They are often in a better position to break down barriers to entry in the market than their foreign counterpart because they are usually already well established in the local market.

Strategic Alliances

A strategic alliance is a co-operative relationship between businesses. It can be informal, such as a pooling of information, or contractual. It may focus on a business function such as marketing or research and development or be comprehensive and involve all the functions in the businesses.

Joyce and Woods (1996) define *strategic alliances* as 'partnership agreements (formal or informal) between two firms who may agree to co-operate in a variety of ways – including joint ventures, joint-product development, transfer of skills, and so on. Horizontal alliances are where the partnership is between competitors.'

A strategic alliance is often created to enter a market. An agreement with a firm that has access to a foreign market may be the best strategy to gain a foothold in that market. Airline companies frequently adopt this strategy in order to build networks across different markets. Marketing alliances allow several airlines to act in some ways as a single carrier, sharing schedules and even profits in what amounts to a virtual merger without any of the financial and employment consolidations of a traditional corporate merger.

By not actually merging, the airlines enjoy the benefits of their new consolidated markets without the need for regulatory approval or having to combine their work forces. Varig, the Brazilian airline has joined the Star Alliance, the benefits of which are described in Box 1.3.

BOX 1.3

VARIG BRAZILIAN AIRLINES JOINS STAR ALLIANCE NETWORK

Global network expands to South America as momentum builds

Air Canada, Lufthansa German Airlines, SAS (Scandinavian Airlines System), Thai Airways International and United Airlines welcome VARIG Brazilian Airlines to the Star Alliance family. With flights to every major destination in South America, VARIG opens up an entire continent to Star Alliance customers, providing increased global recognition and a wide range of other benefits.

VARIG frequent flyers will be able to accumulate and redeem mileage points whenever they fly on any scheduled flight operated by any Star Alliance airline. Likewise, members of any Star Alliance frequent flyer programme will be able to accumulate and redeem mileage points on all scheduled flights operated by VARIG. Mileage points accumulated on Star Alliance flights qualify toward elite-level status in the frequent flyer programme of a traveller's choice.

Qualified passengers will now enjoy access to over 185 Star Alliance airport lounges around the world. With the addition of VARIG today, no other airline or airline group offers the scope of elite-level mileage benefits or lounge access available to Star Alliance customers.

VARIG will participate in the introduction of further customer benefits, including simplified ticketing and reservations, more convenient connections and through check-in, and better baggage and ground services.

VARIG Brazilian Airlines is the largest airline in Latin America, serving every major city on the continent, as well as major capital cities on four others. Total revenue for VARIG in 1996 was US$3.4 billion. VARIG has 18,100 employees and serves 24 countries. VARIG transports 9.7 million passengers annually, with 390 daily departures to 122 cities, on 82 aircraft. With the addition of VARIG, the six Star Alliance airlines now employ more than 230,000 people and serve 642 destinations around the world. Total revenue for the six Star Alliance airlines in 1996 was $45.7 billion. The Star Alliance airlines transport 184 million passengers annually, with 6692 daily departures on 1446 aircraft.

Source: Canada News Wire, 1998.

Exporting

Countries lacking the required skills base to develop and run their tourism industry often rely on expertise from abroad. Consultants in economic development, construction, architects, land use, marketing, management, banking and so on provide know-how and professional services. These services may be imported directly by governments or provided by international institutions in the form of technical assistance such as the World Tourism Organisation (WTO) as illustrated in Box 1.4.

BOX 1.4

WORLD TOURISM ORGANISATION: CO-OPERATION FOR DEVELOPMENT

The transfer of tourism know-how to developing countries is one of the World Tourism Organisation's fundamental tasks.

As an executing agency of the United Nations Development Programme, WTO contributes decades of experience in tourism to the sustainable development goals of nations throughout the world.

Acting on requests from member governments, WTO secures financing, locates the world's leading experts, and carries out all types of tourism development projects, large and small.

In the operating period 1996–97, the World Tourism Organisation carried out development activities in 42 countries worth US$4.4 million.

Practical Projects

Development projects carried out by WTO often encompass the entire tourism sector of a nation and involve many months of work, such as the strategy for environmentally sustainable development of India's Andaman Islands completed in 1996. Other examples of long-term projects include:

■ Tourism Master Plan in Ghana (1996).

■ Reconstruction and Development Plan in Lebanon (1997).

■ Action Plan for Sustainable Tourism Development in Uzbekistan (1997).

Projects can also be short and targeted to address an immediate need. A sectoral support mission to assess the economic impact of tourism in Egypt in 1996, is one example. Other recent short-term projects have included:

■ A pilot eco-tourism development in Congo.

■ Hotel classification system in Ecuador.

■ New tourism laws for Nicaragua.

■ Resort management in the Maldives.

■ Analysis of air transport in Costa Rica.

■ Protection of historic sites in the Philippines.

■ Statistics training for the United Arab Emirates.

■ Resort marketing in China.

Sustainable Development

In opening up new tourism destinations and improving existing ones, the World Tourism Organisation is a vital link in the transfer of tourism technology from West to East and from North to South.

BOX 1.4 (cont'd)

All WTO projects are based on the policy of sustainability, ensuring that the economic benefits of tourism development are not offset by damage to the environment or to local cultures. Projects also ensure that local communities share in the planning process and in the prosperity achieved through increased tourism.

Working hand-in-hand with our member governments, donor agencies and the private sector, WTO's objective is to make sure that income and jobs generated by new tourism development will last for generations to come.

Source: WTO, 1998.

Hotel corporations export services and labour at all professional levels to firms in countries that do not have the available expertise to run and operate establishments aimed at the international clientele (see Box 1.2).

Labour is also exported as a commodity. For instance, several international hotels in the Middle East employ operational staff from Asia, particularly from the Philippines, because of their reputation for providing good service and for their technical ability.

Destinations in the Global Market

All destinations compete with others in the global market for international tourists. Seaton and Bennett (1996) explain that destinations are both physical entities and socio-cultural entities and their tourism image is influenced deliberately by the marketing efforts of the authorities and tourism firms (induced sources) and by personal experience of consumers, word of mouth, history, the media and so on (organic sources).

The international marketing of destinations occurs on several levels. The public sector is usually involved at national level but also at regional and local level. Cooper (1997) states that 'At these levels the lead agency tends to be the public sector and this in turn has a number of implications for the marketing process. For example, the public sector often is not able to sell products, rather it relies on overall promotion of the destination to "pull" consumers to points of sale provided by the private sector.'

The private sector has it own interests to put forward, but as 90 per cent of tourism firms are small and medium-sized enterprises (SMEs) with limited resources, they benefit from and often rely on marketing efforts co-ordinated and directed by the public sector. The public sector can represent them abroad through the overseas offices of the tourist boards.

Successful destination marketing rests on strong partnerships between the different stakeholders and on a coherent, consistent and collaborative marketing approach to create identities that are unique. Destinations must find identities that differentiate them from other destinations in the global marketplace. Therefore all public sector and private sector organisations must work in partnership to pursue differentiation strategies.

Partnerships can also be created at international level. For instance, the tourist boards of Scandinavian countries collaborate to bring tourists to the region by joint marketing actions (see Box 1.5). Once the tourists have decided to come to the area, then the countries compete with each other to convince them to visit their respective countries. In other words, they collaborate to create a market and compete to divide it up. This is the concept of co-opetition (co-operation and competition) which is developed in Chapter 2.

BOX 1.5

THE SCANDINAVIAN TOURIST BOARDS: INFORMATION FOR NORTH AMERICAN TRAVEL AGENTS

The entire Scandinavian tourism industry emphasises value. Airlines, cruise lines, hotels, tour operators, local transportation, sightseeing, shopping have come together in a commitment to help visitors capitalise even further on the current, still favourable currency exchange rates. Opportunities abound for American visitors to enjoy more of Denmark, Finland, Iceland, Norway and Sweden.

Most of all, Scandinavia is year round opportunities for you. For the travel agent, the potentials are boundless. The emphasis on value and affordability mean increased business for you… and profits. The Scandinavian Tourist Boards of Denmark, Finland, Iceland, Norway and Sweden are here to assist you to maximise your Scandinavian sales efforts and results.

As part of our efforts to provide information to travel agents in North America, the Scandinavian Tourist Board publishes the yearly *Scandinavia Agents' Manual.* This comprehensive, 400-page guide is the 'A–Z' of travel in Scandinavia, and it provides information on everything from travel discounts and packages to individual tour operators. It will save you hours of research.

STAR – Scandinavia Travel Agents' Registry is a referral system giving consumers more than 40,000 STAR agents referrals each year. The referral system is undergoing restructuring in 1998.

In 1997 we added an extra 24-hour service for ordering brochures and fax-bax information. An automated and easy-to-use telephone and fax-on-demand system has been installed to serve the public, and trade with improved and sufficient information and support services.

Source: The Scandinavian Tourist Boards, 1998.

GLOBALISATION, DEREGULATION AND TECHNOLOGICAL ADVANCES

Globalisation is more than just internationalisation of firms. Borders are becoming increasingly difficult to define or to maintain. The world is shifting from distinct national economies to a global economy. Technological advances in areas such as transport and communications are helping to overcome physical distance and barriers and sustain the trend towards a global economy. Capital flows freely between countries, production is internationalised and populations are travelling to other countries for work and leisure. Barriers to entry are declining and communication costs are shrinking. As a result, business is internationalising and tourism is a leading industry in the globalisation process. The most successful businesses are those that understand how to operate in the international arena.

Globalisation and International Competition

Deregulation has strongly increased competition between firms as well as between states. Firms do not base their policies only on the individual countries they operate in but also on pursuing global policies. These policies rely on free access to the market in each country. For this reason, the air transport sector has been transformed since deregulation.

Advances in communication technology, which enable firms to pursue global strategies, have greatly intensified international competition. These innovations are particularly significant for the tourism sector.

Globalisation and Industrial Strategy

To cope with globalisation and intensive competition, companies are adopting new industrial strategies and adapting traditional methods and techniques for the global arena. Diversification and sectoral strategies are no longer just applied within countries but also across borders.

Large tourism firms such as American Express follow globalisation strategies.

American Express focuses on diagonal integration. The company operates in 130 countries, employs 73,000 staff and had a turnover on US$17.1 in 1997. American Express developed its strategy focusing on two core businesses:

- Its travel agency network which comprises 3,200 outlets world-wide including those that it acquired from Thomas Cook, Havas Voyage in France, Nyman & Schultz in Sweden, Schenker Reinus in Germany, Life Co in the United States and a joint venture with BBL Travel Amex in Belgium.
- Its financial services (such as travellers' cheques and credit cards) with the American Express Bank and the American Express Financial Advisors. American Express has been involved in the tourism industry for a long time and has offered travellers' cheques for many years.

American Express has become the largest business tourism operator in the USA, Australia, Canada, Mexico and France. It also has an important position in Great Britain and Germany.

The focus has been on a leadership strategy in national markets, aiming for at least 30 per cent of the market and it has succeeded in reaching its objectives in 25 countries of the world. By following this strategy, American Express has become a global company.

Globalisation and Alliances

However, it is increasingly difficult for individual companies to grow organically in the global arena without seeking partners and allies to develop their strategies. Alliances are in a better position to control the market.

With an increase in equity participation between firms, alliances can result in concentration on a global scale.

Globalisation and Marketing

Globalisation can, however, lead to monopolies. Giving alliance partners the power to set prices and conditions can result in closing the market to competition.

In effect, there is a risk of returning to regulation. For instance, in the air transport sector, rules have been introduced to control the operation of global distribution systems (GDS) to prevent certain companies or alliances enjoying unfair advantages over their competitors.

Paradoxically, a return to regulation will make it more difficult for firms to pursue globalisation strategies, which is what made them very profitable in the first place. As Brown (1998) observes: 'If true globalisation is to take place, future patterns will feature the downscaling of companies so that core large firms are increasingly unable to dominate the producers marketing globally.'

The Impact of Globalisation on Small and Medium-sized Enterprises (SMEs)

According to the European Union conference, Agenda 2010, held in Wales in May 1998:

> In European tourism, SMEs account for 90 per cent of all businesses and more than 94 per cent of them are micro operators employing less than 10 individuals. There are some 2.7 million SMEs in tourism (West Central and Eastern Europe) employing some 17 million people. This compares with a only a few hundred large organisations defined as employing more than 250 people each, although collectively the turnover of large firms represents an important share of most tourism markets.

Smeral (1998) warns that globalisation is increasing the pressure on SMEs. He explains that:

> The potential of SMEs for realising economies of scale is very low and the use of computer reservation systems (CRS) has not spread significantly. Many restaurant and hotel businesses are sources of side income for people engaged in the agriculture sector.

Furthermore, SMEs are disadvantaged because of 'their high unit average costs with respect to production'.

Because of the preponderance of SMEs in the industry, European tourism is particularly vulnerable. International receipts per arrival in Europe are approximately 20 per cent lower than the world average. Although Europe is the largest of the world's tourism regions, it is losing market share. The region's share of world tourism arrivals will have fallen from 73 per cent in 1960 to 45 per cent by the year 2020 (WTO, 1998).

Smeral explains that this is a result of the market expanding. In the last two decades, many new destinations have entered the tourism market and developed their industry. 'The traditional customers of the European SMEs – originating from domestic and the (neighbouring) abroad markets – have more options on how to spend their vacation (mostly in the form of the consumption of standardised mass products with a rough degree of differentiation).' He points out that it is the destinations with the highest number of SMEs that are suffering the most. 'In terms of international revenues (tourism exports) Denmark (–27 per cent), Austria (–23 per cent), Germany (–17 per cent), Switzerland (–16 per cent), suffered in the period from 1990 to 1996 with the greatest losses in market share; Europe as a whole lost only 10 per cent of its market share in the same period.'

To compete in the global tourism market, SMEs must be integrated in a destination management system which is supported by public tourism policies. Smeral concludes:

> In order to alleviate the impacts of globalisation on SMEs, the public and private sector should implement flexible production technologies, as well as holistic destination management policies aimed at delivering innovative and 'commodifiable' experiences to meet 'post-modern' tourism demand. The support for building highly integrated destinations with flexible operating network alliances is an important measure to help SMEs compete with global players and restore their capabilities to deliver significant contributions to income and employment creation.

THE EVOLUTION OF MARKETING AND TOURISM MARKETING

It is generally accepted that modern marketing has evolved through four stages:

- Product-led marketing
- Sales-led marketing
- Consumer-led marketing
- Consumer-led marketing with environmental, social and cultural concerns.

Marketing has now entered a fifth stage with a firm focus on strategy.

Product-led Marketing – the Focus is Orientated on the Product

Historically, tourism marketing has been product orientated. The focus of the marketing effort was to provide the best beaches, the best rooms and so on, and to assume that, because these were the best (or quite often the only ones), tourists would automatically visit or buy goods or services from the tourism firm. Product-led companies succeed in conditions where there are no sales problems – they are in a sellers' market. The focus is on increasing output.

Sales-led Marketing – the Focus is on Selling the Product

The emphasis is on convincing tourists to purchase the good or service or to visit the destination. Usually the condition for this is that supply is greater than demand. For instance, mass market destinations need volume to survive. The focus is on the needs of the producer to sell rather than on the needs of the tourist to buy.

Historically, this was fuelled by technological progress resulting in an increase in productivity and higher real incomes. Buyers first purchased consumables, then consumer durables and then services.

In this condition, it is a buyers' market and supply is in excess of demand. A sales orientation prevails.

Consumer-led Marketing – the Focus is on Consumer Needs

The marketing orientation focuses on the consumer. What does the tourist or the customer want? Can the organisation provide it? This is a true marketing focus ensuring that the consumer is at the centre of the effort and using techniques to identify and anticipate what the customer needs and wants. A strong emphasis is put on communicating with the customer and the focus is on customer service.

Consumer-led Marketing with Environmental, Social and Cultural Concerns

During the 1980s and 90s, the marketing emphasis turned towards awareness of the environment and towards social and cultural concerns. In 1992, the Earth Summit in Rio de Janeiro highlighted the depletion of the earth's natural resources and the threat of economic development to the future of the environment. The conference recommended a series of actions and commitments that governments and businesses should adopt to ensure the sustainability of the resources.

The growing awareness of the effects of consumerism on the environment as well as on society and on cultures means that consumers now examine the products they purchase and want to know that their production has had no negative impacts. By its very nature, the tourism industry interacts with the environment, society and culture. Furthermore, tourists – the consumers – are part of the production process – production and consumption are inseparable. Tourists can cause damage directly by merely being at the destination and consuming tourism products.

Tourism marketers have responded to this new consumer need and have tailored their products, images and communication accordingly. They have realised that it is in their interest to protect tourism destinations and sites, as this is what originally attracted tourists to visit. Therefore they must ensure the sustainability of their products.

Because of the impacts of globalisation, the growth in the number of players operating in the market and rapid advances in technology, tourism marketing has entered a fifth stage.

Consumer-led Marketing and Strategic Thinking – Focus on Internationalisation, Strategic Alliances and Leading Through the Use of New Technologies

In an economy that is becoming increasingly global, it is not enough that tourism organisations and destinations concentrate on satisfying the needs of their clientele. In order to survive and compete they must identify new opportunities and niches, often in co-operation with other players, while still attending to the needs of their traditional customers. Therefore, successful organisations are driven to adopt a strategic focus taking advantage of new tools and technologies and seeking economies of scope in an international market rather than just economies of scale.

Success is based on three key concepts that are inter-related:

- Strategic Thinking
- Internationalisation
- The Use of New Technologies.

Therefore, the backbone of present-day tourism marketing is to develop strategies to compete globally using the latest technologies.

STRATEGY

John Tribe in *Corporate Strategy for Tourism* (1997) analyses different definitions of strategy and concludes that 'Strategy is a master plan which has certain key features. It is medium- to long-term and is concerned with aims... look(ing) towards and hit(ting) some target... the planning of a desirable future and the design of suitable ways to bring it about.'

An organisation will operate at three strategic levels: the corporate level, the business unit level and the operational level, although at the operational level the orientation is mostly tactical. Tactics and strategy are discussed below.

SBU = Strategic Business Unit

Figure 1.4   The different strategic levels (adapted from Asch and Bowman, 1989)

Strategy and Policy

Baker (discussing Igor Ansoff's analysis in *Corporate Strategy*) notes that policy and strategy are often used interchangeably. However, he explains that there is a clear distinction between the two concepts.

Business policies are standard procedures that have been developed by decision-makers in conditions of certainty and which can be delegated to employees of the organisation. In other words, when the outcome of a situation is known in advance, a set of rules and preferred responses can be developed for the staff to follow.

Business strategies are devised for situations where the outcome is uncertain. Techniques and judgement must be used to decide the course of action that is going to be followed.

In short, policies are followed in situations of certainty and strategies are devised for situations of uncertainty.

Strategy and Tactics

Strategy and tactics are complementary. To survive and achieve success, an organisation must devise effective strategies supported by efficient tactics. Consider this statement: 'The army was highly trained and superb at fighting in the mountains: unfortunately it was positioned in the wrong mountains and it lost the war' (Hardy, 1987). Tactically the army was well prepared and skilled at warfare but failed because its leadership made the wrong strategic choice.

Drucker (cited in McDonald, 1995) remarked that strategy is 'doing the right thing' and tactics are 'doing things right' and McDonald (1995) designed a matrix, represented in Figure 1.5, describing the outcome of different combinations of effective and ineffective strategies and efficient and inefficient tactics.

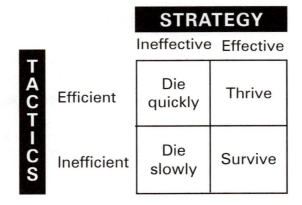

Figure 1.5   Strategy and tactics are complementary (adapted from McDonald, 1995)

It is clear from this matrix that it is better to have effective strategies even if the tactics are inefficient. At best, the organisation will thrive; at worst it will survive. Choosing the wrong strategy will lead to failure either slowly if the tactics are inefficient or quickly if the tactics are efficient because it will arrive at its fate all that much quicker.

This would suggest that strategy is more important in terms of survival than tactics.

Corporate Strategy

At the corporate level, the organisation deals with situations affecting the organisation as a whole. These relate to areas such as company structure, mergers and acquisitions, analysis of the range of different businesses and products belonging to the organisation and decisions about future direction. Marketing strategy supports corporate strategy and guides the organisation in a chosen direction. Corporate strategy may also be determined by marketing strategy from other sectors. For instance, modern airports are now designed and laid-out in such a way to allow airlines to pursue 'hub and spoke' strategies (see Chapter 9).

According to Koch (1995), value is created at the business unit level. He warns that corporate strategy should be implemented with care as it may destroy more value than it creates:

> Corporate strategy should be developed to deal with situations which are beyond the ability or vision of business units and individual parts of the organisation to see what is happening and react effectively to it... It is required to exploit potential advantages on the proper scale or to survive in the face of how competitors operate in a growing and changing market place.

Changes decided at the corporate level affect the business as a whole and can jeopardise strategies at the business unit level. Corporate centres are expensive to run and consume profits generated by business units.

In the tourism industry, corporate strategy for larger tourism firms is increasingly important. There are several factors that determine corporate strategy:

- Regional and global economies of scale
- Brand benefits
- International competition
- The convergence of consumer tastes
- The enlargement of markets and the reduction of import barriers
- The strive for technological and know-how lead.

Koch identifies six principal corporate strategies, which are applied in different business situations or conditions:

1. *Emergency*: when a firm is being threatened from external factors, is in financial difficulties or its business units cannot cope with a given situation.

Hands-off Strategies

2. *Olympian*: a hands-off strategy where the centre has little involvement with the business units.

Interventionist Strategies

3. *Mergers and acquisitions*: this strategy is especially favoured in the tourism industry (see Box 1.6), particularly by tour operators, hotel chains and the airlines. It is usually a high-risk strategy.

4. *Market expansion*: a strategy focused on gaining market share in the business segments that they operate in. This strategy relies strongly on marketing techniques and may include strategic alliances with other players in the market.

5. *Competence and culture building*: the focus of the organisation is on its staff and their skills. Success depends on quality and motivation.

6. *Performance control:* the organisation concentrates on the 'bottom line' and on tight budgetary control. Targets are set and managers are held responsible for achieving them.

Table 1.1 relates the business conditions and the cultural environment and skills within the organisation for each of these strategies.

BOX 1.6

MERGERS AND GLOBALISATION: THE CASE OF CARLSON COMPANIES AND THOMAS COOK

The British travel industry continues to consolidate. Minneapolis-based CARLSON COMPANIES, a privately held travel group, and THOMAS COOK, a venerable travel and financial-services group, are merging their British travel-service operations. The joint venture will operate as Thomas Cook in more than 100 countries and generate annual sales of 25 billion pounds ($42 billion). Germany's Westdeutsche Landesbank, Thomas Cook's owner, will hold a majority stake in the new venture.

Source: The Economist, 9 October 1998.

Vertical, Horizontal and Diagonal Integration

Organisation may expand and grow by acquiring other organisations and operating related businesses. They integrate either vertically, horizontally or diagonally depending on the form that this expansion takes.

Vertical Integration

By integrating vertically, the organisation aims to control every step a product takes from its source to the consumer. When the organisation acquires suppliers,

Table 1.1   **Koch's corporate strategies**

Strategy	Business conditions	Cultural environment and skills within the organisation
Emergency	■ Firm in disarray ■ Financial crisis – and/or expectations gap ■ Divisions cannot/will not take appropriate action ■ Threat of take-over/ dismemberment	■ Centre must be willing to suspend normal relations with businesses and intervene ■ Centre must be able to establish 'the facts' ■ Centre must be decisive and ruthless
Olympian	■ Stable market and competitive environment ■ Attractive market ■ Similar key success factors in all businesses ■ Internationalisation is not a major issue	■ Centre not respected ■ Centre's costs exceed benefit ■ Good operating management
Mergers and acquisitions	■ Industry with wide range of profitability ■ Targets exist where it is clear performance could be greatly improved	■ Good EPS (earnings per share) record on high PE (price earnings ratio) ■ Chief executive and financial director very experienced in take-overs ■ Excellent financial control ■ In-house corporate finance team ■ Operating management good and could run bigger firm
Market expansion	■ Good business to be in ■ Global businesses with 2–3 main competitors ■ Plenty of cash for expansion	■ Powerful culture throughout firm stressing internally led expansion ■ Little political game-playing ■ Top management obsessed with market leadership ■ Firm marketing led, not finance led ■ Long-termist managers and owners
Competence and culture building	■ Culture and competencies are more important than micro-strategy in explaining relative competitor performance... and in improving firm's short to medium-term financial performance	■ Truly united board and top management ■ Visionary chief executive ■ Well-regarded head office ■ Business interdependencies recognised and co-operative ethic in place ■ Change programme will be given many years to work
Performance control	■ Market predictable ■ Stable competitive environment	■ Above average EPS growth ■ Culture of continuous profit improvement ■ Centre highly respected and adds insights ■ Sophisticated financial controls throughout the firm

Source: Based on Koch, 1995.

this is known as *backward integration* and when it acquires distributors *forward integration*.

Tour operators are most likely to integrate vertically in the tourism industry. By integrating backwards, they acquire and control the basic elements that make up the packages that they sell such as hotels, airlines and travel services at the destination thus ensuring that there is an adequate supply at a controllable cost. By integrating forwards, they control how their packages are sold, usually by acquiring travel agencies. For instance, Thomson, the largest UK tour operator owns the largest charter airline in the world – Britannia Airways – and the travel agency chain Lunn Poly.

Horizontal Integration

By integrating horizontally the firm's objective is to gain market share and maximise usage of its assets. It usually does this by acquiring other firms in the sector, either direct competitors or firms that will complement and augment its range of products or services. Horizontal integration can be defined as combining institutions at the same level of operation under one management.

Both vertical integration and horizontal integration provide economies of scale. As the firm grows, unit costs fall because shared resources are employed, there is better control of supplies and distribution and a stronger negotiating position.

Diagonal Integration

According to Poon (1993), the objective of diagonal integration:

> Is not to produce a single service and market it to a supermarket of clients. Rather, the objective is to produce a range of services and to sell them to a target group of consumers… The essence of diagonal integration is that: 2 + 2 = 5. In other words, the benefits of integrating activities are greater than providing each activity separately.

She continues to explain that firms benefit in the form of lower costs through *synergies, systems gains* and *economies of scope*.

Davis and Devinney (1997) describe the advantages of economies of scope:

> Economies of scope arise because of the ability to spread production and service technologies across products. Part of the impact of economies of scope comes from the more efficient utilisation of capacity (in a sense economies of scales). However, the true value of economies of scope is in the ability to share assets, be they physical plant and equipment, technical knowledge or intangible brand assets.

In the tourism industry, firms such as American Express provide a number of services to consumers across several traditional sectors. The firm describes itself as 'the world's leading travel service company with over 1800 offices in 120 countries, employing thousands of career professionals'. It offers financial services, travel agency services, tour operator services, insurance products as well as training at the American Express Travel School with campuses in Arizona and California.

Business Level Strategy

Markets are developed and exploited at the business unit level. Depending on its size, an organisation may have several strategic business units. A strategic business unit is an autonomous business centre, which has its own value network (suppliers, related businesses (complementors), clients and competitors). Small and medium-sized firms may have just one business unit (in other words the whole firm is the business unit).

At the business unit level and operational level, strategy focuses on identifying customers and their needs, on the development and quality of products, and on the marketing environment for these products, their competitive position, and profitability.

This chapter has considered definitions of marketing and tourism marketing. It reviews the international aspect of tourism marketing and concludes that marketing has evolved to the stage of internationalisation, strategic alliances and leading through the use of new technologies.

Chapter 2 focuses on the strategic marketing process applied to tourism and examines techniques used in business strategy.

REFERENCES AND FURTHER READING

Ansoff, I. (1968) *Corporate Strategy*, Penguin, Harmondsworth.

Asch, D. and Bowman, C. (eds) (1989) *Readings in Strategic Management*, Macmillan: Basingstoke.

Baker, M. (1992) *Marketing Strategy and Management*, Macmillan: Basingstoke.

Bradley, F. (1991) *International Marketing Strategy*, Prentice Hall: Hemel Hempstead.

Brown, F. (1998) *Tourism Reassessed. Blight or Blessing?*, Butterworth-Heinemann: Oxford.

Canada News Wire, Press Releases Accessed (accessed autumn 1998) http://www.newswire.ca/

Cooper, C. (1997) 'Strategic Perspectives on the Planning and Evolution of Destinations: Lessons for the Mediterranean?' Conference Paper presented to the seminar Tourism in the Mediterranean, University of Westminster, December.

Davis, G. and Devinney, T. (1997) *The Essence of Corporate Strategy*, Allen & Unwin: St Leonards, NSW, Australia.

Diamantis, D. (1998) Ecotourism: Characteristics and Involvement Pattern of its Consumers in the UK. Unpublished PhD thesis, Bournemouth University.

Drucker, P. (1968) *The Practice of Management*, Heinemann: London.

Fayos-Solá, E. (1996) Human Capital in the Tourism Industry of the 21th Century. Paper presented at the conference, Madrid, 21–23 January.

Hardy, L. (1987) *Successful Business Strategy: How to Win in the Marketplace*, Kogan Page: London.

Holloway, C. and Robinson, C. (1995) *Marketing for Tourism*, 3rd edn, Longman: London.

Jarrillo, J.C. (1993) *Strategic Networks: Creating the Borderless Organisation*, Butterworth-Heinemann: Oxford.

Joyce, P. and Woods, A. (1996) *Essential Strategic Management: From Modernism to Pragmatism*, Butterworth-Heinemann: Oxford.

Koch, R. (1995) *Strategy*, Pitman Publishing: London.

Lumsdon, L. (1997) *Tourism Marketing*, International Thomson Business Press: London.

McDonald, M. (1995) *Marketing Plans – How to Prepare Them – How to Use Them*, Butterworth-Heinemann: Oxford.

Middleton, V.T.C. (1998) A Proposed Framework for Action in Support of SMEs in Tourism. Agenda 2010. A Tourism Conference held at Llandudno in May 1998 under the UK Presidency of the EU, with the support of the EC (DGXXIII). Final Conference Communiqué – revised 30 June.

Poon, A. (1993) *Tourism, Technology and Competitive Strategies*, CAB: Oxford.

Porter, M. (1980) *Competitive Strategy: Techniques for Analyzing Industries and Competitors*, Free Press: New York.

Porter, M. (1985) *Competitive Advantage: Creating and Sustaining Superior. Performance*, Free Press: New York.

Scandinavian Tourist Boards web site (accessed November, 1998) http://www.go.scandinavia.com, interknowledge Corp.

Seaton, A.V. and Bennett, M.M. (1996) *The Marketing of Tourism Products: Concepts, Issues and Cases*, International Thomson Business Press: London.

Smeral, E. (1998) 'The impact of globalisazation on small and medium enterprises: new challenges for tourism policies in European countries', *Tourism Management*, 19(**4**): 371–80.

Terpstra, V. and Sarathy, R. (1991) *International Marketing*, 5th edn, Dryden Press: Orlando.

The Economist, Business this Week, E-mail information service from http://www.economist.com 9–15 October, 1998.

Tribe, J. (1997) *Corporate Strategy for Tourism*, International Thomson Business Press: London

UK BusinessPark Company Search Web site; Airtours page (accessed November, 1998) http://www.ukbusinesspark.co.uk/airtours.htm

Walsh, L.S. (1993) *International Marketing*, 3rd edn, Pitman: London.

WTO (1998) *Tourism 2020 Vision*, WTO: Madrid.

WTO web site: http://www.world-tourism.org/, (accessed autumn 1998).

CHAPTER 2 Strategic analysis and strategy formulation

CONTENTS

STRATEGIC ANALYSIS AND STRATEGY FORMULATION

LIONEL BÉCHEREL

The objective of this chapter is to provide a broad overview of the stages of the strategic marketing process and to introduce a few of the techniques used in developing a strategic plan. In the last two decades, this topic has been extensively covered and a list of references is included the end of the chapter to guide the reader towards sources for further reading.

Whereas strategy at the corporate level is concerned with the future direction of the organisation as a whole, strategy at the business level focuses on products and markets – it is strategy 'on the front line'. Marketing is directed by the goals that the centre has set for the organisation. However, marketing plays a guiding role in the elaboration of corporate strategy. Baker (1992) asserts that 'corporate strategists *must* be marketing strategists for without the market there is no purpose for the corporation and no role for the corporate strategist, which would not deny any claims that the corporate strategist takes a broader view than the firm's activity in the market place.'

Strategists all start with a *clear framework* of what they want done – and of where they want to be in future. Of course, for every company, the future means something different The future for high-tech industries is short – 6 months, for capital-intensive industries such as forestry the future is long – several years (Farkas *et al.*, 1995).

Therefore, if strategy is to achieve goals set in the future, the methods used to achieve these goals must be set out in a well-thought out and systematic plan.

The plan should consider the basic questions: Why? What? How? When? Where? and Who?

STRATEGIC MARKETING PLANNING

Where no plan is laid, where the disposal of time is surrendered merely to the chance of incidence, chaos will soon reign. (Victor Hugo)

Organisations exist and operate in constantly changing environments. To survive and prosper they must cope with change and select the right course to follow, and this requires planning. Change creates uncertainty and plans are produced to reduce uncertainty.

Plans vary in scope – some focus on an entire organisation (corporate plans), others focus on a sub-set of organisational activities (business/divisional level plans) and yet others focus on day-to-day activities (unit/functional level plans). Planning is needed to meet both short- and long-term goals.

Planning is deciding and laying down objectives to be achieved over a defined time period and selecting the best methods to achieve these objectives in function of the resources available and external forces. It should aim to achieve results that are measurable and the process must be constantly monitored to ensure that the goals are reached within the desired time scale.

Strategic marketing takes a long-term view, which normally spans a five-year period. The purpose of the strategic plan is to provide broad guidelines for the marketing organisation. Gilbert (cited in Cooper *et al.*, 1993) explains that the plan is designed to help management of the organisation consider a number of questions: What is it we want? Where are we now? Where do we want to go? How do we get there? Where did we get to?

These questions relate to different stages of the planning process. The planning process is depicted in Figure 2.1. It comprises a number of logical steps:

1. The organisation's business and its reasons for operating in this business are defined.
2. Research is carried out to understand how the industry is expected to perform in the future, what will influence it and how well the organisation is equipped to cope with and profit from developments.
3. Possible future scenarios are identified which consider different strategies and the most appropriate are selected.
4. Operational plans to implement the strategies are developed.
5. The strategies are implemented.
6. The plan is constantly monitored to ensure that it is on target and, if not, to take the appropriate actions to bring it back on course.

Marketers use established techniques at each stage of the planning process.

The marketing techniques used in the strategic planning process are represented in Figure 2.2 and described in the following sections. Small diagrams of the process are provided at the beginning of each section to guide the reader.

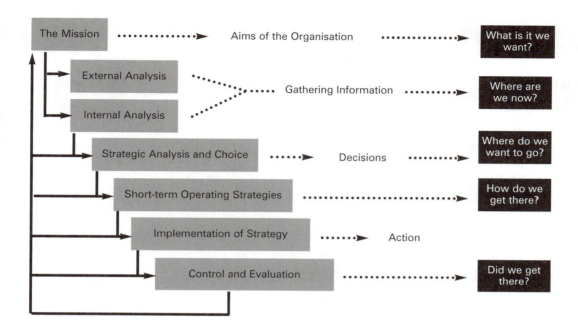

Figure 2.1   The strategic planning process (adapted from McDonald, 1995)

Figure 2.2   The strategic marketing planning process (adapted from McDonald, 1995)

UNDERSTANDING THE BUSINESS AND DEFINING THE ORGANISATION'S MISSION – THE CORPORATE MISSION STATEMENT – WHAT IS IT THAT WE WANT?

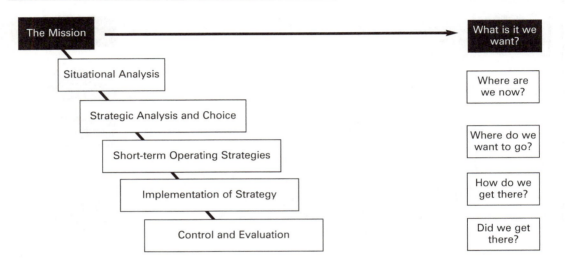

The most successful strategies are visions, not plans. (Henry Mintzberg, 1994)

The organisation's corporate mission statement announces why the organisation exists, what are its values, its strategies and its behaviour standards. It answers the questions: What is it that we want? What is it we stand for?

The mission statement allows the organisation to think about and define the business that it is in. It should be a true reflection of the organisation's purpose rather than a public relations statement. It provides vision and direction and serves to inform customers and guide employees about the organisation's values and aspirations. It is important that the staff identify with and 'own' the mission. If they do not, the mission is unlikely to be achieved, particularly if services are being offered (which depend on high commitment of staff). Other stakeholders (customers, funding bodies and so on) should also be able to fit the mission to their idea of what the organisation is about.

Andrew Campbell at the Ashridge Strategic Management Centre (1991) identified the elements that should be present in a mission statement. His model is represented in Figure 2.3. In his view, the mission statement should comprise four parts:

- *Purpose:* defines why the organisation exists
- *Values:* declares what the organisation believes in and its moral principles
- *Strategy:* explains the organisation's position *vis-à-vis* the competition and its competitive advantages

● *Standards and behaviour:* sets out how the organisation's staff operates, their competencies and the way they act.

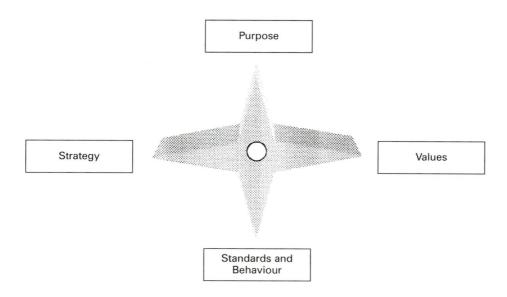

Figure 2.3   The Ashridge mission model (Campbell *et al.*, 1990)

The mission statement is a very important stage of the strategic process. The strategic marketing mission statement should reflect the corporate mission statement and emphasise the marketing orientation of the organisation.

Hamal and Prahalad (1994) explain that *visioning* provides the organisation with a sense of destiny. 'Getting to the future first is more a function of resourcefulness than resources. Resourcefulness stems not from an elegantly structured strategic architecture, but from a deeply felt sense of purpose, a broadly shared dream, a truly seductive view of tomorrow's opportunity.'

Box 2.1 sets out the overall vision for the future of tourism in Hawaii. Vision statements 2, 4 and 5 are concerned with the broad marketing mission. Box 2.2 sets out the marketing mission in greater detail.

BOX 2.1

THE FUTURE OF HAWAII'S VISITOR INDUSTRY: A VISION

While this strategic plan maps out goals and strategies for Hawaii's visitor industry in the next five years, it has an even longer term vision about the kind of visitor industry we would like to have in the distant future. This plan takes us in the direction of that vision in the next five years. Our vision is captured in the following six statements:

Vision Statement 1:
Tourism should not be Hawaii's only industry. It is important that the State continue to make efforts to diversify Hawaii's economy as its long-term economic development strategy. Nonetheless, we foresee that the State's economy will continue to rely on tourism to provide its share of new jobs for our growing population.

Vision Statement 2:
As a mature destination, Hawaii cannot continue to host unlimited numbers of visitors in the future. Instead, we need to focus on 'yield' rather than 'volume.' Thus, we aim to embrace a quality tourism development strategy. This means attracting high spending visitors.

Vision Statement 3:
To minimise the environmental and cultural-socio impact of tourism, Hawaii aims to encourage the development of low-impact tourism.

Vision Statement 4:
To take advantage of our unique qualities, we aim to make Hawaiian culture and our multicultural heritage a central theme in our tourism development strategy. Not only is this good strategy, it also promotes local pride and enhances our own cultural and heritage awareness.

Vision Statement 5:
Hawaii will continue to diversify the geographic source of our visitors. This means placing more emphasis in developing international tourism. Diversifying our tourism markets can provide greater economic stability in Hawaii and reduce volatility in employment and tax revenues.

Vision Statement 6:
The State shall continue to pursue a strategy of directing tourism's growth to the Neighbor Islands, particularly the Big Island that has more capacity to accommodate tourism growth.

Source: Hawaii Tourism Office, 1998.

BOX 2.2

HAWAII'S TOURISM MARKETING MISSION STATEMENT

Product development

■ To develop Hawaii as the world's most desirable visitor destination with a unique and diverse range of facilities, services and activities that reflect the host Hawaiian culture and the multi-ethnic population of the islands.

■ To identify and develop new sustainable competitive products compatible with the host Hawaiian culture and the multi-ethnic population of Hawaii.

Research

■ To establish a well co-ordinated statistical and research program designed to drive the direction of strategic planning efforts, guide future marketing activities, and monitor the impacts of tourism and product development issues.

■ To develop a comprehensive industry and community-supported statewide tourism strategic (5-year) plan that is regularly reviewed and updated.

Promotion

1. To identify specific desired promotional outcomes and relate them to visitor growth objectives.

2. To capitalize on the individual personalities for each of the Neighbor Islands.

3. To refocus the current promotional message and campaign strategy to include the culture and natural environment in Hawaii.

4. To diversify markets and cultivate new and developing markets.

5. To evaluate and identify specific market segments.

6. To assess and evaluate competitive messages and methodologies of delivering messages.

7. To develop a measurement and evaluation system for promotional programs.

8. To develop and implement a promotional program for the planned Waikiki Convention Center.

9. To develop and market the Hawaii tourism industry in such a manner as to complement and enhance other economic development programs.

10. To develop a comprehensive industry-supported multi-year promotional program and identify a dedicated funding source.

Source: Hawaii Tourism Office, 1998.

Mission statements vary in length. Some are just one sentence others may be several pages long. The leisure corporation Bass has a mission statement that encompasses the wide range of its values in a pithy statement: 'Our mission is to deliver excellent value by achieving a unique breadth of hospitality, leisure and drinks businesses which bring increasing numbers of people together across the world to share great leisure moments.'

Mission statements may also serve as a code of business conduct. The mission statement of the State of Victoria in Australia is a good example of how it can serve as a code of conduct not only for the organisation but also other tourism stakeholders (see Box 2.3).

BOX 2.3

STATE OF VICTORIA – MISSION STATEMENT

Tourism Victoria's mission *in partnership with industry*, is to:

'Maximise employment and the long-term economic benefit of tourism to Victoria by developing and marketing the State as a competitive tourism destination.'

To achieve this mission, the Board of Tourism Victoria has set the organisation four broad goals:

Marketing Goals: Increase visitor numbers, length of stay and visitor expenditure by positioning Victoria as a distinct and competitive tourism destination.

Leadership Goals: Take a leadership role in the tourism industry, encourage professional standards and the development of co-operative arrangements, which maximise industry effectiveness.

Infrastructure Goals: Improve the tourism assets of Victoria by identifying infrastructure opportunities and facilitating development projects.

Management Goals: Maximise the effective use of resources by conducting the business of Tourism Victoria in accordance with professional commercial management principles.

Source: Tourism Victoria, 1998.

THE MARKETING AUDIT – UNDERSTANDING THE EXISTING SITUATION – WHERE ARE WE NOW?

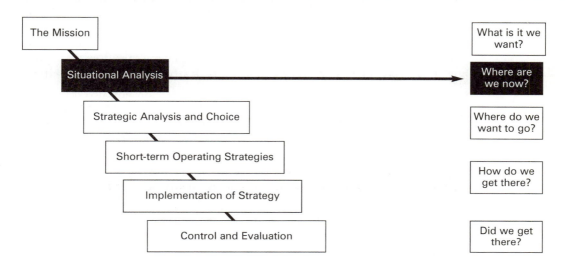

The next step in the strategic marketing process is to consider the question: 'Where are we now?'

This involves a thorough audit of the factors that influence and impact on the organisation – the situational analysis. It should be comprehensive and analyse the marketing environment, existing strategies, the structure and efficiency of the marketing organisation, the marketing systems used, productivity and the different marketing functions (products, prices, distribution, promotion and so on).

Several techniques are applied to understand the existing situation:

- The PEST analysis examines the macro-environment – the uncontrollable factors
- The market analysis looks at trends in the market
- The competitive analysis looks at the competitive situation of the organisation
- The product analysis looks at the organisation's products with respect to the market and the competition
- Consumer analysis studies the organisation's customers and consumers, their characteristics and their behaviour
- The SWOT analysis examines the way the organisation relates to the external environment and how well it is equipped to cope. It sums up and presents logically the information collected and processed in the analytical process.

It is said that 'information is power' and strategists need information to select strategies. The marketing audit informs the strategic plan. With the intelligence collected, strategists are able to anticipate the opportunities and threats that will arise in the future, evaluate different scenarios and select the direction to follow and the appropriate actions.

The PEST Analysis

The PEST analysis is a study of the elements that may influence the organisation at the macro-level. PEST is an acronym that stands for 'Political, Economic, Socio-Cultural and Technological' and refers to the external environment. The technique provides an in-depth look at the forces and trends that affect the organisation. In many cases, these are forces that the organisation cannot control but must be aware of to avoid pitfalls and take advantage of opportunities that may arise.

As a global industry, the tourism industry is particularly vulnerable to variations at the macro-level. Changes in one country or region have a knock-on effect and usually affect the tourism industry in neighbouring countries and in generating countries.

The political environment consists of laws affecting the operation of tourism business (for example the introduction of visa restrictions or barriers to entry in the market such as taxation); changes in political system (for example Eastern Europe), political instability (for example the Gulf War, Serbia); political boycott (for example Iraq, Myanmar) and the closure of borders to tourism (for example Afghanistan). Political changes may bring new opportunities for tourism. Since the peace treaty, the Lebanon has been rebuilding its tourism industry and tour operators in generating countries are now offering the destination. Box 2.4 describes the new ventures to re-establish tourism in a country which was once one of the most successful destinations in the Mediterranean.

An analysis of the political environment must be carried out for each of the countries where the organisation operates and from where customers and suppliers originate. It should examine such factors as:

- the type of government and ideology
- government stability
- government philosophy towards business
- government disposition towards foreign firms
- regulation (money transfer; people transfers; technology transfer; possibility of arbitrage and so on)
- political risk (confiscation; expropriation; nationalisation)
- political harassment (licensing restrictions; taxation on foreign firms; social unrest, terrorism and so on)
- nationalism (patriotism, chauvinism and so on).

The economic environment encompasses the economic situation in the home country as well as in the country of operation and where tourists originate. The analysis should cover areas such as fluctuations in exchange rates, in the cost of operation and in the cost of purchasing raw materials (that is, fuel), inflation, credit risks, changes in value of investments (that is, land; building such as hotels), labour costs and unemployment.

BOX 2.4

THE TOURISM REBIRTH OF BEIRUT

If you look down from the lofty balconies that once doubled as snipers' vantage points, you will see signs of rebirth. Beirut's hotels have long been a barometer of the country's prosperity and in the immense junkyard below several multi-million dollar projects are at the forefront of the Government's drive to lure back the tourists that once flooded to 'the Paris of the Middle East'. The rebuilding of The Phoenicia Hotel at a cost of $60 million is one of the most ambitious projects. The Government is planning to build a huge conference centre with a 600-room hotel.

International hotel chains have already returned to Beirut: Le Vendôme Intercontinental is a 70-room oasis of luxury; a Marriott has opened near the airport and a Holiday Inn is going up in the upmarket shopping area of Verdun, where Emperio Armani and Planet Hollywood are thriving.

Hotels scheduled to open their doors in early 2000 include the Hilton, Ritz Carlton and Meridien. A billionaire Saudi prince is spending £72 million on a new Four Seasons hotel on a prized piece of land with access to a new marina.

Source: Adapted from Kathryn Westcott – *The Times*, 1998.

The socio-cultural environment is particularly important for tourism firms operating in other countries and/or dealing with people for other countries:

> The term 'socio-cultural environment' is used to refer to all those factors behind a country's international marketing prowess, which are of a learned nature. This makes it a rather omnibus term, covering attitudes, sociology, behaviour, psychology and the cultural development of, and within the country as a whole, and the various sub-populations which go to make up that country. (Bradley, 1991)

For tourism, this refers to demography; tourist attitudes and holiday-taking habits; consumer preferences, behaviour and values; ethnic factors; cultural systems and social organisation; social, religious and family values; the role of women; communication (that is, language) and perception; and material culture.

Advances in the technological environment have transformed the tourism industry and organisations must monitor closely how technology affects their business. They must ensure that they are not left behind and that they take advantage of opportunities presented by the introduction of new technology. Developments in communication are changing distribution, promotion and operation of tourism products and services. These include global distribution systems, the Internet, electronic communication, electronic ticketing and electronic funds transfer. Labour-saving technology is increasing productivity particularly in the hotel and catering sectors (that is, yield management); advances in transport technology are increasing efficiency, bringing down costs and providing convenience and comfort; and tourist attractions use sophisticated technology in the activities they offer (theme parks) and in the interpretation of heritage (historical, heritage and natural centres).

The Market Analysis

Before entering into the discussion on market analysis, it is useful to define three concepts: the market, market share and market growth.

The Market

The market for a product can be thought of being made up of four elements:

- People with a need or a desire for the product
- People with purchasing power
- A place where people buy the product – the marketplace
- People with the willingness to purchase.

Therefore, the market has a size (a number of people) which can grow or contract, a geographical location (physical or virtual) and people with at least one thing in common – they want to buy the product. Markets change over time as preferences and desires change and new products are introduced.

The definition of the market is 'the aggregation of all the products that appear to satisfy the same need' (McDonald, 1995).

Market structure determines the competitive relations between sellers. The most important of these characteristics are:

- the size distribution of firms
- the size distribution of buyers
- the barriers to entry for new buyers and sellers
- the degree of product differentiation
- the degree of vertical integration
- the capital intensity of production
- the stability of demand for the product on the market
- the spatial distribution of buyers and sellers. (Bannock *et al.*, 1973)

Market Share

Markets have dimensions and it is important not to define them too broadly or too narrowly. For example, a four-star hotel chain is classified in the accommodation sector, a sub-sector of the tourism sector, but in terms of measurement this is far too broad a categorisation to be useful to the marketer. McDonald provides a framework to measure market share, which can be applied to the four-star hotel chain in our example. The four-star hotel chain is in the hotel subcategory of the accommodation sector – this is *the product class*. It is in the four-star category – *the product sub-class*; and *its product brand* is Holiday Inn. 'A brand, for the purpose of measuring the market share is only concerned with the aggregates of all other brands that satisfy the same group of customer wants' (McDonald, 1995). However, the marketing manager of Holiday Inn must also monitor trends in the accommodation sector as a whole.

Measuring the size of the market is the basis for understanding its composition – the customers, the competition and the complementors.

Market share can refer to:

- the sales of the product or products of a firm (organisation) as a proportion of the sales of the product or products of the industry as a whole
- the sales of a particular commodity compared with the total sales for the class of commodity of which the particular commodity is a member.

Markets are not static, they grow and contract over time.

Market Growth

The rate at which a market expands (or contracts) is a contributing factor to its attractiveness. *Market attractiveness* considers market growth, the degree of competition, relative market size and corporate competencies.

The *product life cycle* (PLC) concept, which is represented in Figure 2.4, shows that the market for a product goes through four distinct stages: introduction, growth, maturity and decline.

When a product is introduced, the market is small as few people know about it or have experienced it and few firms offer it. At this stage the product may be heavily promoted to increase awareness and profits are usually very low or non-existent. Once the product becomes successful in the marketplace, the market grows and new firms are attracted to enter. Profits are high at this stage but so are costs. The level of competition is starting to increase and firms are vying for market share to secure their position in the growing market. At the maturity stage, market growth slows down as the market reaches its optimum size. As competition intensifies, firms that have become well established defend their position to secure profits and to survive. At the decline stage, the market is contracting and profits are falling. The decision may be taken either to exit the market or to rejuvenate the product by perhaps modernising it, augmenting it or repositioning it. This has the effect of extending the PLC of the product.

Butler (1980) adapted the PLC model to the tourist destination. Strategies to overturn the decline stage are particularly important for destinations. A major area of current tourism marketing research focuses on devising and adapting new strategies to regenerate destinations, particularly in the ageing European resorts such as those on the British coast.

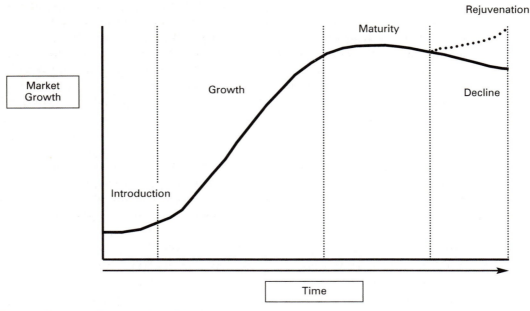

Figure 2.4   The product life cycle

Although the PLC model has been criticised for being too simplistic, it is still a useful tool to describe how industries evolve and how markets develop over time. According to Lele (1992):

The major concerns about the model are:

- It is hard to distinguish between the industry life cycle and individual product life cycles, especially when the industry is large and includes several major innovations.
- We cannot predict the duration of individual stages or the total life cycle with any accuracy.
- Some industries may even 'skip' a stage, going from growth abruptly into decline.
- Structural changes do not always follow the same pattern; for example some industries may consolidate rapidly quite early in their life cycle, while others stay fragmented late into maturity or even decline.

Nevertheless, the life cycle framework provides marketers with an indication of how fast the market is growing and contracting (now and in the future) and the likely degree of competition.

The Competitive Analysis

Research is carried out to identify and analyse the position and the strengths and weaknesses of competitors and complementors.

Every firm or organisation has a value net. The value net comprises the organisation's suppliers and customers as well as its competitors and complementors. A complementor provides a product or service that complements the organisation's product and therefore adds value to it. For instance, a tour operator may deliberately choose a hotel where nightly entertainment is available to amuse its clients. Although this is not part of the original package, the convenience of having entertainment at hand adds value to the tour operator's product. In Mauritius, Sega musicians and dancers perform each night at different hotels on the island and therefore add value to the product of the hotels that have hired them as well as to that of the tour operators that use the hotels.

The concept of complementors is particularly important for destination marketing. For a destination to be successful all the actors at the destination must complement each other and work in a concerted manner.

At times, competitors become complementors. For instance, competing airlines enter into strategic alliances and share codes and loyalty programmes for greater market coverage (see Chapter 9 on Airline Marketing Strategies). Destinations in a region such as the Caribbean Islands and the Scandinavian countries co-ordinate their marketing efforts to bring tourists to their area. They work together to create a market and, once it is created, compete to divide it up (see Box 1.5).

As the industry evolves and markets develop, the level of rivalry increases, as depicted in Figure 2.5. Different strategies are deployed at different stages of the life cycle.

Porter (1980) provides a framework for analysing competition and identifies five competitive forces in a market:

- *The intensity of the competition among organisations servicing the market:* When the industry has reached the maturity and decline stage of the life cycle, rivalry becomes intense.
- *The threat of new entrants into the market:* New entrants are particularly attracted to the market when it is in the growth stage. The cost of entry tends to increase as the industry evolves. Firms already in the market erect barriers to dissuade other firms from entering.
- *The threat from substitutes using different technology:* This can occur at any time during the evolution of the industry but is most likely at the maturity and decline stage when the market has been fully developed.
- *The bargaining power of customers:* As competition becomes more intense, customers have greater choice and are in a position to select the best products for their circumstance.
- *The bargaining power of suppliers:* The fewer the number of suppliers in the market, the greater their bargaining power. At the introduction phase and the growth stage, there are usually fewer suppliers and therefore, their bargaining power will often be greater than at the maturity and decline stage.

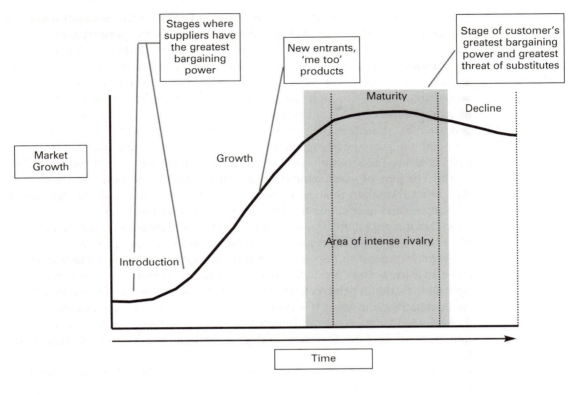

Figure 2.5   The intensity of rivalry and the industry life cycle

Kotler (1988) explains that organisations must know at least five things about competitors:

- Who they are
- Their strategies
- Their objectives
- Their strength and weaknesses
- Their reaction patterns.

The Product Analysis

A product as defined by Kotler 'is anything that can be offered to a market for attention, acquisition or consumption. It includes physical objects, services, personalities, places, organisations and ideas'.

However, the character of the product may be seen differently by the buyer and the seller. It is useful to distinguish three concepts of the product:

- Formal product
- Core product
- Augmented product.

Formal Product: this is a good or a service that is offered to the target market. It will be recognised by the market as having up to five characteristics:

- a quality level
- features
- styling
- a brand name
- packaging.

Core product: The essential benefit that is being offered to, or sought by, the buyer. The person purchasing a holiday is not buying transport and accommodation for their own sake, he or she is buying relaxation, a cultural experience, a change of scene and so on. The formal product is simply the packaging of a core product or benefit. The marketer's job is to sell benefits, not features. He or she must find a way to create benefits for the product.

Augmented product: All the benefits that a person receives or experiences in obtaining the formal product, for example the augmented product of the tour operator, is not only the basic package but a whole set of accompanying services, including guided tours, complementary carry-on luggage, welcome drinks, maps and so on. This leads the seller to look at the buyer's total consumption system. As a result sellers are able to recognise many opportunities for augmenting their product offer. It is not the actual product that causes competition between sellers but what is added in terms of packages, services and so on. Therefore competition is at the augmented level rather than at the core product level.

The Product Portfolio and Competitive Position

The product portfolio comprises the range of products offered by the organisation. Product are categorised into three levels:

1. The *product item* is the individual product
2. The *product line* is composed of closely related products either because they satisfy a need; or they are sold to the same customer group; or they are marketed through the same outlets; or, they fall within the same price range
3. The *product mix* is the combination of products offered by a firm or a business unit.

Organisations should develop a mix of products to ensure a wider market base. This can be done by *diversification* into different products or by *adaptation* of an existing product to enter new segments of the market. The product mix of a company can be described as having *width*, *depth* and *consistency*:

- *Width* refers to how many different product lines are found within the firm or organisation. Through increasing the width, the company hopes to capitalise on its good reputation and skills in markets it operates in.

  The British tour operator Thomson sells over 4 million holidays a year. Its summer 1999 programme is presented in 13 different brochures for different market segments *(A la Carte; All Inclusive; Club Freestyle; Cruises; Cyprus; Faraway Shores; Florida; Thomson Gold; Greece; Small and Friendly; Summer Sun; Superfamily; Turkey)*. It also offers an extensive winter programme as well as specific holiday concepts such as *Young at Heart* designed for the older consumers and *Weddings in Paradise*.

- *Depth* describes the number of items offered by the company within each product line. By increasing depth, the company hopes to ensure the loyalty of buyers of widely different tastes and needs.

- *Consistency* refers to how closely related the various product lines are in end use, production requirements, distribution channels or in some other way. Through increasing consistency, the company hopes to acquire a reputation in one category of product.

Several models have been devised to analyse the product portfolio, the most famous being the Boston Consulting Group's (BCG) growth/share matrix developed in the 1960s. The technique uses a combination of the product life cycle (PLC) and market share. It classifies a product according to its market share relative to that of the market leader and the growth rate of the market.

Four classes of products are identified:

1. *A product in a growing market with a large market share – A STAR*
    A star product has great potential and is already producing good returns. Because it is in a growing market it requires a high level of investment to ensure that the product maintains and gains market share during the growth period. The aim is to be in a dominant position in the market by the time this reaches the maturity stage of the life cycle.

2. *A product in a growing market with a small market share – A QUESTION MARK*
    A question mark is a product with a weak competitive position in a growing market. The future of the product is not easy to predict and the marketer has to be confident in the future success of the product if he or she decides to commit resources to convert it into a star product. Normally, this will be an expensive venture.

3. *A product with a large market share in a mature market – A CASH COW*
    Cash cows are well-established products in mature and stable markets. They are usually market leaders and their marketing outlay is small and focused on defending their position rather than trying to gain share from competitors in a market that is not growing anymore. Cash cows generate cash for the firm and can be milked easily – hence the name.

4. *A product with a small market share in a declining market – A DOG*

   A dog is a product in the decline phase of the life cycle that requires investment but generally produces little return. The market is declining and there is therefore little future for the product. It has very little market share and is usually a drain on the firm's resources.

The growth/share model has had its critics. It has been pointed out that not all dogs lose money or they may be in a period of transition before moving back to more productive times; and not all products with low market share necessarily cost more to produce than those with high market share. Furthermore, it has also been criticised for using just two variables (market growth and market share). Nevertheless, it is still a useful model to apply to gain a general feel for how products are performing.

Other models have been developed to analyse product portfolios, in particular the General Electric model (Figure 2.6) which uses industry attractiveness and competitive position as variables. Both these variables comprise a number of factors and therefore this model is seen to be more comprehensive than the BCG model.

According to the model, market attractiveness includes overall market size; annual market growth rate; historical profit margin; competitive intensity; technological requirement; inflationary vulnerability; energy requirements; environmental impacts; and the social, political and legal environment.

Competitive position includes such factors as market share; share growth; product quality; brand reputation; distribution network; promotional effectiveness; productive capacity; productive efficiency; unit costs; material supplies; research and development and managerial personnel.

To calculate the position of a product or a SBU in a market, each factor that makes up market attractiveness and competitive position is listed and given a weighting according to its perceived importance for the particular market. Each factor is evaluated and given a grade on a scale of 1 to 5. The grades are multiplied by their respective weighting, added together and the results are plotted on a matrix divided into nine areas or blocks.

For instance, one of the factors of market attractiveness – overall market size – is given a weighting of 0.20. The perceived importance of this factor for the product is ranked 4 out of a possible 5. Therefore, the value of overall market size is: 0.20 x 4 = 0.80.

Similarly, a factor of competitive position – brand reputation – is given a weighting of 0.10. The ranking for the product is given a ranking of 3. Therefore, the value of this factor is 0.20 multiplied by 3 = 0.60.

Once the values of all the factors have been calculated, they are aggregated to give an overall ranking for both market attractiveness and competitive position (see Box 2.5).

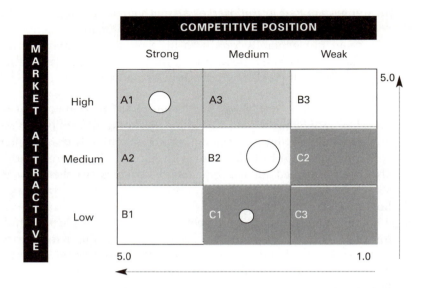

Figure 2.6   General Electric product portfolio analysis model (adapted from Day, 1986)

The matrix is not only useful to analyse the strength of the portfolio it also offers an indication of the appropriate strategies to pursue. These include whether to invest in a product to manage its growth, hold and protect it to preserve market share, harvest it to increase cash flow or divest to relieve the drain on company resources if it is producing little returns.

The nine blocks in the matrix can be divided into three broad categories. 'A' category products or SBUs (located in the top left-hand corner of the matrix) are strong and an appropriate strategy would be to invest for growth. Strategies for the 'B' blocks (diagonally from the top right-hand block to the bottom left-hand block) focus on selecting the right products to develop and on maximising earnings from them. 'C' category products (bottom right-hand corner) are not very attractive and a decision must be taken about whether to milk them for as much revenue that can still be generated or divest (Kotler, 1988).

Day (1986) described the different strategies for each block in the market attractiveness/competitive position matrix. These are represented in Table 2.1.

The Calgary Model of Competitiveness for Tourism Destinations

The World Tourism Education and Research Centre based at the University of Calgary in Canada devised a model to understand and analyse the competitiveness of tourism destinations. Based on the World Economic Forum Model for competitiveness of nations in the global economy, it focuses on the tourism sector in greater detail to provide a tool for managerial analysis, planning and decision-making.

Table 2.1   **Strategies applied in the market attractiveness/competitive position matrix**

SBU/Product Category	Strategy
A1	*Protect Position*: Invest to grow at maximum digestible rate; concentrate effort on maintaining strength
A2	*Build Selectively*: Invest heavily in the most attractive segments; build up the ability to counter competition; emphasise profitability by raising productivity
A3	*Invest to Build*: challenge for leadership; build selectively on strengths; reinforce vulnerable areas
B1	*Protect and Refocus*: Manage for current earnings; concentrate on attractive segments; defend strengths
B2	*Selectivity/Manage for Earnings*: Protect existing programmes; concentrate investments in segments where profitability is good and risk is relatively low
B3	*Build Selectively*: Specialise around limited strengths; seek ways to overcome weaknesses; withdraw if indications of sustainable growth are lacking
C1	*Manage for Earnings*: Protect in most profitable segments; upgrade product line; minimise investment
C2	*Limited Expansion or Harvest*: Look for ways to expand without high risk; otherwise, minimise investment and rationalise operation
C3	*Divest*: Sell at time that will maximise cash value; cut fixed costs and avoid investment meanwhile

Source: Day, 1986 and Kotler, 1988.

A distinction is made between *competitive advantage* which includes tourism infrastructures, the quality of management, the skills of the workforce, government policy and so on and *comparative advantage* which includes climate, beautiful scenery, attractive beaches, wildlife and so on (Ritchie and Crouch, 1993).

The Calgary team argues that *destination prosperity* is a function of the competitiveness of different sectors in the destination, including the tourism sector. Tourism competitiveness is made up of a number of determinants that must be identified and evaluated.

The determinants of competitiveness are:

- *Destination appeal* – both the destination's attractiveness and the destination's deterrents must be considered
- *Destination management* – this includes marketing efforts and managerial efforts
- *Destination organisation* – the capabilities of destination management organisations and the impact of strategic alliances
- *Destination information* – internal management information systems and research capabilities
- *Destination efficiency* – productivity and integrity of experience. (Ritchie and Crouch, 1993)

BOX 2.5

AN EXAMPLE OF MARKET ATTRACTIVENESS/COMPETITIVE POSITION MATRIX – A TOUR OPERATOR'S PORTFOLIO

An adventure tour operator evaluates the firm's product portfolio, which comprises three strategic business units:

1. Trekking tours in Nepal
2. Walking tours in the Sierra Nevada in Southern Spain
3. Mountaineering in the Alps in France.

Each of these SBUs has different markets and different competitors. The market attractiveness and the competitive position for each SBU are calculated and plotted on the market attractiveness/competitive position matrix.

The company is the market leader for trekking tours to Nepal and has an excellent reputation. Its competitive position scores very high at 4.7. Trekking in Nepal has become very popular and this market is developing at a fast rate. The market attractiveness for trekking in Nepal is calculated at 3.8.

The walking tours in Spain are a new addition to the company's portfolio. This is also a growing market served by large companies. The market attractiveness for this SBU is 2.5 and the competitive position is ranked at 2.3.

Mountaineering holidays in the Alps were the first products offered by the company. Unfortunately, the company has moved on, it has lost its best employees to competitors and its equipment is old. This is a small market and there is high competition from other mountaineering destinations. The firm's competitive position is low at just 1.2 and the market attractiveness is also fairly low at 1.8.

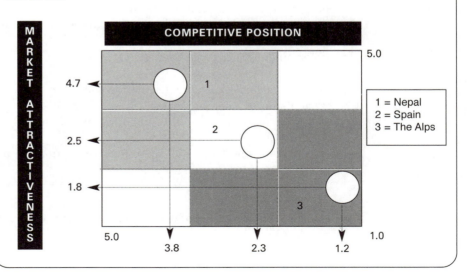

BOX 2.5 (cont'd)

The analysis shows that the range of trekking products in Nepal is very healthy and that its position should be protected. All marketing efforts and expenditure should be concentrated on maintaining the strength of the SBU.

The walking tours in Spain fall in the 'selectivity/manage for earnings' block. There is good potential for the market to grow although it is being well covered by larger companies. However, the tour operator has a good presence in the market with a loyal clientele. It must protect these products and invest in growth.

The company's mountaineering SBU in the Alps is at the end of its life cycle. With heavy investment, it may be turned around although it is more likely that if the company wanted to revive the product it would choose other popular mountaineering destinations. The strategy here would be to stop investing in this SBU and concentrate on businesses that are growing and/or producing healthy returns.

The next step is to define standard measurements to grade these factors so that comparison between destinations can be made. The model is still being perfected and further research must be undertaken to refine the methods of measuring the determinants. However, this is already proving to be a valuable tool in benchmarking the competitiveness of tourism destinations.

Analysing Customers

'Customers are the only profit centre' (Drucker, 1968). Customers matter more than anything else to a business. Therefore, the organisation must understand:

- who its customers are
- where to find them
- what they want
- how and why they purchase.

Most markets are too large for the organisation to provide all the products and services needed by all the buyers in that market. The market must be sub-divided into group of consumers with similar characteristics, which the organisation can target. These are known as target markets.

At the centre of marketing strategy lies the analysis of market segments. In a market or market segment, the marketer has three targeting options:

- *Undifferentiated marketing*: introducing a product hoping to get as many people to want and buy it as possible. Mass market tour operators compete on volume and offer products with the broadest appeal to attract as many people as possible. The organisation practising undifferentiated marketing often aims at one large segment of the market.

- *Differentiated marketing*: The organisation operates in two or more segments of the market but designs separate products and marketing programmes for each segment, for example a hotel serving the business market during the week has weekend packages to attract the leisure market. The effect of this type of marketing is to produce more total sales over the whole market. However the costs of doing this are greater than undifferentiated marketing. These costs are product modification costs; production costs; administrative costs; inventory control and promotion costs.

- *Concentrated marketing*: The organisation concentrates on one segment and develops the ideal product for the consumers of that segment. Instead of trying to cover the entire market, it concentrates on achieving a good market position in a few targeted segments by focusing on the segment's needs and acquiring a reputation for being a specialist. The marketer must decide which are the attractive segments of the market. Attractive segments must be *measurable, accessible, sustainable, unique and stable*. (Frank *et al.*, 1972; Thomas, 1980; Kotler, 1988)

Segmentation

Segmentation is the technique of dividing the market into several distinct groups according to customer characteristics and reasons for buying so that separate marketing mixes can be devised. It is a process of gathering and interpreting market information. Identifying common specific characteristics creates potential customers.

The overall objective of using market segmentation is to improve competitive position and better serve the needs of customers.

Segmentation is used by marketers both proactively and reactively (Baker, 1992). Proactively, segmentation allows the marketer to understand customer characteristics, identify prospects, find niches and elaborate marketing strategy to develop and capitalise on the organisation's competitive position in the chosen niches. Reactively, segmentation is used to determine the response of different market segments to marketing strategy.

A market segment is composed of customers that have characteristics in common. There are two types of criterion that can be used to segment the market: consumer characteristics and consumer responses.

Consumer characteristics can be sub-divided into various types:

- geographic (region, climate, urban and rural areas and so on)
- demographic (age, sex, social class, ethnic origin, religion and so on)
- psychographic: (lifestyle, social class, personality, feelings and so on).

Box 2.6 describes a classification by age and identifies the Canadian 'baby boomer' market segment.

BOX 2.6

BABY BOOMERS DOMINATE CANADIAN DOMESTIC TRAVEL

The distribution of domestic trips by age mirrors the demographic makeup of the population. Canadians aged 31 to 50 (baby boomers) dominated the populations as well as the share of one-or-more-night domestic trips in 1996. In fact, they accounted for a greater share of trips relative to their population. In contrast, the share of travel among younger (under 15 years) and older age groups (aged 61 and over) dropped below their proportion of population, particularly among travellers aged 71 and over.

Source: Travel-log, Summer 1998.

Consumer responses include:

- benefits sought by buyers (health, attractiveness, quality and so on)
- occasion and usage (frequency of purchase, rate and volume of usage)
- attitude towards the product (positive, hostile, indifferent and so on)
- purchase habit.

Each variable has its own factors. Purchase habits, for example, may be evaluated according to a number of variables. You can use the number of alternative products, the number of ultimate decision-makers, the number of needs and wants, price, degree of product loyalty and ease of purchase to explain the purchase decision.

The advocates of product standardisation and mass marketing argue that consumers do not all fit into precise market segments and standardised products are cheaper to produce so there is a greater likelihood of purchase. While this may hold true for certain *low involvement* products where the consumer make decisions on whether or not to purchase on little information (such as buying safety matches), consumers have a large choice of tourism products which they consider in great detail and evaluate before purchase. Customers are more sophisticated in their tourism consumption and choose products that reflect exactly what they want from a trip or a holiday.

Box 2.7 describes the travel habits and characteristics of different US market segments.

BOX 2.7

CHARACTERISTICS OF US TRAVELLERS

Personal travel ranks high in life priority for the US and travel is increasing. There are different market segments:

Life enhancer
- Dominant traveller in the USA; 40 per cent of total market;
- Seeks new adventures, friends, experiences; travel is purposeful to broaden the mind;
- Single middle-aged men and women earning less than US$35,000;
- Little foreign travel.

Sun-seekers
- 25 per cent of the market;
- Typical destinations: California, Florida, Hawaii, Caribbean, Europe;
- Younger, single;
- High income (over $40,000 per household);
- Can be further subdivided into:

    Sophisticates: more inclined to foreign travel, highest propensity to spend; travel in groups to non-traditional locations; exotic tastes – Far East/South Pacific, also Europe;

    Pleasure-seekers: very affluent; seeks good climate, good beaches, swimming vital; fantasy resorts important for this group; however, only 1 in 3 travel outside Continental US; impulse group, planning very little ahead.

Glitter set
- Older; blue collar; less educated;
- Climate conscious; all-in luxury resorts; water sports, beaches, clubs and gambling;
- Typical destinations: Caribbean, Las Vegas and Reno.

The Play-it-safers
- 15 per cent of the market;
- Nuclear family; cautious;
- Mainly domestic travel.

The seasoned traveller

- Activity based;
- 59 per cent of all foreign trips;

> ## BOX 2.7 (cont'd)
>
> ■ Travels more frequently (average 2 trips a year);
>
> ■ Typical destinations: West Pacific coast, Hawaii, Caribbean, Mexico, Europe;
>
> ■ More inclined to take a risk, rough it to see something exotic, wants to visit new places;
>
> ■ Usually stay at mid-range to economy hotels.
>
> ---
>
> *Source*: Based on BTA Country Profiles 1994–95.

Segmentation techniques

Several techniques are used to identify and isolate market segments.

Cluster Analysis

Cluster analysis identifies and classifies individuals or variables on the basis of similarities of their characteristics so that a concise and understandable description of the groups can be developed with minimal loss of information (Hair, *et al.*, 1987).

Each cluster has recognisable characteristics and attributes, which are distinct from the other clusters and are the bases for identifying market segments.

Cluster analysis is a statistical technique which aims to group or sort items into a number of homogeneous groups. The aim is to minimise 'within group variance', while maximising 'between group variance' (Bailey, 1994). This suggests that an arrangement is taking place in which sets of entities are placed into groups with the condition that each group is different and unique for all other groups as well as internally homogeneous (Bailey, 1994; Hammond, 1995). The application of cluster analysis spans a variety of market segmentation studies like the development of new product opportunities, identification of relatively homogeneous and comparable test markets and tourism studies (Ryan, 1995). Looking at the usage of cluster analysis in greater detail the main aim is to explore a given relationship between objects and subjects without a dependent variable being selected (Diamantis, 1998).

Perceptual Segmentation

Perceptual segmentation analyses customer valuation of a product. It is based on how people evaluate different products according to their specific attributes and seeks to fragment the market by consumer taste and expectations. Using a technique known as perceptual mapping, products are rated according to attributes on two sliding scales such as cheap to expensive and low quality to high quality. The results are plotted on a graph and the products are grouped around 'ideal points'. An ideal point is the centre of a particular cluster. This is illustrated in Figure 2.7.

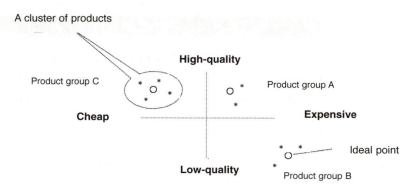

Figure 2.7   A perceptual map (adapted from Holloway and Robinson, 1995)

The concept of perceptual maps is described in greater detail later in this chapter.

Data-mining
Data-mining has been defined as:

> The process of discovering meaningful new correlations, patterns and trends by sifting through large amounts of data stored in repositories, using pattern recognition technologies as well as statistical and mathematical techniques. (Gartner Group, 1997)

Data-mining is made possible by technological developments and the large increases in computing power. Information collected by the organisation and stored on databases is analysed to discover relationships and patterns, associations between sets of apparently unrelated data and to uncover clusters of potential customers.

Data-mining transforms new information into strategic knowledge. It allows organisations to identify valuable customers, support management decisions and consolidate customer service. Inter-Continental Hotel and Resorts' data-mining strategy is described in Box 2.8.

BOX 2.8

WINNING WITH YOUR BEST CUSTOMERS

Report on The International Hotel and Restaurant Association's Congress: *Impact For Hotels Of New Marketing Revolution*

John Cahill, Senior Vice-President Information Technology, Inter-Continental Hotels and Resorts

Of all the major changes taking place in the marketplace, perhaps the most important is that the customer now knows the meaning of 'lifetime' value. Not only is the customer king, but he knows his current value and also expects added value. Neither segment nor mass marketing can prove adequate to reach this type of customer. Competition is extensive, it is both local and global, information is ubiquitous, change is rapid, competitor response is rapid, new media channels are appearing, and marketing funds are both finite and fragmented.

In the face of this, Inter-Continental's approach to customer management is divided into three tiers: Alliance Databases, Global 2000 and the Six Continents Club.

Alliance databases give Inter-Con access to more than 15 million potential customers in travel and non-travel areas, including financial, retail, telecommunications and media. Just from the airline alliances alone, Inter-Con had generated 677,600 room nights in global mileage awards, and there was considerable potential for exploiting those further.

One tier up, Inter-Con has its database of Global 2000 guests, a total of about two million occasional guests with over 12 million stay records. Inter-Con has access to their reservation records, travel agent data, frequent flyer information and spend information, all of which could be used for data analysis and mining. Some of the information could also be shared with partners and alliances.

The Six Continents Club, of about 250,000 members, constitutes the top tier of the target market. These hold considerable promise for further marketing efforts to maintain their loyalty through continued research even while maintaining the global integrity of the programme and the exclusivity of the membership.

For them, the short-term object is to move from mass to tailored communication based on known travel patterns, known needs or past behaviour and, more importantly, incentivise further loyalty/spend levels.

To gain overall success a comprehensive customer management strategy has to be integrated with both the overall business and technological strategies, and have a strong belief in the value it generates vs. the cost it involves. Moreover, there has to be a long-term commitment as well as willingness to change, Mr Cahill said.

Source: John Cahill's presentation at The International Hotel and Restaurant Association's Congress, 1998.

It is important for the marketer to understand how and why customers act and react.

Consumer Behaviour

Consumer behaviour studies analyse the factors that influence consumer choice of particular products or brands. Tourism products compete with each other and it is important to understand why and how consumers choose particular products or specific brands. For instance, a family decides to take a holiday. They may decide to take a beach holiday, a walking holiday or a sports activity holiday. They may decide to buy an all-inclusive package or go self-catering. These are different products. Once the product has been chosen, then they will evaluate different brands before selecting and purchasing the holiday they require. In the following section, the terms 'product' and 'brand' are used interchangeably.

Three principal factors influence consumer choice:

- Needs of consumers, perception and evaluation of information about a product and attitude to alternatives
- Environmental influence (culture, social class, peer group, family and so on)
- Marketing mix strategies (product, price, advertising and distribution).

Consumer decision-making

There are four types of consumer purchase processes which depend on how 'involved' the consumer is with the product and the complexity of the decision making process.

High involvement products: the purchase of these products offer an element of risk to the consumer. This may be financial risk, social risk or psychological risk. The consumer spends time and effort evaluating different products before choosing the most appropriate one for his or her needs. Brands are particularly important. Tourism products are mostly high involvement products.

Low involvement products: The consumer does not need to spend much time evaluating different low involvement products or brands. There is little risk and decisions to purchase are generally based on convenience and availability.

Complex decision making: The decision making process starts with need arousal as illustrated in Figure 2.8. This may originate from the consumer's psychological set such as attitudes, desires and personality, from the consumer's lifestyle and peer group influence and from external stimulation such as advertising and economic needs. An example of consumer attitude is described in Box 2.9.

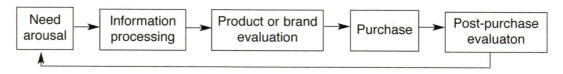

Figure 2.8   The complex decision-making process (adapted from Assael, 1987)

Once the consumer's interest has been stimulated, he or she seeks and processes information about the product. This is a selective process as consumers will tend to choose the information that most closely matches their needs and convictions. Based on the evaluation of the information he or she will select a brand and purchase it. The evaluation is rigorous for high involvement products. Clearly, the marketer must attempt to understand what makes consumers pick one brand over another.

The process does not end with the purchase. Once the product has been consumed or the service been experienced, post-purchase evaluation occurs. The consumer evaluates whether the choice of product was right or not and this will influence future purchasing behaviour.

BOX 2.9

CONSUMERS WITH ATTITUDE

Today's traveller certainly has attitude when it comes to choosing where to holiday and which, or whose, product to buy. Research shows that 'environmental responsibility' is one area where attitude is turning to action, with consumers increasingly wanting to ensure that the people they do business with are switched on to environmentally sustainable management practices.

In a UK survey, around 5 in 10 people said they would be willing to pay more for their holiday or business trip to ensure the tour operator, transport company, hotel, tourist attraction, caterer or retailer were committed to environmental protection (Mori/Green Globe Survey, 1995).

In a 1996 British Airways Survey, nearly 37 per cent of respondents said they had a great deal of concern for environmental issues when travelling for leisure purposes, with 53 per cent saying they would prefer to do business with an airline or tour operator who took environmental issues into account over one who did not.

Demand by corporations for environmentally responsible travel services is already significant in Europe, with Douglas Greenwood (Scandic Hotels International Sales Director) believing that environmental awareness ranks in importance alongside price and location.

Source: Consumers with Attitude, Australian Government Publication, 1998.

Whereas consumers make decisions after serious consideration when they buy high-involvement products, it is easier for them to change brands when buying low-involvement products. Because the risk is low, consumers experiment and try out new products.

'Habit' buying: When a consumer is satisfied with a product or a brand, he or she is likely to purchase it again. For high involvement products, satisfaction provides *safety* and therefore reduces the risk of making bad choices. For low-involvement products, *inertia* may lead consumers to repeat purchasing. When they have found a suitable brand, it is not worth the effort to look for a better one. Decision-making is a difficult process for the consumer. It requires effort and causes turbulence in the mind, which is uncomfortable. The consumer learns from past experience and finding the brand that satisfies her or his requirements reduces the uncertainty and therefore the anxiety of having to evaluate and choose other brands.

Marketers must build *brand loyalty*. They must understand how their clientele learn and find information about a brand and what will make them buy it again. Marketers use techniques to encourage brand loyalty. In tourism, these have become very sophisticated with a multiplication of loyalty programmes. Airlines lead the way and frequent flyer programmes are discussed in Chapter 9. Points can also be accumulated by staying at hotels with loyalty programmes and all major car hire firms are linked into airline programmes. Tour operators offer discounts to past clients.

This is a growing field of marketing called *relationship marketing*. Research has shown that it cost five times more to acquire a new customer than to keep an existing one. Therefore, the objective is to build one-to-one relationships with existing customers by opening two-way interactive dialogue with them and establishing a system to understand the customer's point of view. Understanding individual requirements means that more business can be created as products can be tailored to the needs detected by the personalised interaction.

Understanding the Consumer

Marketers must understand how consumers perceive and process information about their products. Perceptions depend on how information is selected and organised in the mind of the consumer. He or she will select the information that relates to a particular need and screen out information that is not relevant. To make sense of the information, the consumer organises and integrates it into groups, categories, contexts, similarity and so on.

Marketers create stimuli to guide consumers toward their products and encourage them to choose them. According to Assael (1987):

> Marketing stimuli are any communication or physical stimuli that are designed to influence the consumer. The product and its components (package, contents, and physical properties) are *primary stimuli*. Communication designed to influence consumer behaviour are *secondary stimuli* that represent the product either through words, pictures, and symbolism, or through stimuli associated with the product (price, store in which purchased, effect of salesperson).

Surveys are carried out to measure perceptions and how information is processed. In fact, they serve to test the effectiveness of advertising messages by understanding where information is seen (exposure), if it caught the eye of consumers (attention), if the information is understandable (comprehension) and if it sticks in the mind (retention).

Therefore, marketers must consider consumer perception in their advertising strategies and product development strategies.

Motivation

Marketers need to understand what motivates people to travel and why they make certain choices. Motivation factors are classified as either 'push factors' or 'pull factors'. Push factors comes from within the individual. They are internal and affected by the individual's psychological processes such as his or her attitudes and social milieu. They are related to wants and needs and the search for benefits to satisfy these. Push factors may include the need to escape the daily routine; the need to relax; and the need to meet new people. Sometimes needs are awoken unconsciously by external sources (see Box 2.10).

BOX 2.10

MOVIE-INDUCED TOURISM

For some people, movies induce them to travel to the locations where they were filmed. The data gathered at 12 US locations supports earlier anecdotal accounts of movie-induced tourism… Data analysis showed at least four years of visitation increases after movies were released.

Source: *Annals of Tourism Research*, **25**(4), 1998, p. 919.

Pull factors are factors that attract people to buy a particular product. For instance the specific attributes of a destination will motivate different types of people to visit. Destinations with natural attractions such as Chile and New Zealand will attract eco-tourists whose motivation is to enjoy the landscape and maybe partake in activities such as trekking or horse riding. Tourists interested in culture and history will be motivated to visit destinations with historical building and museums such as Venice and Paris. Pull factors for a destination include beautiful scenery; friendly people; inexpensive entertainment and so on.

Environmental Factors that influence Consumer Choice

Consumers have attitudes that influence the way they behave and their disposition towards the product. Williams (1985) explains that attitudes are made up of three components:

1. The *cognitive* or knowledge component, which refers to belief or disbelief.
2. The *affective* or emotional component, which embodies positive and negative feelings.
3. The *conative* or behaviour-tendency component, which embodies a tendency to behave in a certain way. This does not mean that a certain behaviour will occur but that a certain action is likely to occur if the opportunity presents itself. An attitude therefore predisposes an individual to act in a certain way towards a person or object.

Attitudes are formed by a number of factors:

- *Personality*: The consumer's personality will affect his or her choice of product. Personality will influence whether a tourist chooses a sports holiday, a holiday where meeting other tourists or meeting the local population is important or a holiday to enjoy a cultural experience. Personality traits include aggression, extroversion, submissiveness or authoritarianism (Assael, 1987).

- *Past experience*: Consumers learn from their past experiences and this conditions their future behaviour.

- *Peer group influence*: What the consumer's peer group thinks influences his or her buying choice. The product has to be acceptable to the consumer's social environment.

- *Family influence*: Families exert strong pressure in purchase decisions. Parental influence shapes the attitudes of children, many of which are carried through to adulthood. It is important for marketers to understand who the customer is, who the consumer is and who make the decisions in the family. The customer is not necessarily the person who chooses the product. For instance, the children will often dictate the type of holiday taken by the family. One parent may choose the firm to go with and the other may pay for the holiday. In such a case, the person who pays for the holiday (the customer) did not choose it. However, the customer may veto the decision if the price is not to his or her liking.

- *Stereotyping*: This is an important concept often used by tourism marketers to reinforce the images and attitudes that consumers have towards destinations.

  Stereotyping is the term given to the human tendency to make over-simplifications and generalisations about people or objects based on limited experience. It should not be thought, however, that stereotyping simplifies the complexity of social interaction. [It] can be helpful for it alleviates ambiguity and enables a fairly rapid and easy evaluation of people and objects. On the other hand, it may give too simplistic an evaluation and lead to the formation of prejudices and to discriminatory behaviour. (Williams, 1981)

Brazil is thought of as a colourful fun-loving destination and this is reflected in the photos, logos and information diffused by tourism marketers selling Brazil. London is known for the pageantry of its monarchy and its historical monuments. The symbols representing London in the marketing literature usually include Big Ben and the Guards protecting Buckingham Palace.

Tourism marketers can adapt their product to appeal to different social groups at different times.

Benidorm in Spain has a bigger programme in winter than it has in summer. It has one of the mildest winter climates in Europe. The tourism sector at the destination has understood that to beat the problem of seasonality suffered by many coastal resorts, they must adapt the product to different market segments at different times of the year.

The local tourism industry organises in such a way as to attract different types of holidaymakers during the year.

Early in the season:	Families
August:	Young people
Late in the season:	Families
From 1 November:	Over 55s

When the different social groups arrive at the destination, the whole resort is ready to receive them. They adapt to the needs of each group and change 'the show' to provide the services and entertainment required. As a result, Benidorm is one of the most successful coastal resorts in Europe (Brackenbury, 1997).

The SWOT Analysis

The information collected and processed in the analysis is the basis for developing a SWOT analysis. It provides a synthesis of all the analysis undertaken in the marketing audit.

SWOT stands for Strengths, Weakness, Opportunities and Threats. It is a technique to provide a framework for identifying systematically the position of the organisation and the way it relates to the external environment and problems and opportunities facing it. The purpose of the SWOT analysis is to isolate key issues and to facilitate a strategic approach. The SWOT analysis should be based on precise data from external as well as internal sources rather than on perceptions (Seaton and Bennett, 1996).

The 'Strengths and Weaknesses' part of the analysis is the internal scan and the 'Opportunities and Threats' part of SWOT is the scan of environmental trends likely to impact on the organisation. Some trends will present opportunities; others will be threats.

The technique is also used to evaluate the position of competitors and identify their weaknesses that can be exploited as well as the potential threats they present.

When used in the context of a country's tourism industry, the SWOT analysis examines conditions that exist within the competitive tourism environment. As a result of the exercise, strategic responses can be formulated to increase the country's competitiveness.

A SWOT analysis of Chile's as a tourism destination was carried out by the consultancy, the Surrey Research Group. It is presented in Box 2.11. The information was based on the perceptions of opinion leaders in the country, an existing report by a government team, the Corporación de Fomento de la Producción ('Analisis Estratégico del Sector Turismo en Chile'), and the conclusions of the Surrey Research Group.

BOX 2.11

SWOT ANALYSIS OF CHILE AS A DESTINATION

Strengths	*Weaknesses*
■ Unique geography and variety of climates	■ Lack of promotion of Chile in tourist generating countries – lack of budget for promotion
■ An absolute advantage: Easter Island, pull factor for visiting Chile	■ Distance from generating markets
■ Strong natural assets: Lake district, the Andes, Patagonia, the northern desert, the Altiplano, Antarctica	■ Access to and transport within Chile
■ Beach product particularly strong for domestic market and for neighbouring countries	■ Cost of travel to Chile
■ Ethnic mix in the North, strong cultural and ethnic presence	■ Holiday period reversed to major generating markets
■ Relatively developed particularly in the metropolitan area	■ Dependency on Argentinian market
■ Good sanitation, fairly healthy environment	■ Long-term economic stability has yet to be assured
■ Safe image compared with other parts of Latin America	■ Strengthening of the peso
■ Inward investment high to develop physical plant	■ Inadequate regulation for safety and quality of tourism services – hotel classification does not look at quality of service, increase in accidents in adventure tourism activities
■ Hospitality of the local population	■ Concentration of tourism servies in the Metropolitan area and the 4th and 5th regions
■ Current political and economic stability	■ No system (private or public) to monitor changes in international tourism demand so as to benefit from opportunities
■ No diseases or plagues	■ Lack of quality in services outside the large tourism establishments, lack of manpower training in the industry

---

BOX 2.11 (cont'd)

Threats	*Opportunities*
■ Perception of the rest of Latin America: dangerous for visitors, economic instability	■ Developing promotion of the destination
■ Danger of being overtaken by competitors, that is, countries with strong classical attributes (Peru)	■ Selling a different destination – long haul – remoteness and new destinations are currently popular
■ Danger of environmental pollution – weak regulatory system to protect the environment	■ Exclusive winter destination
■ Lack of urban regulatory plans in many regions	■ Possibility and ability to develop eco-assets
■ Low importance placed on tourism activity at national level and a lack of a strategic vision for the sector	■ Possibility of developing skiing product
■ Potential conflicts between the tourism sector and new investment projects in natural resources (infrastructure, forests and others)	■ Possibility of developing activities with other Latin American destinations
■ Lack of co-ordination and consensus between different players in the industry on regulations necessary for tourism and on new development initiatives	■ Development of new tourism centre

■ Development of the timeshare market
■ Obtaining international funding to protect the environment
■ Growing interest by foreign investors and international operators in Chile's tourism
■ Developing the awareness and understanding of the local population of the benefits of tourism
■ Better capacity of regional governments to promote tourism activities
■ Opportunity for training in the sectors

Source: Surrey Research Group, 1996.

The consultants concluded that Chile has great potential to develop its tourism sector. However, several factors must be taken into account and some serious threats avoided if it is to reach 3 million international tourists by the year 2002 as planned by the National Tourism Organisation (NTO) and if domestic tourism is to continue to grow.

A number of areas for improvement were identified as a starting point for achieving the NTO aims. These included:

1. increasing international promotion to maintain current markets and to develop new ones
2. developing infrastructure and in some cases modernising superstructure
3. adopting measures to protect the environment

4.   increasing the quality of service in the industry; and preparing a well-trained and qualified workforce for predicted increased levels of tourism activity.

FORECASTING THE FUTURE AND MAKING ASSUMPTIONS. SETTING MARKETING OBJECTIVES – WHERE DO WE WANT TO GO?

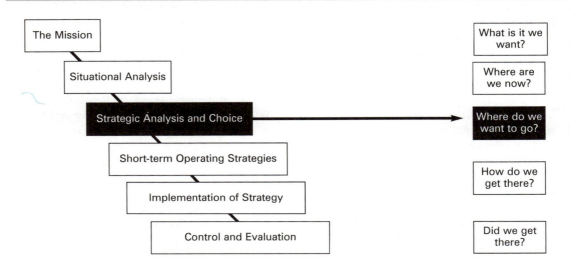

The analysis of the internal and external environment is complete and the information has highlighted opportunities for the organisation to exploit and threats to defend against. The next stage of the strategic process is to consider the question: *Where do we want to go?*

Forecasting the Future and Making Assumptions

The future is like another country. They do things differently there. (Arthur C. Clarke)

A strategic plan is normally drawn up for a five-year period. It is important to estimate what will happen over the five years before selecting strategies to pursue. Therefore demand for the organisation's products and developments in the external and internal environments must be forecasted.

There are several forecasting methods:

- *Surveys of buyer intentions:* Surveys are carried out with a selected sample of consumers to find out whether they intend to buy the product in the future. Industrial buyers may also be surveyed to collect information on their forecasts for the future. For instance, an airline increasing its fleet of aircraft is a clear indication that they expect a greater volume of passengers in the future. The survey would show the routes on which it expects to do more business and to which destinations. This information would be useful for marketers elaborating the destination's strategic plan as well as for tourism firms at the destination (for example hotels) and tour operators. Box 2.12 describes a telephone survey of buyer intentions carried out in Canada.

- *Expert opinion:* Opinions about the future are sought from people knowledgeable about the industry such as dealers, distributors, suppliers, marketing consultants, and trade associations (Kotler, 1988).

- *Market test method:* New products are introduced in a small area, buying patterns are analysed and forecasts are extrapolated for the potential of the total market.

- *Time series analysis:* This technique is used to forecast sales, to analyse demand, and in econometric studies. Projections are based on past trends and are a function of time.

- *Statistical demand analysis*: This method considers different variables that historically have influenced demand for the product and uses a statistical technique called multiple-regression analysis.

BOX 2.12

SURVEY OF BUYER INTENTIONS

The Conference Board of Canada reports that Canadians plan to take some 12.1 million trips this year, compared to 11.5 million planned trips last year. The figures were compiled from a random telephone survey, which also showed that 58 per cent of Canadians intend to take a vacation this summer.

Source: GSA, **4**(81), June 16–July 6, 1998.

Marketers must make assumptions about what they expect will happen in the market in future and these must be in agreement with the expectations of other managers in the organisation. However, assumptions can be dangerous and unexpected changes in conditions can destroy even the best thought out plans. For instance, despite buoyant growth in the early 1990s and forecasts of continued growth, the Asian economic crisis of the late 1990s took many tourism businesses by surprise. Box 2.13 shows how Australia and New Zealand in particular suffered from a drop in arrivals from Asia.

BOX 2.13

JTB SURVEY ON SUMMER TRAVEL – 1998

For the first time in 18 years, the number of Japanese going overseas during the summer travel season (July 1–Aug 31) will drop, mainly the result of concern over the outlook of the economy. According to the annual survey Travel Trends for Summer by the JTB Foundation, the number will fall 2.4 per cent from 3.184 million in 1997 to 3.107 million.

Source: *Travel Journal International*, July 27 1998, **21**(14).

Therefore, strategic plans must be flexible and monitored regularly to adapt to unforeseen circumstances.

Setting Objectives

The analysis has identified possibilities and dangers in the future. The organisation must set precise goals to be accomplished over the life of the strategic plan. The mission statement sets out the broad aims of organisation. The objectives translate the overall mission into attainable goals. These must take into account the opportunities and threats uncovered by the situational analysis and the resources the organisations will have in the future. Objectives are still fairly broad and specific quantifiable aims are described in sub-objectives.

For instance, the mission statement of a tour operator may be 'to provide high quality cultural experiences for a discerning clientele'. An objective related to the mission may state: 'to become the leading provider of *wine tours* in Eastern Europe within the next five years.' A sub-objective may be 'to increase market share in Romania by 10 per cent a year to cover 60 per cent of the total market in five years'.

Sub-objectives cover shorter time scales providing milestones along the way to achieving the stated objective (see Box 2.14). They are the goals that guide operational plans.

In his famous work *Corporate Strategy* (1968), Igor Ansoff devised a matrix, represented in Figure 2.9, which considers expansion into markets in which an organisation already operates as well as expansion into new markets. McDonald (1995) suggests that it is a useful device for thinking about marketing strategies.

BOX 2.14

TOURISM DURBAN
MARKETING AUTHORITY FOR THE CITY OF DURBAN
COMMITTED OBJECTIVES FOR 1997/1998

- To secure conference and convention business for the metropolitan Durban region with a positive annual economic impact of at least R175 million.

- To secure and promote sports and other events for the metropolitan Durban region which will attract visitors to the region, and generate an annual economic impact of at least R100 million.

- With a 29 per cent market share of the KwaZulu-Natal domestic leisure tourism visitors compared with 24.6 per cent 2 years ago (an increase of 16.4 per cent), our aim is to increase our market share to 30.45 per cent by December 1998. Total tourism visitors to the city, including overseas and business, generate R4,042 billion into the local economy. Specific figures for Metro Durban will be extracted during the year.

- To maintain the present level of international holiday visitors from our traditional markets, and to also aggressively explore the leisure tourism potential in identified new markets.

- To provide a level of visitor information and reservation services that is comparable with the best in the world.

- To assertively promote the vibrant cultural diversity of the Metropolitan region, and project Durban as a truly African city.

- Through all initiatives, to actively promote the positive aspects and potential of the region to its citizens, to create a sense of awareness, pride and ownership.

R = Rand

Source: Marketing Authority for the City of Durban, South Africa – 1997.

The matrix is based on two variables: product and market.

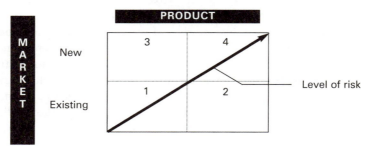

Figure 2.9   Ansoff's market expansion matrix (based on Ansoff, 1968)

According to this model, four marketing objectives are possible with different levels of risk.

The least risky option for an organisation is to continue offering established products to the market that it already services (block 1 on the matrix). The objective here is to increase market share and the decision to do this will be based on the portfolio and life cycle analysis carried out during the product analysis. This is referred to as *market penetration*.

Blocks 2 and 3 are both equally as risky. Block 2 involves introducing a well-established and tried out product to a new market and is known as *market extension*. In block 3, the objective is *product development* where new products are offered to the organisation's existing clientele. These objectives will involve higher market research costs and promotion costs without the guarantee of success.

The riskiest option is *diversification* (block 4). This involves introducing new products to new markets. Here the organisation is attempting to enter unknown territories and situations. This corresponds to the introduction stage of the product life cycle. It must invest heavily in market research and promotion to ensure that the product becomes established in the select market.

Positioning and Branding

Positioning

According to Kotler (1988), 'positioning is the act of designing the company's image and value offer so that the segment's customers understand and appreciate what the company stands for in relation to its competitors'. Assael (1988) explains that products can be positioned with respect to consumers and with respect to competitors. This is endorsed by Burke and Resnick (1991, also in Seaton and Bennett, 1996) who identify four positioning strategies: with respect to target markets, by price and quality, relative to a product class and relative to competitors.

A number of authors have noted that positioning is finding a niche in the mind of the consumer and occupying it (Ries and Trout, 1981; Woodside, 1982; Baker, 1992). Chaco (1997) describes positioning of tourism destinations in the following way:

> The objective of positioning is to create a distinctive place in the minds of potential customers. A position that evokes images of a destination in the customers mind; images that differentiate the destination from the competition and also as a place that can satisfy their needs and wants. Positioning is a communications strategy that is the natural follow-through of market segmentation and target marketing. Since market segmentation is based on the notion that different tourism destinations appeal to different types of tourists, target market segments must be selected before tourism marketers can begin to entice these potential customers. An effective positioning strategy provides a competitive edge to a destination that is trying to convey its attractiveness to the target market.

Marketers use a technique called *perceptual mapping* to understand where products are positioned in the market and to identify opportunities (see Figure 2.10).

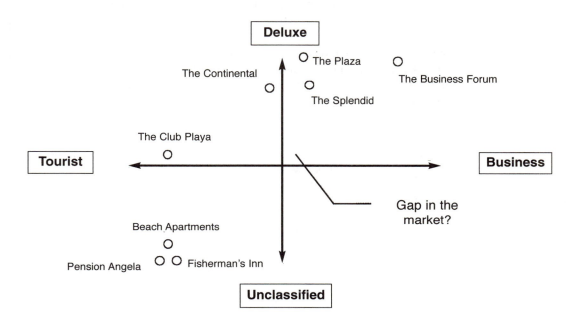

Figure 2.10   Example of a perceptual map of hotels at a destination

Figure 2.10 is an example of how hotels at a destination would be represented on a perceptual map. Two sets of variables are used in this particular map: type of clientele served and star rating. The destination serves both the business and leisure markets. The Business Forum Hotel is aimed solely at the business market and provides a deluxe service. The Plaza, the Splendid and the Continental are four- and five-star hotels and cater to both markets. The Club Playa is a medium category hotel and is exclusively used by the leisure market. At the lower end, there are a number of unclassified apart-hotels and inns also used by the leisure market.

The perceptual map shows clusters of competitors and gaps in the market. For instance, there is no medium-category hotel serving the business market. This could mean that there is an opportunity to open a three-star hotel for the business market (the case study in Box 2.15 describes such a situation). However, a gap may also mean that there is no demand for the product at this level and is therefore not an opportunity. This would need to be tested by market research.

BOX 2.15

NEW BRANDS ARE CHEAPER AND JUST AS CHEERFUL FORGING NEW GROUND: THE SHANGRI-LA GROUP'S TRADERS HOTEL

A new brand of hotels has emerged in Singapore: the business hotel without unnecessary frills. These hotels cater to the busy executive, offering basic amenities without compromising quality service and international standards.

Trademarks of these new entrants include empty mini-bars, vending machines and laundrettes. These hotels bring new meaning to the word 'no-frills', which has been associated in the past with budget hotels.

The Shangri-La Group's Traders Hotel pioneered this concept in Singapore, and has enjoyed high occupancy since its soft opening in 1995. Traders Hotel general manager Lothar Nessmann said, 'A year ago, we received mainly middle management guests.

'Now we have a huge amount of top management executives staying with us. We cannot compete in certain aspects with large hotels but where we can, we do. We are very diligent about that.'

The no-frills formula has also proved successful for the four-star Raffles Hotels International's Merchant Court Hotel. General manager Tan Choon Kwang said, 'The Merchant Court Hotel is designed for discerning, value-oriented travellers, a market segment that is fast growing throughout the Asia-Pacific region. We provide only the necessary and essential facilities and services that travellers need and appreciate so as to give them value for their money.'

Both general managers see the no-frills concept growing in Singapore. Said Tan, 'The planned conversion of several mid-range hotels to condominiums will continue to keep the demand for quality business hotels buoyant. In addition, the tight labour market in Singapore makes it difficult and costly for hotels to offer guests frills and fanfare in their services.'

Nessmann however admitted the competition was still very tough. 'If a guest has the choice between a no-frills hotel and a four- or five-star hotel offering all perks imaginable at the same or similar rate, where do you think they'll stay?'

Source: Ollie Quiniquini, Singapore – *Travel News Asia*, October 1997.

Products often need to be repositioned during their life cycle to contend with changes in the environment, particularly during the decline phase. This requires radical changes and a large financial investment with no guarantee of success (see Box 2.16). Destinations are particularly difficult to reposition for the same reason that they are difficult to brand in the first place.

REPOSITIONING CLUB MEDITERRANEE: FROM PRODUCT FOCUS TO BRAND MANAGEMENT

Club Med was founded in 1950 by an Olympic sports association as a vacation village where members could enjoy sporting activities in a camping site setting. The philosophy of the Club was based on the premise that people living in urban environments are looking for a totally different experience when on holiday. This is a time for city dwellers to escape from their everyday lives. Therefore, at a Club Med holiday village, reminders of daily routine are kept to a minimum: no telephones, no newspapers, plenty of entertainment (especially sporting activities), casual dress, and a payment system for extras based on tokens with bills to be settled at the end of the stay... in short, all the facilities for full enjoyment in relaxed surroundings.

The concept was a great success and by the early 1980s, the Club had around 80 villages in 24 countries. These included summer villages, winter villages as well as year-round villages located away from large centres in isolated sites, selected for their natural beauty and the recreational possibilities – these were totally self-contained communities with excellent facilities. In total, the villages offered 60,000 beds, employed 12,000 staff and counted a membership of over 1 million. The Club offered packages that included round-trip transportation on its charter airline, airport transfers, accommodation in hotels or in purposely-built lodges, bungalows or huts, all meals, and use of sporting facilities with expert instruction. Entertainment was organised by staff members referred to as 'Gentil Organisateur' (Nice Organisers) who were encouraged to mingle with the guests on a basis of friendship rather than just providing a service as Club Med employees. This was a unique all-inclusive operator offering an original product.

The company was particularly strong with the French and US markets, relying on heavy print advertising, repeat clients and word-of-mouth promotion. The President of Club Mediterranée North America, Mr Jean Lallement, felt that the Club Med product was its strength and the concept distinguished the Club Med package from other packages on the market. He admitted that little research had been carried out to understand the profile of the company's customer-base but supposed that the average client came from the higher social strata, was aged between 20 and 40 and that one in three was single. He felt that the company must be getting it right as 70 per cent of its customers were repeat clients which suggests a high degree of satisfaction with the product.

Over the next two decades, several other operators copied the all-inclusive holiday village concept particularly on Caribbean islands, however selecting and targeting specific market segments. In an increasingly segmented market, the Club Med brand seemed to be losing its originality and, although the company was still successful in its traditional markets (France and USA) its reputation for quality was becoming eroded and its holidays were perceived as being expensive. By the end of the 1990s, the company was in financial crisis.

BOX 2.16 (cont'd)

In 1997, Club Med recruited Philippe Bourguignon from Eurodisney to turn the company around and his first task was to perform a comprehensive evaluation of the its strengths and weaknesses. He found a product-led company: 'Today, the focus of the Club is on the management of holiday villages. In the future, we must focus on managing the brand… This implies a mini-revolution from operations towards marketing…'

He recognised that the concept and the core product were not obsolete but that the image of the company was and that productivity was very low. Therefore, he recommended pursuing a new strategy based on repositioning the company and on increasing efficiency.

Productivity and Efficiency Measures
- The first task to increase productivity and efficiency has been to close down the Club's subsidiary brand, Aquarius, which offered simpler, lower priced products and to refocus on the original concept: the all-inclusive holiday. Mr Bourguignon realised that the traditional Club's client expects quality at a reasonable price and since cutting out elements of the product in order to make it cheaper went against the original concept, the Aquarius offer did not fit in with the Club's image. In the future, he plans to introduce a range of products at different price levels but all with one feature in common: all-inclusive facilities.

- Next his team re-examined each village to evaluate the areas that needed up-grading. By 1999, all the villages will have been renovated. To increase profitability, the company has introduced measures to lengthen the season in certain villages, some of which had been open for only 3 months a year.

- A new human resources strategy has been put in place to reduce personnel and to bring wages in line with those of other employees in the sector. In some villages, Club employees were being paid two-and-a-half times more than employees in competing hotels in the area were. Performance-related pay and a system of incentives have been introduced.

The Repositioning Process
- The first task in the repositioning process is to recapture the Club traditional clientele: the young and the family market. Once the marketing effort is firmly focused on the core business, only then can measures be adopted to attract other market segments.

- The focus is now on marketing the brand rather than concentrating on acquiring more real estate and assets for the company – a move away from product-focus to brand management.

- Once the core brand has been re-established, the company plans to offer a range of new products such as cultural tours, business meetings and conventions under the Club Med Business label, events with the Club Med

---

BOX 2.16 (cont'd)

Business label, events with the Club Med Events label and the development of the Club Med World, an entertainment and shopping complex, with discotheques and cinemas as well as retail outlets and travel agencies.

Thus, Philippe Bourguignon understood that the strength of the Club lies in its effective brand and the concept and lifestyle that are associated with it. But he also realises that the key to survival is diversification. So the strategy is clear: protect and enhance the brand and create a range of new products under it umbrella.

Strengths

- Brand identification is strong
- Concept is still viable
- Professionalism of frontline staff at the villages and resorts
- Appeals to the family market
- Competitive price positioning in the US market
- Competitive prices in the winter holiday market (although this is not well known)

Weaknesses

Management at head office

- Lack of management training at head office
- Unclear definition of responsibilities at management level
- Vague and inaccurate forecasts
- Lack of a budgetary process

The Product

- One third of the villages in a mediocre state – need for renovation
- Too short a season for certain villages because they are expensive to run
- Comparatively high staff wages
- Perceived to be expensive in France

Current Marketing Effort

- Ineffective brand management
- Ineffective communication
- Unclear image
- Lack of clear understanding of the customer profile ('We want to touch everyone but we touch no one!')

Source: based on information from *Le Monde*, February 1998, and Harvard Business School, 1978.

Branding

> In the positioning era, the single most important marketing decision you can make is what to name the product. (Ries and Trout, 1981)

Branding is a method used to differentiate a product or range of products from those of competitors. According to Holloway and Plant (1988), 'A brand may be defined as a name, sign, symbol or design, or a combination of these, intended to identify the products of an organisation and distinguish them from those of competitors.' It is manifested in the way the product is packaged and the logos and slogans used.

Branding provides a consistent image which makes the product stand out and easy to identify. Thus branding adds value to the product. Many tourism products offered by the larger tourism firms are branded. Increasingly, destinations are also being branded Box 2.17 describes Australia's branding of Queensland and Victoria and Box 2.18 explains a new destination branding strategy – *mood marketing*. However, branding destinations presents a number of difficulties. These have been noted by Seaton and Bennett (1996): destinations do not have a homogeneous product; there is little control over the design of the product; prices are not set; there is little control over the distribution system; and promotion is to all comers rather than to selected market segments.

BOX 2.17

TOURIST BELT TO LEAD AUSTRALIA

The tourist regions of Queensland and Victoria will lead Australia's marketing charge at the Arabian Travel Market this year, although the Australian Tourist Commission (ATC) will not be participating at the market.

However, ATC spokeswoman Renata Gombac said Australian products would be well represented at a booth organised by the Queensland Tourist and Travel Corporation (QTTC) and Tourism Victoria, which will showcase its new marketing strategy focused on the state's five key tourism regions.

Cairns and Port Douglas have been branded 'Tropical North Queensland', while Australia's oldest and most popular beach resort area, the Gold Coast, is getting a makeover as 'The Ever Changing Always Amazing Gold Coast'. Other brands have been created for Brisbane, the Sunshine Coast and the Whitsundays.

Source: Chris Tolhurst, Sydney – *Travel News Asia*, 1998.

BOX 2.18

'MOOD MARKETING'
THE NEW DESTINATION BRANDING STRATEGY

In the ever more competitive tourism market-place, destinations – from resorts to countries – are increasingly adopting branding techniques in an effort to craft and differentiate an identity which emphasises the uniqueness of their product. It has been argued that there are significant problems facing destination brand managers, however successful branding brings enormous rewards. Destinations are adopting strategies that involve the development of an emotional relationship with the consumer through highly choreographed and focused communications campaigns. Branding activities must be credible, plausible, durable and deliverable and most critically, must meet the tourists' expectations.

Source: *Journal of Vacation Marketing*, June 1998.

Formulating and Implementing Strategy – How do we get there?

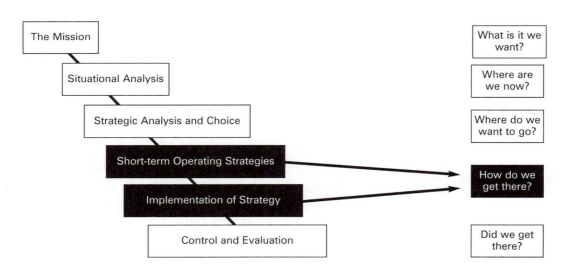

An objective is what you want to achieve. A strategy is how you plan to achieve your objectives. (McDonald, 1995)

This is the crux of the strategic plan. The organisation has considered its current position and has decided where it wants to be in the future. Now it must decide how it is going to get there. It must elaborate a plan of activities, which will achieve the desired results.

Traditionally, strategic option formulation was based on the strengths, weaknesses, opportunities and threats identified in the situational analysis. For instance, portfolio analysis indicated when it was most appropriate to maintain, improve, harvest or stop investing a product to exit the market. However, several new approaches to formulating strategy have been put forward in recent years.

In the following sections four approaches are discussed:

● Porter's 'generic' strategies and derivatives
● Strategies related to competitive position
● Game theory
● Global marketing strategies.

Porter's Generic Strategies

Perhaps the most famous writer of recent times on competitive strategies is Michael Porter who published his theories in *Competitive Strategy* in 1980, which he developed further in 1985 in *Competitive Advantage*. He contends that there are two routes that an organisation can follow to achieve advantage over the competition:

1. Producing the product at the lower cost than the competition – achieving cost leadership
2. Offering unique and superior quality products and services that are charged at a premium price – differentiation.

Porter proposed three 'generic' strategies:

● Overall cost leadership
● Differentiation
● Focus.

● *Overall cost leadership*: The emphasis is on efficiency to ensure that costs are kept to a minimum. Costs are lowered by investing in technology and in facilities and introducing labour-saving devices. The strategy does not rely on offering unique features but concentrates on producing the product at a lower price than competitors and therefore being in the position to sell it at a lower price for the same profit margin while maintaining the same quality. When pursuing an overall cost leadership strategy, the product is offered to the major market segments and not targeted towards specific market segments. The organisation has a broad scope.

● *Differentiation*: The scope here is also broad and the product is offered to the major market segments. However, the product is distinct from others on the markets either because of superior quality, extra or distinct features, or all three. It will generally have a strong brand or name identity in the marketplace and is valued by the buyers. The organisation needs to charge a higher price to fund the extra investment in the product.

- *Focus*: The product is aimed at specific segments of the market and is designed to satisfy the requirements of these segments. Competition is on a narrow rather than a broad front. The organisation concentrates its strategy on either cost reduction or diversification (or both). Compared with broad differentiation where extra or different benefits are emphasised in the product, focus differentiation is based on what a particular segment of the market needs and the product is designed with this in mind. The objective is to find a niche and occupying it. For example, Box 2.19 presents the American Frontier Motorcycle Tours, Inc. – a tour operator offering tours on Harley Davidson motorcycles in the South West of the USA. The company has targeted wealthy executives who want to live (or re-live) the 'Easy Rider' lifestyle and provides a high-quality personalised service. Luxury is emphasised. Although there are other tour operators offering motorcycle tour in the USA, American Frontier Motorcycle Tours has concentrated its efforts on a specific market segment.

According to Porter, organisations that do not follow either cost reduction or differentiation strategies are 'stuck in the middle'. These firms may be successful in a market that is growing but when competition increases as the market becomes mature, they will be vulnerable as they have no strategic position.

BOX 2.19

AN EXAMPLE OF FOCUS DIFFERENTIATION
AMERICAN FRONTIER MOTORCYCLE TOURS, INC.

Blue skies, green mountains, red mesas, small groups, day tours, first class accommodations, gourmet dining and Harley-Davidson® motorcycles. This is what you will experience when you tour with American Frontier Motorcycle Tours, Inc.

Come visit a slice of the American Frontier and discover why the Santa Fe area is one of the most popular destinations in the world.

Hear the Thunder in the Southwest as you ride through the breathtaking landscape of New Mexico on a Harley-Davidson®. Our tours are based in Santa Fe, New Mexico, one of the top 5 vacation destinations in the United States. Experience the Southwest. From the ancient Indian ruins at Bandelier to the Wild West Cowboy Town of Las Vegas, from Canyon Country to the Coal Mines and the Turquoise Trail.

American Frontier Motorcycle Tours, Inc. is the sole provider of personalized, all-inclusive luxury motorcycle tours in the United States. We take care of everything, right down to the gas in your tank. Tour groups are small, limited to only six

---

BOX 2.19 (cont'd)

motorcycles, so we are able to give each of our guests the individual attention that will make this vacation unique. We are committed to offering a level of service and comfort not found with any other motorcycle tour company. American Frontier Motorcycle Tours, Inc. invites you to join us for the ultimate luxury motorcycling experience in the Southwest. Hear the Thunder in the Southwest.

While we are on the road, we cater to you. A gourmet picnic and your preference in snacks and beverages are always available. Whether it's sparkling water and fresh fruit or a soft drink and a candy bar at a rest stop, we have them.

All of the tours are lead by an experienced guide on a Harley and followed by an escort in a Jeep. We even bring an extra motorcycle in case there are any problems or you just want to ride something different. You can even ride with our escort in the Jeep!

Source: American Frontier Motorcycle Tours, Inc. advertising, 1998.

However, writers have questioned Porter's generic theories. Tribe (1997) explains that competitors of the firm pursuing a cost leadership strategy can also reduce costs and challenge for leadership. Furthermore, quality may be compromised, particularly if products are unbundled in an effort to reduce costs (broken down to their basic elements which are then sold separately). He points out that Porter often confuses 'cost' with 'price' (costs are what the firm pays to develop and sell products, and prices are what consumers pay to acquire them). Finally, Porter suggests that firms choose either cost leadership strategy or differentiation strategy, but not normally both. According to Tribe, many try to pursue both strategies at the same time – low cost as well as differentiation. He favours Kotler's (1988) and Bowman's (1992) adaptation of the generic strategies which looks at strategy from the consumer's perspective. Several variations on the generic strategies are proposed:

- *'Price-based strategy'* focuses on passing on cost reductions to the customer in the form of lower prices.
- *'Differentiation-based strategy'* emphasises value-added based on quality and investment in research and development is advocated.
- A *'hybrid strategy'* is a combination of both low cost and differentiation. Economies of scale and high-load factors are methods adopted in the tourism industry to achieve quality and low cost leadership.
- Finally, in conditions of monopoly (for example public transport) or where there is little information available on other products for customers to compare, an organisation may adopt the short-term (and risky) *'zone X strategy'* where high prices are charged for low-quality products. In such a situation, customers will only return if there is no other alternative. (Tribe, 1997)

Strategies Related to Competitive Position

Organisations may select strategies according to their competitive position in the market.

- The firm with the largest market share is the *market leader.*
- Firms with large market share and in a position to threaten the market leader are *market challengers.*
- *Market followers* are firms that do not aspire to challenge for leadership. They are happy to compete in the market and their market share is large enough to provide adequate profits. Generally they copy the leaders' and challengers' products, on occasion offering some improvements or slight differentiation.
- *Market nichers* are smaller firms or divisions of larger organisations that compete in selected areas of the market not covered by larger firms. They offer specialised products geared to the market segments they are targeting.

Market leader strategies

Organisations in dominant positions in the market want to maintain their leadership. They adopt strategies to secure their status such as expanding total market demand; defending market share; and expanding market share.

Market challenger strategies

Market challengers adopt attacking strategies to increase market share and rival the supremacy of market leaders. To achieve this they may choose to attack market leaders, other market challengers or smaller companies.

Market follower strategies

Market followers seek to maintain their share of the market and defend against market challengers. Kotler (1988) distinguishes three market follower strategies:

- following the market leader closely without attacking or blocking it by imitating its marketing mix strategies and servicing the same market segment
- following at a distance by operating in the same market segments but introducing a degree of differentiation
- following selectively by choosing the most advantageous market segments to follow the market leader but also picking other segments and marketing mixes to develop.

Market nicher strategies

Smaller organisations and firms avoid larger firms by tailoring their marketing mix very precisely to the target segments. They select potential markets that are large enough to exploit, preferably growing and for which they can provide a specialist service. According to Kotler, there are at least ten specialist roles they can adopt (Kotler, 1988; Baker, 1992):

- *End-user specialist*: specialising in targeting one type of end-use customer; for instance, a tour operator can specialise in incentive travel for firms in the financial sector.

- *Vertical level specialist*: firms specialising in providing a section of the production process; for instance, a firm that specialises in meeting tourists at the airport and transferring them to hotels on behalf of tour operators.
- *Customer-size specialist*: specialists in particular markets which larger firms do not deem worth exploiting; for example a tour operator specialising in bird watching holidays.
- *Specific-customers specialist*: firms that specialise in providing a service for one or two major customer; for instance, an agency exclusively providing local guides in a city for a large tour operator.
- *Geographic specialist*: focusing on a specific geographical area; for instance a tour operator that specialises in a particular country.
- *Product or product line specialist*: the firm offers a single product or product line; for example a restaurant in a tourist area famous for a particular speciality.
- *Product feature specialist*: a firm specialising in offering a particular product or product feature; for example bicycle hire at a tourist destination
- *Job-shop specialist*: specialist in tailor-made products; for example a travel agent or tour operator who designs a tour based on a client's specifications.
- *Quality/price specialist*: firms that specialise at a particular quality/price level (high or low end of the market).
- *Service specialist*: firms providing specialist services not offered by other firms; for example, a tour operator specialising in 'singles' holidays without charging a 'single' surplus.
- *Channel specialist*: a firm specialising in using a particular channel to distribute its products. For instance, an implant travel agent in a business that concentrates on providing all the travel services required by the business.

Game Theory

In 1944, mathematician John Von Neumann and economist Oskar Morgenstern developed a method for studying the strategic behaviour of economic decision makers. This method is based on understanding how opponents who play parlour games such as chess, bridge, and poker adopt strategies. They developed game theory, which has been adapted to many fields:

> To date, the largest single area of application has been economics; other important connections are with political science (on both national and international levels), evolutionary biology, computer science, the foundation of mathematics, statistics, accounting, law, social psychology. and branches of philosophy such as epistemology and ethics. (Aumann and Hart, 1992)

In 1994, John Nash, John Harsanyi, and Reinhart Selten were awarded the Nobel Prize for their work on adapting game theory to business.

Business in the marketplace is akin to playing a game. The game has a size (the pie), a scope (depth and width and linkages with other games), a number of players and a set of rules. The game can be *co-operative* where players collaborate with each other, come to agreements and commitments that are binding or it can be *non-co-operative* where the strategic choices are down to individual choices.

Game theory is the study of rational behaviour, however, it is important to be aware that organisations do not always act rationally in business.

The following section leans heavily on the work by Nalebuff and Brandenburger (1996) who developed a framework based on game theory to analyse the complexity of the game. They proposed the concept of 'co-opetition' explaining that 'business is co-operation when it comes to creating a pie and competition when it comes to dividing it up... "You have to compete and co-operate at the same time" (Noorda, 1993)... This makes for a more dynamic relationship than the words "competition" and "co-operation" suggest individually.' To describe this relationship, they adopted the term 'co-opetition', first coined by Ray Noorda, the founder of Novell, the software company.

Nalebuff and Brandenburger suggest that success in business does not necessarily mean that opponents have to fail. If situations are managed properly and the correct strategies are adopted, there can be 'multiple winners'. Sometimes it is appropriate to compete but there are many instances when co-operation will be more effective. These are known as win–win situations where all players in the game win. At other times, just the threat of competition is enough to gain an advantage that may lead to a mutually advantageous solution. This has the effect of increasing the pie.

It is important to understand the *value net* of the organisation. These are all the players in the organisation's environment that are involved in shaping the game. Figure 2.11 represents a value net.

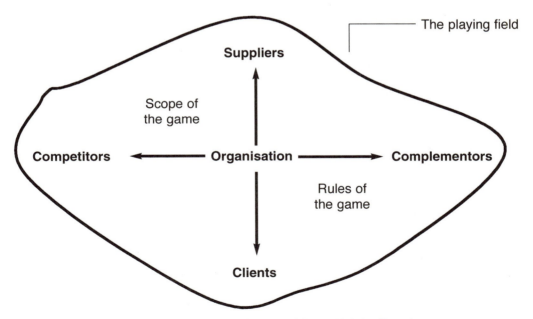

Figure 2.11   The game and the value net (adapted from Nalebuff and Brandenburger, 1996)

The complementors' product offer increases the attractiveness of organisation's product and, because the added value appeals to a greater number of customers, this has the effect of increasing the pie. According to Nalebuff and Brandenburger, successful organisations understand how to make the pie bigger to make business more profitable. Often it is better to let competitors do well rather than expend energy and resources attempting to impede their progress.

The authors claim that the frequent flyer programme concept first introduced by American Airline is a very good example of a win–win situation for airline companies and their customers. The primary objective of the frequent flyer programme is to create customer loyalty. The beauty of the concept is that the cost of doing this is very low. The airline rewards passengers for their loyalty by offering them free flights. Passengers take up seats that have remained unsold (the airline ensures that free passengers do not displace fee-paying passengers).

After American's AAdvantage programme had become established, other airlines copied the concept and launched their own affinity programmes. This initially reduced American's advantage but once each competing airline had built up a loyal client base, the effect of reducing or increasing prices was less-ened. In fact, clients will generally stick with the airline they select and are less likely to switch so as to not lose the advantages of membership. Furthermore, competitors join forces in marketing tie-ups to ensure that they maintain market share and that they are in favourable positions to enter and exploit new markets (see Chapter 8).

Nalebuff and Brandenburger propose a framework to analyse the elements of the game – the *PARTS* of strategy. An organisation must look at changing the game to its advantage. Each PARTS element is a strategic lever that can change the game. According to Lele (1992): 'A comprehensive knowledge of leverage is essential for determining which tactics and strategies are feasible, which objec-tives are attainable, what resources and skills (competencies) are necessary, and how to 'creatively disrupt' an industry for the company's benefit.' Changing one PART of the game changes the whole game.

The PARTS that can change the game are:

- Players
- Added Value
- Rules
- Tactics
- Scope.

Players
The players and their relationship to each other are represented in the value net. Each player adds value to the game and changes it when entering. Players must evaluate whether it is worth the cost of entering the game (such as development and marketing costs).

Bringing in more players changes the game. Increasing the number of customers has two benefits: on the one hand the pie gets bigger, therefore there is more profit, on the other the importance (or added value) of each customer is reduced. The organisation's reliance on its customers is lessened, as there are more customers to service. It sometimes pays to pay customers to enter the game by creating the right incentives. For instance, bars, discotheques and restaurants may offer a 'happy hour' where drinks are half-price or the customer receives two drinks for the price of one for a period outside peak time. The objective is to encourage customers to patronise the establishment rather than that of competitors and stay on during peak time.

Increasing the number of suppliers also means that the organisation is in a stronger bargaining position because dependency on any one supplier is reduced. Organisations can pool their resources to form buying coalitions to be in a stronger bargaining position.

Bringing in more complementors increases the value added of the product. The more complements to the product the more sophisticated, complete, easy to use or comfortable it is. The organisation may develop its own complements thus augmenting the original product.

There are occasions when increasing the number of competitors is beneficial to the organisation as this obliges it to maintain quality and standards and may diffuse an accusation of monopoly levelled against it.

Added value

The added value is the value a player brings to the game. Consider the following situation. A destination has two hotels both with 500 rooms. These two hotels represent the total accommodation stock. If one hotel closes, the whole destination will suffer because only half the number of tourists can be accommodated. This will affect business for local tourism firms and tour operators featuring the destination. There will be fewer opportunities for tourists to find holiday availability at the destination. As time goes by and businesses lose interest because of the constraints, they close or stop featuring the destination – the destination starts declining.

Therefore, the added value of the hotel is the size of the pie when it is operating minus the size of the pie when it is closed. It is important for the organisation to understand its own added value and those of the other players in the value net to recognise its negotiating position.

Rules

Rules in business are established through laws, customs, market discipline and contracts drawn up with customers and suppliers. However, these can change and small changes often provoke shifts in the balance of power. It is important for the organisation to ensure that the balance is in its favour.

Contracts can be re-negotiated. If a rule cannot be controlled, it is risky to base strategy on it. In the marketplace, it is the party with the power that makes the rules.

Rules may be introduced in contracts to ensure that suppliers and customers comply with the organisation's plans. For instance a hotel may guarantee a tour operator the best price for accommodation and complementary facilities if the operator commits to a certain capacity before the season. By contractual agreement, the operator is accorded *Most-Favoured-Customer* status and receives all the benefits that this entails as long as he or she abides by the hotel's business rules. Other such rules include *Meet the Competition* clauses where the operator is given the option to match any price offered by the competition.

Tactics

Changing people's perception can change the game. An image is created and built on every time an organisation is featured in the media, when its policies are made public and through the actions that it takes or does not take. The signals that it sends shape people's perception of the game. The organisation needs to take perceptions into account to really know what game it is in and to be in control of how to change it. Understanding the perceptions held by buyers, suppliers and competitors is an essential part of the negotiation process. When it comes to dividing the pie, different players may want different slices. It is important to understand what the other actors in the value net require from the game. Often, it is possible to divide the pie in such a way as to satisfy everybody in the game. They each receive what they want without having to resort to conflict situations.

Tactics are used to change perception. Tactics in this case are 'actions that players take to shape the perceptions of other players. Some tactics are designed to lift a fog, others to preserve a fog, and yet others to stir up new fog' (Nalebuff and Brandenburger, 1996).

'*Lifting the fog*' involves ensuring that other players understand exactly what is being offered. In other words, establishing credibility. The quality and the superiority of the product can be communicated in a number of ways such as displaying quality standards (for example ISO Quality Standards), running information campaigns about the product, seeking sponsorship and support from respected opinion leaders and offering free trials ('try the product'). Guarantees or the promise of large compensations should anything go wrong shows the organisation's belief in its product and inspires confidence.

'*Preserving the fog*' entails hiding mistakes, bad decisions and missed opportunities. In negotiation it is important to only reveal that which will put the product and the organisation in a good light.

'*Stirring up new fog*' involves confusing other players so that the actions taken by the organisation cannot be easily anticipated. This sometimes involves creating complexity out of simple situations. Pricing techniques are often used to create fog. For instance, to hide price increases over a holiday weekend, a hotel may put together a package that includes a number of features and insist that only people taking the whole package can make reservations. The price of the individual elements comprising the package has been masked by the various add-ons that have been integrated into the package.

The Scope

The game has boundaries, which are drawn up by people in order to understand and analyse it. These are mental boundaries and are therefore artificial. In reality, all games are knitted into one large game. However, it is difficult to make sense of a large complex system so boundaries are drawn up which break down the large game into understandable smaller interrelated games such as a national economy, an economic sector, a competitive market and so on. When a game is defined and accepted rules are created to control it.

However, boundaries are not always evident. For instance, the actual definition of what makes up the destination is often unclear. Is the boundary of a destination the resort? The country? The region? Defining the destination boundary is often the first problem the destination marketer must resolve (see Chapter 7).

It is important to understand and identify the links between games and how one game relates to another. For instance, a change in the cost of flying to a destination changes the game for many of the firms and organisations operating in the tourism sector related to that destination. Tour operator prices change and the destination may lose or gain competitiveness and may attract different tourist segments.

Different players perceive the game in different ways. Often this is because they have different needs and are in the game for a variety of reasons. It is important to understand how other games are linked to the game the organisation is in. Opportunities can be exploited. For instance, a typical Spanish restaurant's main business is over the lunch time period, which in Spain normally starts after 2pm. Substantial meals are generally served at this seating, as lunch is the main meal in Spain. However, North Americans on sightseeing tours tend to want a light lunch at 12am or 1pm. By opening early and creating extra options on the menu, the restaurant has an opportunity to organise an extra seating to cater for North American sightseers. As seating timings are different, the restaurant's traditional business will not be affected. This adds value to the firm providing the sightseeing tours as it wants to be in the position of satisfying the needs of their clients and to the restaurant in the form of increased profits and more efficient use of the restaurant.

Nalebuff and Brandenburger explain that each of the PARTS can link games together and that links are strategic levers to change games.

Players can operate in different games at the same time thus linking them. Complementors can also link games. For instance a newspaper offering package tours with a tour operator at a reduced price if readers collect tokens over a period of time creates a link and adds value to both organisations. Rules can be manipulated to link games. For example, some tour operators provide a discount on their packages but insist that clients take out the insurance they recommend. Finally games can be linked just because they are perceived to be linked. Therefore changing perceptions can change links between games.

Game theory allows business strategist to make decisions by looking at business from other firms' or organisations' perspectives – literally putting themselves in their shoes. However, not everyone reacts in the same way – some may even appear to react irrationally. It is therefore important to understand what motivates other organisations in the value net to anticipate their reaction pattern and identify potential strategic responses.

Global Marketing Strategy

In global marketing strategy, the decision must be made between *standardisation* and *adaptation* to local markets. Generally, a degree of adaptation is necessary as consumers differ across borders (tastes, behaviour, culture, income levels and so on) and the marketing infrastructure (media, type of advertising, transportation, distribution and so on) varies from country to country as does the legal environment. The question facing marketers in the global environment is how much they should adapt to local markets and which of the following elements should be adapted: packaging, pricing, sales promotion and media decisions, distribution channels and after-sales service. Furthermore, decisions must be made on the market position: whether to market to the same segment in each country adapting the product to the requirements of this segment or whether to sell to different market segments in different countries.

Standardisation is attractive as it generally brings economies of scale and therefore reduced costs. Some elements such as the basic product, the brand name and often also the advertising message are more likely to be standardised.

Hotel chains, particularly those aimed at the business traveller, often have standard furnishings that are fitted in all the hotels in the chain. The traveller knows the standards to expect and the chain benefits from economies of scales in designing and producing the furnishings. Staff training is also facilitated as the equipment is the same throughout the group and training programmes can be standardised and easily transferred.

Sometimes, a standardisation strategy may be used to create a concept or a theme such as the Hard Rock Cafés and Planet Hollywood restaurants. One of the most successful concepts has been the development of Irish pubs around the world as illustrated in Box 2.20.

According to Doz and Prahalad (1987), the global marketing system relies on three components:

1. presence in multiple markets – revenue from markets where the firm is strong are used to subsidise penetration in new markets
2. global brand presence and strong distribution systems
3. extended product lines across countries to gain economies of scope and greater competitive strength and allow cross-subsidisation across business and across national markets.

Terpstra and Sarathy (1991) explain that 'co-ordinating the global marketing system is a complex task. Some common methods include using similar marketing approaches across countries, transferring marketing know-how and experience, sequencing marketing programmes across countries, and integrating approaches to multinational clients.'

BOX 2.20

THE IRISH PUB CONCEPT

Since Guinness launched its Irish Pub Concept in 1992, more than 1,200 Irish pubs have opened in 35 countries and the current average is one per day all over the world, most recently O'Malley's in Shanghai. Germany has the greatest number of Irish pubs. Differing from the traditional rough-cut, Irish-emigrant watering holes that dot cities around the world, the trendy new pubs are designed and staffed in Dublin.

Guinness helped set up two companies to create these instant pubs: the Irish Pub Co., which employs architects, and Action Recruitment, which trains bar staff. Along with videos and brochures, they provide all that's needed to set up a pub – no matter where.

'Essentially, we offer a turn-key service. You tell us where, and we can have a typical Irish bar decked out and ready for you to open in a matter of 12 weeks,' said Brendan Buckley of the Irish Pub Co.

Guinness makes no investment in the pubs but prospective publicans are vetted, given advice and certain rules are imposed: dartboards are encouraged because darts is convivial; pinball machines are banned because they are solitary, noisy and ugly. No carpeting or neon lights, and the head on a glass of beer must measure between 17 and 22 millimetres. And, most important, there must be at least two Irish bartenders to create atmosphere.

To be part of the Guinness Irish Pub Concept, the candidate must have about $175,000 available and high motivation. Guinness provides advice on sites, legal and architectural counselling and marketing tools such as St. Patrick's and Halloween kits.

Through a design company, investors can choose between five pub types, available in kit form and suitable for use throughout the world, and they can also get a manual of recipes and the Guinness Guide to Irish music. Trained Irish staff, live Celtic music or a course in cooking Irish stew and other dishes can be arranged.

Source: Adapted from Mary Blume, *International Herald Tribune* (15.3.97) and Ciaran Giles, the Seattle Times Company (30.7.96).

DEFINING OPERATIONAL STRATEGIES: THE MARKETING MIX – OPERATIONAL PROGRAMMES – BUDGETS AND RESOURCES

Once the marketing objectives have been set, action plans must be devised taking into account the resources available to implement them.

The Marketing Mix – the 4 Ps and the 4 Cs – and Marketing Mix Strategies

The marketing mix is at the centre of the strategic marketing process. It is the mechanism used to implement strategic plans. Kotler (1988) defines the marketing mix as 'the set of marketing tools that the firm uses to pursue its marketing objectives in the target markets'.

The 4 Ps Framework (7 Ps for Services)

The marketing mix is based around the 4 Ps structure first devised by McCarthy in 1978. He identified elements that can be influenced and manipulated in the way a product is marketed and provided a framework to systematically analyse each of these elements: Product, Price, Promotion and Place/Distribution.

- *Product* refers to the development of the product or service. Product attributes include: quality; features and options; style; brand name; positioning; product perception; packaging; warranty; service support; range; cost; and patent, trademark or copyright.
- *Price* refers to the cost of producing the product or service and is determined by market demand. Competitive positioning influences pricing decisions. Price attributes include price level; discount policy; credit terms; and payment methods.
- *Promotion* consists of all of the methods of communicating the product offering to the target market. Promotional tools include above-the-line advertising – for which a fee has been paid such as television, radio, press advertising; advertising in cinemas as well as poster campaigns; below-the-line advertising – also referred to as sales promotion which includes giving away free samples of the product, discount coupons, competitions, point-of-sale, and direct mailing; personal selling, and publicity – public relations and sponsorship.
- *Place* (or distribution) is the task of getting the goods to market. Advances in electronic reservation and communication systems are transforming the way tourism products are being distributed. Box 2.21 describes the self-service check-in kiosks that Air Canada is introducing at Canadian airports. Distribution includes distribution channels; distribution coverage; outlet location; sales territories; inventory levels and locations; and transportation.

The '4Ps' are elements in the marketers armoury – aspects that can be manipulated to keep ahead of the competition. (Dibb and Simkin, 1994)

The 'mix' is how these element are combined together to produce action plans tailor-made for the target market. Each of the elements requires marketing decisions, which are set out in marketing programmes. Different markets require different marketing mixes at different times of their life cycle.

BOX 2.21

AIR CANADA DEVELOPS SELF-CHECK-IN KIOSKS FOR AIRPORTS, FOCUSES ON TECHNOLOGY TO SIMPLIFY TRAVEL EXPERIENCE

MONTREAL – Air Canada announced today that it is in the final stages of developing a self-service airport check-in kiosk for its customers. The first check-in kiosks will be pilot-tested at selected Canadian airports in the fall of 1998. Air Canada becomes the first airline in Canada to bring the timesaving convenience of self-service check-in to air travellers.

'Self-service kiosks are part of Air Canada's electronic distribution "Value Proposition",' said Marc Rosenberg, Vice President, Sales and Product Distribution on the occasion of the opening of Travel Technology '98 Conference and Trade Show. 'Based on extensive customer relationship management research, we know what value added products our customers want. Our objective is to continue to develop new technology-based products, such as the self-service kiosk, the Personal Ticket Office and the CallMall/Vista 350 phone information system, to respond to customer demand and strengthen our competitive position.'

Air Canada's self-service check-in kiosk will provide a convenient alternative to the traditional process for checking in at the airport. Customers will have the option to choose to go to the regular check-in counter or the self-service kiosk.

The bilingual English and French self-service kiosk will consist of a PC, boarding pass printer and a card reader all attractively packaged in a streamlined kiosk. The user-friendly product features an easy-to-follow software interface and touch sensitive monitor.

This is how Air Canada's new self-service check-in kiosk will work. Customers who have purchased a paper or electronic ticket activate the self-service kiosk by inserting into the card reader their Aeroplan card with a magnetic strip or the credit card used to purchase the ticket.

The customer will then be led through a series of user-friendly screens and will be prompted to: confirm their itinerary, confirm or select their seat through use of interactive seat maps, confirm special services, stand by for an earlier flight, request an upgrade or check baggage. A bar coded boarding pass will then be printed and instructions on how to proceed will be displayed.

Customers travelling with hand luggage only may then proceed directly to the boarding gate. Passengers with baggage will be asked to proceed to a dedicated baggage control counter where their luggage will be tagged.

Prototypes of Air Canada's new technology-based products including the self-service check-in kiosk, its Personal Ticket Office and the Vista 350 CallMall telephone service, are on display at the Air Canada booth at Travel Technology '98 Conference and Trade Show in Toronto April 1 and 2.

Source: Canada News Wire, Air Canada Press Release, April 1, 1998.

Services have specific attributes and, to address these, a further 3 Ps have been proposed:

- *People:* focusing on the quality of the human resources involved with the product – their skills, knowledge, motivation and customer care. Employee attributes include friendliness; how well they presented themselves; helpfulness; approachability; politeness; knowledge; and competence.
- *Physical evidence:* consideration is given to the decor, environment and ambience of the product or where the product is consumed (particularly important in tourism). The features of physical evidence include size; premises; corporate image; ambience; comfort; facilities; and cleanliness.
- *Process:* the efficiency and performance of the process is evaluated. The attributes of process include speed; efficiency; service time; waiting time; appointment system; and forms and documents.

If the Ps framework compels marketers to examine each of the elements of the mix, the Cs framework reminds them that the focus of the marketing effort is the customer.

The 4 Cs Framework
The 4 Cs relate to the 4 Ps while strongly emphasising the customer:

- *Consumer* relates to Product. It focuses on the needs of the consumer and the benefits that he or she expects. The product must match the expectations and satisfy needs.
- *Cost* relates to Price and refers to the cost to the customer. The marketer must be aware that the price is not the only cost that the customer must bear. There may be the cost associated with time and expenditure involved in travelling to consume the product, the cost of guilt or embarrassment in front of the consumer's peer group and so on.
- *Convenience* relates to Place (distribution). Methods of distribution are becoming widespread, varied, faster and more sophisticated. Marketers must take into account how easy it is for the customer to obtain the product: location, access, speed of service, transaction time and availability.
- *Communication* relates to Promotion. Promotion is a one-way process; the communication process must include a feedback mechanism to allow two-way communication. The building of relationships with customers is becoming a vital element of the marketing process.

Marketing Mix Strategies
Marketing mix strategies are closely related to the life cycle concept.

At the introduction stage of the life cycle: Few consumers have heard of the product, which must be tested to ensure its viability. Generally, it has to be heavily promoted until it has gained market acceptance and therefore costs are high at this stage. Several pricing strategies can be adopted, including *skimming strategies* and *penetration strategies*.

Skimming involves launching a product at a high price to maximise revenue. Buyers in this situation are not generally price sensitive. Skimming can either be rapid or slow depending on how heavily the new product is promoted. Organisation will adopt fast skimming to maximise returns from high spending buyers before the competition attacks the market. Promotion is used to ensure that potential buyers are quickly made aware of the product. Brand preference is created giving the organisation a competitive advantage over competitors who have not yet entered the market. Slow skimming strategies involve charging high prices but using little promotion because consumers are already aware of the product and there are few or no competitors in the market. The returns are even higher than in fast skimming strategy because of the saving on promotion costs.

Alternatively, penetration strategy involves charging low prices to attract consumers, particularly those that are price sensitive, and securing market share. As with skimming, the level of promotion determines the speed of penetration strategy. Fast penetration strategy is adopted in large markets where consumers are unaware of the product so it is strongly promoted, and when there is a strong threat of competition. Slow penetration strategy uses a low level of promotion because there is high awareness of the product, so costs are kept down.

At the introduction stage of the life cycle, advertising and publicity and, to a lesser extent, personal selling are the most effective methods of promotion. Distribution strategy will be determined by the number of competitors in the market and the channels available to get the product to the market. In highly competitive environments, it makes sense to multiply the number of distribution outlets, as competitors' products are widely available to buyers. Favourable conditions such as higher commissions, incentives and competitions are alloted to distributors such as travel agents to ensure that they promote the product above others. If there are few competitors, distribution is selective and based on the most cost-effective methods.

At the growth stage: The focus is on gaining market share to ensure that the product becomes established in the market – market penetration. The cost of promotion falls as sales increase and the message concentrates on explaining the benefits to potential buyers, many of who are already aware of the product and on reinforcing the loyalty of the existing client base. Word-of-mouth promotion is very effective at this stage. Several competitors copy the product and enter the market (the 'me too' syndrome). Resources are spent on product enhancement, new features are added to the product and quality is improved. Distribution becomes increasingly important and new channels are developed to reach the growing market. Prices remain high and this is a period of high profit, however, some pricing strategies are employed to bring in new consumers (or different market segments) and to react to the growing competition.

The strategic emphasis at this stage is to compete for a dominant position, which is important to arrive at before entering the maturity stage of the life cycle.

The maturity stage is generally the longest stage of the life cycle (except for products that quickly go out of fashion). There are three distinct phases – when the market is still growing, but slowly; when the market has stopped growing and is stable and when the market starts to decline. Market leaders are in a good position to reap profits and dictate how the market progress but have to contend with challengers trying to take over. They must invest in defending their position. There are many competitors competing for a piece of a pie that has stopped growing and may be already contracting. Market leaders and challengers may threaten followers and nichers to capture market share. Advertising is heavy and concentrates on differentiation by emphasising the unique features of the product and differences with those of competitors.

The product may be modified to differentiate it and to convert new types of users. For instance, tour operators offering trekking holidays originally aimed at the young market may modify their holidays to attract older trekkers. This may involve providing more comfortable facilities en route, porters to carry the backpacks, less strenuous itineraries and the preparation of more elaborate meals.

As competition intensifies, the most effective method of promotion is sales promotion (discounts, free gifts, competition and so on). The pressure of competition brings down prices and profits are reduced, with the danger of instigating price wars. This also has the effect of attracting new price-sensitive buyers to consume the product. Volume becomes an objective to secure profits. Many distribution channels and outlets are used to efficiently cover the market.

The strategic emphasis at this stage is to defend the product's position in the market and to retain (and increase if possible) market share to maximise the profits by increasing the sales volume.

At the decline stage: There are fewer competitors as sales are declining and the market is contracting. There is over-capacity and new products and substitutes come onto the market. Competition is very strong and prices are deliberately set low to sell volume. Sales promotion is the most effective promotion method.

At this stage, the organisation must decide whether to keep the product or whether to divest. Several options are available depending on the situation. By investing in the product, the objective is to extend its life cycle – re-inventing the product.

If the product is still strong in the market, the strategy may be to invest selectively in market segments that have still potential but abandoning those that are not promising for the future.

The analysis may have lead to the conclusion that 'harvesting' is the appropriate strategy. The product is milked dry of all possible benefits. The objective is to get the most out of the product before it declines out of existence.

Finally, the strategic option may be to divest the business. There is no potential for growth any more and the cost of producing and managing the product is a drain on company resources. The objective is to get as much from the assets as possible. However, it should be noted that strategies solely based on the product life cycle must be pursued with caution. As noted in the next chapter, the product life cycle has its critics. It is often difficult to know exactly at which stage in its life cycle the product is. It may experience several lulls and new leases of life, thus it may not follow the predicted curve.

Furthermore, there is also the notion of 'self-fulfilling prophecy'. By attempting to follow the life cycle too closely, investment to support the product may be withdrawn too early thus precipitating its decline.

Operational Programmes, Budgets and Resources

Operational programmes are schedules of actions and activities designed to achieve the objectives and sub-objectives of the plan. Sequences of events are set out in precise timetables and responsibilities are assigned to carry them out. The success of the plan will depend on the budgets that have been allocated and how will these are managed and on the resources and competencies available to the organisation.

Budgets are divided into *operating budgets* to finance the planned activities and *opportunity budgets*, which are kept for tactical actions to respond to changes and opportunities that may arise during the life of the plan. For instance, tour operators allocate a budget for brochure production. The cost of producing and distributing brochures is very high. During periods of intense competition, they must budget to bring out several brochures to react to price cuts by their competitors. If they can anticipate the cost of doing this in advance then it is accounted for in the operating budget. If they are taken by surprise and have to find funds to bring out an extra brochure, then they use the contingency opportunity budget.

The plan, the operating programmes and the budget must be monitored constantly to ensure that what has been planned is being achieved within the agreed time scale and employing the resources available.

MONITORING AND CONTROLLING THE PLAN

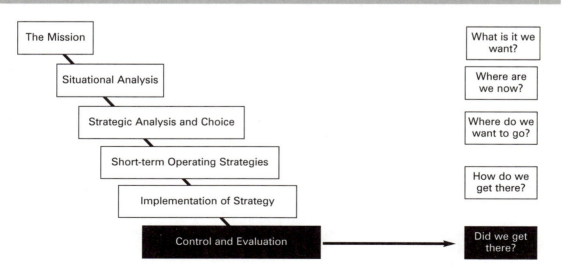

The Mission	What is it we want?
Situational Analysis	Where are we now?
Strategic Analysis and Choice	Where do we want to go?
Short-term Operating Strategies	
Implementation of Strategy	How do we get there?
Control and Evaluation	Did we get there?

During the life of the plan, there will many changes in the environment, both external and internal. The organisation must react to these changes but never lose sight of the original mission – although, if necessary, the mission itself may have to be re-evaluated. The importance of monitoring the plan and controlling it is often ignored by organisations as it is seen to be an extra expense and use of resources. However, it can make the difference between the success and failure of the plan. Plans are built on forecasts and assumptions. Often during the implementation phase, it becomes apparent that the assumptions or forecasts were not quite right and need to be revised. Accordingly, the strategic options and the operating programmes may also need to be revised if the mission is going to be achieved.

The implementation stage of the plan must be monitored on a constant basis to ensure that the actions are achieving the desired results within the scheduled time scale and that the budget is being used efficiently and will stretch.

According to Kotler, there are four types of control:

- *Annual plan control* to ensure that the objectives set out for the year are on track
- *Profitability control* to ensure that the organisation is making money
- *Efficiency control* to measure the efficiency of marketing expenditure
- *Strategic control* to ensure that the appropriate strategies were selected.

Systems and procedures should be put into place and communicated to everybody in the organisation. These should be checked on a regular basis at several points during the process in order to pinpoint where schedules are being missed or where there is a possible gap in the information gathering and analytical process. Responsibility should be allocated to ensure that all procedures are followed and that problems are rectified as soon as they are detected.

Finally, each stage of the strategic marketing plan should be set out in detail in writing and it must be easily available for concerned members of the organisation to consult. It should be consulted often to ensure that it remains relevant.

This chapter has presented the strategic marketing process applied to the tourism industry and has explained some of the techniques that are used in developing a strategic marketing plan. The marketing of travel and tourism products is continually evolving because of pressures from trends in the industry. Part 2 considers some of the most important issues and trends in contemporary tourism marketing.

REFERENCES AND FURTHER READING

American Frontier Motorcycle Tours Inc., web site advertising (accessed autumn 1998) http://www.americanfrontiermc.com/, P.O. Box 29241, Santa Fe, New Mexico, 87592, USA

Ansoff, I. (1968) *Corporate Strategy*, Penguin: Harmondsworth.

Assael, H (1987) *Consumer Behaviour and Marketing Action*, 3rd edn, Wadsworth: California.

Aumann, R. J. and Hart, S. (1992) *Handbook of Game Theory With Economic Applications* (Handbooks in Economics, No. 11), Elsevier Science: North Holland.

Bailey, K.D. (1994) *Methods of Social Research*, 4th edn, Free Press, New York.

Baker, M. (1992) *Marketing Strategy and Management*, 2nd edn, Macmillan: London.

Blum, M. *International Herald Tribune* 15 March, 1997 and Giles, C., the *Seattle Times*, 30 July, 1996, Articles on the Development of Irish Pubs Around the World.

Bowman, C. (1992) Charting Competitive Strategy, in D. Faulkner and G. Johnson (eds) *The Challenge of Strategic Management*, Kogan Page: London.

Bradley, F. (1995) *International Marketing Strategy*, Prentice Hall: Hemel Hempstead.

Brakenbury, M. (1997) IFTO's Perspective on Holidays to the Mediterranean. Paper presented to the seminar Tourism in the Mediterranean, University of Westminster, December.

BTA Marketing Guide, Market Guides 1995, British Tourist Authority: London.

Burke, J. F. and Resnick, B.P. (1991) *Marketing and Selling the Travel Product*, South Western Publishing: Cincinnati.

Butler, R. (1980) 'The concept of a tourist area life cycle: implications for management of resources', *Canadian Geographer*, **24**: 5–12.

Cahill, J., Senior Vice-President, Information Technology, InterContinental Hotels and Resorts. Paper presented at the International Hotel and Restaurants Association Congress in 1998, the Impact for Hotels of the New Marketing Revolution.

Campbell, A., Devine, M., and Young, D. (1990) *A Sense of Mission*, Financial Times/Pitman Press: London.

Canada News Wire, Air Canada Press Release: Air Canada Develops Self Check-in for Airports, Focuses on Technology to Simplify Travel Experience, http://www. newswire.ca/ April 1, 1998.

Cooper, C., Fletcher, J., Gilbert, D. and Wanhill, S. (1993) *Tourism Principles and Practice,* Pitman: London.

Day, G. (1986) *Strategic Marketing Decisions*, West Publisher: USA.

Diamantis, D (1998) Ecotourism: Characteristics and Involvement Patterns of its Consumers in the UK, unpublished PhD Thesis, Bournemouth University.

Dibb, S. and Simkin, L. (1994) *The Marketing Casebook*, Routledge: London.

Doz, Y. and Prahalad, C.K. (1987) *The Multinational Mission*, Free Press: New York.

Drucker, P. (1968) *The Practice of Management*, Heinemann: London.

Farkas, C., de Backer, P. and Sheppard, A. (1995) *Maximum Leadership*, Orion: London.

Frank, R.R., Massy, R. and Wind, Y. (1972) *Market Segmentation*, Prentice Hall: Englewood Cliffs, NJ.

Gartner Group (1997) Glossary of Information Technology, Acronyms and Terms, Gartner Group: USA.

GSA's Business and Finance Information Page, Survey of Buyer Intentions, www.gsa.gov/commerce.htm , v.4, issue 81, 16 June–6 July 1998.

Hair, J., Anderson, R.E. and Tatham, R.L. (1987) *Multivariate Data Analysis,* 2nd edn, Macmillan: New York.

Hamal, G. and Prahalad, C.K. (1994) *Competing for the Future*, Harvard Business School Press: Boston.

Hammond, S. (1995) Introduction to multivariate data analysis, in G.M. Breakwell, S. Hammond and C. Fife-Schaw (eds) *Research Methods in Psychology*, Sage, London, pp. 360–85.

Havard Business School (1978) Club Méditerranée, HBS Case Services, Harvard Business School: Boston.

Hawaii Tourism Office web site http://www. hawaii.gov/tourism/library (accessed 1998).

Holloway, C.J. and Plant R.V. (1988) *Marketing for Tourism*, Pitman Publishing: London

Holloway, C.J. and Robinson, C. (1995) *Marketing for Tourism*, 3rd edn, Addison Wesley Longman: Harlow.

Journal of Vacation Marketing, (1998) Mood Marketing – The New Destination Branding Strategy: a Case Study of Wales the Brand, June, Henry Stewart Publications.

Koch, R. (1995) *Strategy*, Pitman: London.

Kotler, P. (1988) *Marketing Management: Analysis, Planning, Implementation and Control*, 6th edn, Prentice-Hall: New Jersey.

Lele, M. (1992) *Creating Strategic Leverage – Matching Company Strengths with Market Opportunity*, Wiley: New York.

Le Monde, (1998) Le Club Méditerranée Mise son Avenir sur la Qualité de sa Marque, Bostnavaron, F. and Rocco, A., 21 February.

McCarthy, E.J. (1978) *Basic Marketing: a Managerial Approach*, Irwin: Homewood, IL.

McDonald, M. (1995) *Marketing Plans – How to Prepare Them – How to Use Them*, Butterworth-Heinemann: Oxford.

Mintzberg, H. (1994) *The Rise and Fall of Strategic Planning*, The Free Press: New York.

Nalebuff, B.J. and Brandenburger, A.M. (1996) *Co-opetition*, HarperCollins Business: London.

Noorda, R. (1993) Electronic Business Buyer, in B.J. Nalebuff and A.M. Brandenburger (1996) *Co-opetition*, HarperCollins Business: London.

Palmer, A. and Hartley, B. (1996) *The Business and Marketing Environment*, Butterworth-Heinemann: Oxford.

Peters, T. (1988) *Thriving on Chaos*, Macmillan: London.

Poon, A. (1993) *Tourism, Technology and Competitive Strategies*, CAB: Oxford.

Porter, M. (1980) *Competitive Strategy: Techniques for Analyzing Industries and Competitors*, Free Press: New York.

Porter, M. (1985) *Competitive Advantage: Creating and Sustaining Superior Performance*, Free Press: New York.

Quiniquini, O. (1997) New Brands are Cheaper and Just as Cheerful. Forging New Ground: The Shangri-La's Group Trader's Hotel, Travel News Asia web site http://web3. asia1.com.sg/timesnet/navigatn/tna.html, October.

Richie, B. amd Crouch, G. (1993) Competitiveness in International Tourism: a Framework for Understanding and Analysis, unpublished paper, World Tourism Education and Research Centre, University of Calgary.

Ries, A. and Trout, J. (1981) *Positioning: The Battle for Your Mind*. McGraw-Hill: New York.

Riley, R., Baker, D. and Van Doren, C.S. (1998) Movie induced tourism, *Annals of Tourism Research* **25**(4): 919–35.

Ryan, C. (1995) *Researching Tourist Satisfaction: Issues, Concepts, Problems*, Routledge: London.

Seaton, A.V. and Bennett, M.M. (1996*) The Marketing of Tourism Products: Concepts, Issues and Cases*, International Thomson Business Press: London.

Surrey Research Group (1996) Pre-feasibility Study for an Education and Training Institute for Tourism and Hospitality Studies in Chile, unpublished consultancy report.

Terpstra, V. and Sarathy, R. (1991) *International Marketing*, 5th edn, Dryden Press: Orlando.

Thomas, M. (1980) 'Market segmentation', *Quartely Review of Marketing*, **6**(1): 22–8.

Tolhurst, C. (1998) Tourist Belt to Lead Australia, Arabian Travel Market Review, *Travel News Asia*, web site http://web3.asia1.com.sg/timesnet/indices/specrp98.html.

Tourism Victoria Internet Site, PO Box 2219T GPO Melbourne, Victoria , Australia 3001, (accessed 1998).

Travel Journal International, (1988) JTB Survey on Summer Travel , www.tjnet.co.jp, **21**(14).

Travel-log (1998) (Touriscope) Ageing Babyboomers and What it Means for Domestic Travel in the 21st Century **17**(3).

Westcott, K. (1998) Shell-shocked and Shattered, Beirut Rises from the Ashes, *The Times Weekend*, Saturday 8 August.

Williams, K.C. (1981) *Behavioural Aspects of Marketing*, Heinemann: London.

Woodside, A.G. (1982) Positioning a Province using travel research, *Journal of Tourism Research*, Winter, pp. 14–18.

PART 2

ISSUES AND TRENDS IN CONTEMPORARY TOURISM MARKETING

Section 2 presents trends that are affecting the way tourism is marketed now and will be in the future. As highlighted in Chapters 1 and 2, technology is changing our way of life and how we conduct business. Chapter 3 considers the impact of technology on tourism marketing.

Since the late 1980s, environmental awareness has become an important marketing factor in business. Tourism is inextricably linked with the environment and measures are taken to protect destinations and sites from the damage that tourism can bring. Chapter 4 describes 'green' initiatives in the tourism and hospitality sectors and analyses 'green' trends and 'green' marketing strategies.

Chapters 5 and 6 consider the human element of the tourism product: tourism employees. Chapter 5 explains how human resources strategies have become an important factor in tourism marketing, both for business and for tourism destinations. Chapter 6 examines service quality and the management of the service encounter and stresses the importance of internal marketing.

CHAPTER 3 The impact of technology on tourism marketing, e-commerce and database marketing

CONTENTS

THE IMPACT OF TECHNOLOGY ON TOURISM MARKETING, E-COMMERCE AND DATABASE MARKETING

PHILIP ALFORD

What impact will technology have on future competitive strategy in the travel, tourism and hospitality industries? What sustainable strategic benefits can technology deliver? In attempting to answer these questions, this section will focus largely on the customer. In other words, how will technology be leveraged to add customer value, both within a business–consumer and business–business context?

Parsons (in Fletcher 1995: 143) identifies three ways in which IT can impact on an organisation's strategy:

- Low-cost leadership
- Product differentiation
- Concentration on market and product niche.

Parsons has borrowed from Porter (1985), who suggests that the three possible generic strategies available to an organisation are cost leadership, differentiation or focus strategy.

It is important to look at technological issues within a strategic context, especially as it is an area prone to much hype. At a Chartered Institute of Marketing Travel Industry Group (CIMTIG) seminar, hosted by British Telecommunications plc, on the role of new media in the travel industry, a BT presenter referred to the range of attitudes towards IT, held by people in an organisation. At one extreme you have 'Gadget Boy' who is likely to advocate the use of the latest technology, regardless of its predicted costs and benefits. This is the person most likely to be fuelling the hype. At the other end of the spectrum there is 'Stone Age Man' who, as the name suggests, is most likely to oppose the implementation of IT because of an innate hostility towards technology. As with most things the answer lies somewhere in the middle ground.

Before examining this middle ground and where IT can impact in the three areas identified above, it is useful to look at some trends in the adoption of technology, both by the consumer and business.

THE GROWTH OF E-COMMERCE

E-commerce is the latest buzzword to have developed as a result of the growth in electronic business. As testimony to the significance of e-commerce, United Airlines has a director of e-commerce. He was a speaker at one of the key tourism and technology conferences, 'Information Management for the Travel Industry', that took place in January 1999 in San Francisco (www.firstconf. com/travel). E-commerce was to occupy one of the four sessions and a glance at the questions and statements in the conference website reveals some of the issues which are likely to focus strategic thinking over the next few years. Can e-commerce help travel suppliers provide the services people want? Do intranets and extranets provide an alternative to existing GDSs (global distribution systems)? Does the traditional airline–GDS–agent relationship have a future? How to cut your company's distribution costs: United's experience. E-commerce to improve the effectiveness and reduce the cost of your marketing.

In order to whet the appetite of the prospective conference delegate, the publicity material (1998) asks the reader to consider these facts:

- In any one week, over 12 per cent of all adults in North America use the Internet. By the year 2000, Internet users will number around 200 million.
- 30 per cent of users access the Net for information about hotels and to make travel arrangements.
- Right now, 8 per cent are prepared to actually buy products on-line. That figure is set to increase rapidly.

Of course whether you embrace these figures or treat them with scepticism, will depend on where you are positioned on the 'stone-age man'/'gadget boy' continuum. The results of a survey conducted by Information Week, however, do indicate that e-commerce is growing (Connolly *et al.*, 1998). The 500 chief information officers who participated in the survey indicated that they spent, on average, 3 per cent of their 1996 information systems budgets on Internet and new media initiatives.

The growth in e-commerce has occurred as businesses realise that people use the Internet. In 1996 it was estimated that 34.8 million households in the US owned a personal computer, 21.6 million had a modem, and 15.1 million had Internet access. However it should be noted that estimates vary widely, ranging anywhere between nine million to 42 million users. ActivMedia estimated 1996 total Internet sales to be $436 million, while Forrester Research put the estimate at $518 million. The extent of these variations illustrates the difficulty in measuring the actual use of the Internet and the rate at which casual 'net surfers' convert into actual buyers. Estimates tend to focus on North American trends, thus reinforcing the opinion, held by some, that the Internet is essentially a US phenomenon. Recent UK figures, however, are similarly variable. An analyst with Salomon Brothers has suggested that more than 50 per cent of US airline sales will be sold through direct channels by the turn of the century, with a significant proportion through electronic distribution channels. This view contrasts with a forecast of 10 per cent of gross sales being spent on-line on flights in the UK by 2002 (Morrell, 1998).

The potential value of e-commerce becomes apparent when business–business transactions are considered. It is predicted that this area of e-commerce will grow from $1 billion in 1995 to $117 billion by 2000.

Travel is often singled out as one of the fastest growth areas of e-commerce. Jupiter Communications predicts that, by 2000, on-line travel bookings will account for approximately 5 to 7 per cent of total e-commerce, representing a figure as high as $6 billion. The value of e-commerce in the accommodation sector will grow from $345 million in 1997 to $2.9 billion by the year 2001, according to Forrester Research.

E-Commerce and Cost Reduction

Can electronic business enable organisations to reduce their costs and assist in the development of a cost leadership strategy? As Internet hysteria dies down, managers will increasingly question the return on e-commerce investment. Forrester Research estimates the average cost of developing and maintaining a web site at $300,000. Development costs for sites capable of electronic booking averages between $840,000 and $1.3 million. A significant portion of this involves staffing costs. Furthermore, the ongoing costs are difficult to project (Connolly, 1998). Questions asked are likely to include the following. What is the distribution share per channel? What is the cost of a reservation per distribution channel and per market segment?

The Corporate Market

One of the growth areas is corporate e-commerce. The corporate electronic booking system jointly developed by Microsoft and American Express now has 60 users in the USA and, although this is a small proportion of total corporate travel, there is evidence that corporate e-commerce is a growth area. Business travellers spend up to one hour planning their travel and accommodation arrangements for each trip. The number of business travellers, as a percentage of total employees, is up 6 per cent from 1994 to 1997 (Connolly *et al.*, 1998). A survey of UK business passengers in 1996, estimated that 25 per cent were connected to the Internet, and that this figure would rise to 60 per cent by 2000 (Morrell, 1998). The development of corporate intranets, which give employees access to specially negotiated rates, not available elsewhere, is set to be a growth area.

Disintermediation

In the corporate market, e-commerce is viewed as a means of disintermediating the booking process, in other words cutting out the traditional agency role. It is argued that this brings responsibility for corporate travel in-house, thereby providing more flexibility and, ultimately, cost savings. Wardell (1998) claims, however, that there is insufficient market-based data to support the claims made by the advocates of e-commerce. He claims that corporations have not accurately costed the time involved in corporate personnel, whose time is likely to be more expensive than agency staff, making their own travel arrangements. This must be factored in when measuring the benefits of disintermediation.

For example, Charles Schwab estimate that the time involved in arranging each business trip costs the company between $55 and $60. By using the Internet, they expect to reduce this time from about one hour to 15 minutes and the cost to $18. Texas Instruments expects to save up to $11 million by providing access to the Internet Travel Network for its 400 most frequent travellers.

Despite these detailed figures, in general terms most organisations are not able to accurately measure return on their Internet investment.

Customer Focus

Organisations will often cite competitive differentiation as one way of justifying investment in e-commerce. For example, British Midland was the first UK airline to provide a complete on-line booking service. This positioned them at the forefront of technology and, in the consumer's opinion, as a technologically advanced airline. Knowing who their customers are, however, will enable organisations to make more informed investment decisions. For example, by understanding their customer base, Southwest Airlines realised that they required a presence on only one of the GDSs, namely, Sabre.

The demise of travel agents and the growth of e-commerce are often linked. There is little evidence, however, to support the notion that customers are happy to replace a visit or telephone call to the travel agent with on-line booking. Only 16 per cent of business passengers in the UK said they would use the World Wide Web for on-line bookings (Morrell, 1998). This is likely to be a result of the high cost of the user's time. It would probably be more cost-effective to give the task to a specialist. This relationship between time and cost is set to assume increasing importance for companies in the future. It would be unwise for the enthusiastic web site designer to assume that the corporate customer will be happy to spend hours arranging his travel on an Internet site. For example, United Airlines' electronic booking system, United Connection, accesses the Apollo computer reservation system through the Internet. The site requests a customer profile, which is a useful means of providing the user with the right service. The entire registration process, however, has to be repeated each time there is even a minor change to the profile. A United Airlines flight schedule will always appear on screen with the other schedules matching the profile, regardless of the fact that the United schedule will often result in a combination of flights that the customer is unlikely to use, and which do not match his requirements. The Internet enquiry and booking service should add value to the customer's experience in the form of more convenience, better quality information, and time and cost savings.

CUSTOMER PROFILING

In addition to poor image quality on the Internet, advertisers complain about the lack of good-quality demographic information on the users of web sites. Increasingly, this is being addressed with the web site registration process. This author recently acquired a copy of the free Internet-access provider, Freeserve, from the high street retailer, Dixons. The software could not be loaded until a range of personal information, including age, income, education and interests, had been submitted during the registration process.

Customer profiles will become an important strategic tool in the future. TravelWeb is one of the largest clearing houses for hotel bookings via the GDSs and the Internet. Recent statistics, published by the company, give an indication of the range of customer data which is available (Connolly *et al.*, 1998: 43):

- the ratio of male to female users is 3.3 to 1
- 14 per cent are executives
- 33 per cent are between the ages of 31 and 40
- 68.5 per cent use TravelWeb from home versus 28.6 per cent from work
- 78 per cent request no-smoking rooms
- the majority book at least one month in advance
- 59 per cent book two guests per room versus 35 per cent who book only one guest per room
- 75 per cent reside in the United States.

This provides some useful demographic and behavioural data, but does not provide the depth of information necessary for detailed target marketing. At present, it is difficult to distinguish between the early adopters and the longer term e-commerce consumer. Strategically, this is an important distinction to make if companies are to invest in e-commerce in the longer term. According to Wardell (1998), there is a specific market which should be targeted for e-commerce. Companies must build accurate profiles of these customers and pursue a proactive strategy to get them on-line.

A more in-depth understanding of the behaviour of this segment would also enable companies to develop a more integrated distribution strategy, where different channels could be used to complement each other. For example, if there is some unused capacity to be sold, a company could use telemarketing or email to inform the customer that last minute bargains are available on the web site. The real-time advantage of the Internet is then used to maximum effect and the customer feels that he is being offered a personal service.

DATABASE MARKETING

Companies now realise that capturing, storing and analysing customer data can provide them with a competitive strategic advantage. The growing power of relational database technology is driving this trend forward. It is difficult to measure the size of the market, because of the number of components involved. A 1996 estimate, from the Direct Marketing Association, values the whole UK market at £4.5 billion. Direct mail is probably the only fully documented sector, worth £1.1 billion in 1995, according to the Direct Mail Information Service (Mintel, 1996). This database technology is fuelling the growth of new marketing paradigms, variously referred to as, 'one-to-one marketing', 'relationship marketing', or 'micro-marketing'. Whatever the term, it is generally accepted that mass marketing is no longer appropriate and that more targeted marketing, involving a customer database, is required. In this section, this form of marketing will be addressed as database marketing, which can be defined as:

An interactive approach to marketing, which uses individually addressable marketing media and channels (such as mail, telephone, and the sales force):

● To extend help to a company's target audience
● To stimulate their demand
● To stay close to them by recording and keeping an electronic database memory of customer, prospect and all communication and commercial contacts, to help improve all future contacts and to ensure more realistic planning of all marketing. (Shaw and Stone, 1988: 3)

Computer Modelling

Opperman (1997) identifies three main objectives of database marketing: customer retention, product promotion and customer creation. His research reveals three potential levels at which database marketing in tourism organisations is practised: basic, applied and advanced. For example, in the area of customer creation, perhaps more commonly referred to as customer acquisition, it is the availability of increasingly sophisticated computer modelling techniques that separates the applied and advanced levels. At the applied level, managers establish, a priori, customer profiles based on inputting a number of variables which they believe are key to purchasing behaviour. At the advanced level, mathematical algorithms are developed, using regression modelling, to search large datasets. Often referred to as predictive modelling, this method identifies variables which are most likely to predict future buying behaviour and can develop a customer profile most likely to produce a better return on marketing investment. This is a labour-saving method which can identify segments the manager may not have even realised existed.

Similar techniques can be used to score customers, according to where they are positioned on the loyalty ladder: advocate, customer, prospect, suspect. This enables marketing resources to be allocated accordingly.

Testing

The ability to test is commonly cited as a key advantage of database marketing. For example, a marketing manager can track responses and conversion rates from two separate small-scale advertising campaigns, prior to national roll out. The database manager could build small cells of customers from different segments and test several customer lists, creative approaches and offers at the same time. The key to testing is effective tracking. This is facilitated with the allocation of codes to each different marketing variable to be analysed.

The database can also be used to test the development of new products and markets. Page & Moy Holidays, a leading direct sell operator in the UK, used this to good effect when it analysed the responses to a press campaign advertising a packaged tour to China. This was new territory to the company, both in geographic and product-type terms. The analysis revealed a customer profile quite different from that traditionally attracted by the company. As a result Page & Moy Holidays subsequently developed a promotional mix based around the needs of this target market.

The growth in database marketing, allied with the advances in digital print, digital television and video production technology, will lead to the demise of the mass mailing and an increase in one-to-few marketing. In the travel trade, this will result in the development of personalised holiday itineraries. Tauck Tours, a US operator already targets the UK market in this fashion. It would be a fallacy, however, to assume that database marketing is applicable in all cases. Deborah Merrifield, Head of Relationship Marketing at Thomson Holidays, acknowledges that it would not be cost-effective to use direct mail on one of their core mass products. She reserves the use of database marketing for niche products with more differentiation, such as the 'Thomson Weddings in Paradise' product or 'Thomson Gold' product, aimed at the couples market (Direct Response 1998: 20). The price-conscious mass tourist will still be looking for the best price. Technology will also favour this type of consumer in the future with the development of 'smart agents' – software which will search the Internet for the product which best fits the customer's pre-specified requirements.

The power of the technology, however, still outstrips the know-how and resources of the manager and the growth in database marketing will only happen as fast as the economic returns can be proven.

REFERENCES AND FURTHER READING

Connolly, D., Olsen, M. and Moore, R. (1998) 'The internet as a distribution channel', *Cornell Hotel and Restaurant Administration Quarterly*, August.

Direct Response (1998) Interview with Deborah Merrifield of Thomson Holidays, **18**(7): July.

Fletcher, K. (1995) *Marketing Management and Information Technology*, 2nd edn, Prentice-Hall: Hemel Hempstead.

Mintel (1996) *Database Marketing*, January.

Morrell, P. (1998) 'Airline sales and distribution channels: the impact of new technology', *Tourism Economics*, **4**(1): 5–19.

Opperman, M. (1997) 'Using databased marketing in the tourism industry – gaining competitive advantage', *Turizam*, **45**(1–2): 13–28.

Porter, M. (1985) *Competitive Advantage*. Free Press: New York.

Shaw, R. and Stone, M. (1988) *Database Marketing*, Gower: Aldershot.

Wardell, D. (1998) 'The impact of electronic distribution on travel agents', *Travel and Tourism Analyst*, 2.

CHAPTER 4   'Green' strategies in the tourism and hospitality industries

CONTENTS

4 'GREEN' STRATEGIES IN THE TOURISM AND HOSPITALITY INDUSTRIES

DIMITRIOS DIAMANTIS AND ADELE LADKIN

GREEN STRATEGIC ISSUES IN TOURISM AND HOSPITALITY

This chapter will examine green strategic issues affecting tourism and hospitality from three perspectives. It will first provide an overview of the sector where a number of initiatives will be discussed. Then, it will outline green trends with particular reference to the significance of environmental indicators and environmental auditing. And finally, green marketing strategies such as green alliances in the tourism and hospitality sectors will be presented.

OVERVIEW OF GREEN INITIATIVES IN THE TOURISM AND HOSPITALITY SECTORS

'Green' or environmental issues became popular during the early 1980s (Berry and Ladkin, 1997). The highlight of this decade was the launch of the Brundtland Report (WCED, 1987) which established and popularised the concept of sustainability. The report declared that sustainable development is an important issue as it aims 'to meet the needs of the present without comprising the ability of future generations to meet their own needs' (WCED, 1987, 43).

At the beginning of the 1990s, a United Nation's conference in Rio de Janeiro introduced a sustainable plan for nations – Agenda 21. This also led to the establishment of a Sustainable Development Commission to monitor the progress of the nations towards sustainability. In 1997, the United Nations reassessed the Rio commitments and evaluated the efforts of the world's industries. These green initiatives created a variety of responses from the tourism and hospitality sectors around the world.

Green Initiatives in the Tourism Sector

In the tourism sector, responses revolved around the concepts of sustainable tourism development and sustainable tourism. Sustainable tourism development focuses on the 'management of all resources in such a way that we can fulfil economic, social, and aesthetic needs, while maintaining cultural integrity, essential ecological processes, biological diversity and life support systems' (Tourism Canada cited in Murphy, 1994: 279).

Defining sustainable tourism is more complex. Many practitioners use this term to describe a form of development, but also 'green' products such as adventure tourism, soft tourism and eco-tourism. These days it would appear that sustainable tourism is a term used to categorise all green tourism products.

Sustainable development according to the World Tourism Organisation (WTO) involves upgrading the quality of life of the local population, providing tourists with a quality experience, and supporting the environmental resources which the tourism system consumes (WTO, 1993, 1997). As a result, the WTO explains that sustainable development must be based on developing a relationship between the tourism industry, environmental supporters and the community (WTO, 1993). This relationship encompass three main principles of sustainable development (WTO, 1993: 10; Mowforth and Munt, 1998: 105–11):

1. *Ecological sustainability* – development that is compatible with the maintenance of essential ecological processes, biological diversity, and biological resources.
2. *Social and cultural sustainability* – development that increases people's control over their lives, that is compatible with the culture and values of people affected by it, and that maintains and strengthens community identity.
3. *Economic sustainability* – development that is economically efficient, with managed resources that can support future generations.

Agenda 21 for travel and tourism (WTO/WTTC/EC, 1995) provides another framework for sustainable development. It outlines twelve guiding principles for sustainable tourism development, nine action steps for the public sector and ten priority areas for the private sector (see Table 4.1). The general principles outlined in the document are applicable at different levels, with a particular focus on the local level. They suggest that tourism products must contain sustainable elements and that the public sector has the responsibility of ensuring progress towards achieving sustainable development.

The European Community's Fifth Action Programme – 'Towards Sustainability' – targets five main sectors, one of which is tourism. Very briefly, the programme advances the concept of *'shared responsibility'* based on three strategies (EC, 1995):

1. reporting the pressures and effects of tourism on the environment
2. emphasising awareness campaigns in order to promote the environmentally friendly use of tourism resources, including modes of transport to and from tourist resorts
3. promoting the implementation of innovative good sustainable tourism development practices.

Table 4.1   The guiding principles for tourism – Agenda 21

1. Travel and tourism assist people in leading healthy and productive lives in harmony with nature

2. Tourism should contribute to the conservation, protection and restoration of the Earth's ecosystem

3. Travel and tourism should be based upon sustainable patterns of production and consumption

4. Nations should co-operate to promote an open economic system in which international trade in travel and tourism services can take place on a sustainable basis

5. Protectionism in trade in Travel and Tourism services should be halted or reversed

6. Tourism, peace, development and environmental protection are interdependent

7. In order to achieve sustainable development, environmental protection shall constitute an integral part of the tourism development process

8. Tourism development issues should be handled with the participation of concerned citizens, with planning decisions being adopted at local level

9. Nations shall warn one another of natural disasters that could affect tourists or tourist areas

10. Since the full participation of women is necessary to achieve sustainable development advantage should be taken of travel and tourism's capacity to create employment for women

11. Tourism development should recognise and support the identity, culture and interests of indigenous peoples

12. International laws protecting the environment should be respected by the world-wide travel and tourism industry

Source: WTO/WTTC/EC, 1995.

These strategies are further developed in the 'Green Paper on Tourism' (EC, 1995) which focuses on creating a positive relationship between economic development and ecology. The paper maintains that the attractiveness of tourism destinations and the economic basis of tourism depend on the conservation and management of natural and cultural resources. It focuses on (EC, 1995):

1. tourist well-being
2. the protection of resources
3. the impulse for growth and more competitive organisations
4. the assessment of costs of tourism's usage of resources.

Several EC countries have now carried out environmental impact studies, formulated codes of good practice and introduced environmental laws (see Table 4.2).

Table 4.2   **Examples of environmental actions at the European Community level**

Member States*	Environmental actions
Netherlands	Studies in forest areas
	Creation of buffer zones around mass tourism areas
	Regular land use plans for decision making
	Environmental impact assessment is required for tourism development projects
Portugal	Studies in national parks
	Studies on tourism impacts on the environment
	Specific land use plans for sensitive environmental areas
Germany	Creation of buffer zones around mass tourism areas
	Environmental impact assessment required for tourism development projects
	Codes of conduct
Sweden	Creation of buffer zones around mass tourism areas
Spain	All coastal zone areas are involved in environmental assessment studies
Finland	Environmental impact assessment is required for tourism development projects
United Kingdom	'Tourism and the Environment: Maintaining the Balance' report
	'Common Inheritance' report
	Environmental indicators studies
	Tourism towards sustainability studies

* Other green initiatives can be seen on the site of the World Travel and Tourism Council, known as ECONETT. The site's address is: www.wttc.org

Green Initiatives in the Hospitality Sector

Environmentally conscious management has been incorporated in the business strategies of many hospitality firms, yet some still have the misguided preconception that their company is immune to environmental problems.

Several organisations such as the Hotel Catering and International Management Association (HCIMA), the International Hotels Environment Initiative (IHEI), Green Globe, and local authorities have recognised the hospitality industry's role in contributing to the protection of the environment. They aim to encourage and upgrade the global performance of the industry, and they often act in unison to achieve these objectives. Notably, they provide guidance in achieving environmental commitment, regularly publishing informative literature in newsletters, and commending environmental successes within the industry (*Green Hotelier*, 1997).

Green Globe is a world-wide environmental management and awareness programme for the travel and tourism industry (Green Globe, 1995). In 1998, Green Globe had 577 members in 107 countries. It assists companies in developing their own environmental programmes. Usually, hospitality initiatives tend to either focus on the minimisation of consumption levels, or on environmental audits which control the performance of hotel operation (see Box 4.1).

Environmental standards manuals form an integral part of the commitment adopted by corporate hotel groups such as the Holiday Inn Hotel Group, Hilton International and Intercontinental Hotels. The Intercontinental Hotels Group regularly monitors the environmental performance of all its hotels through 'environmental audits', and sets targets for each of its participating hotel managers to achieve. In order to ensure that the manual is used, the environmental performance of managers is tied into their performance appraisal. The underlying principle behind these practices is to minimise environmental damage by targeting not only regular guests but also green consumers – an increasing segment of the Intercontinental's target market.

BOX 4.1

EXAMPLES OF GREEN INITIATIVES IN THE HOSPITALITY SECTOR

Countries | **Environmental actions**
Denmark | **Green Key scheme by the Danish Hotel Association:**

40 hotels are currently members of this scheme, all of which have to fulfil 55 environmental criteria. Essential qualifications include:

1. providing information for guests about Green Key

2. limiting water and electricity consumption

3. using eco-friendly detergent

4. waste separation at source

5. no-smoking rooms

6. provision of at least two organic products at breakfast.

USA — **Good Earthkeeping cards:**

The American Hotel and Motel Association and the US Environmental Protection Agency produce in-room guest cards to promote water and energy conservation.
The card has the following message:

PLEASE UNDERSTAND

■ As a new guest, your towels are freshly laundered.

BOX 4.1 (cont'd)

■ As part of our commitment to the environment, we offer you the option of reusing your towels.

YOU DECIDE

■ A towel on the rack or hook means 'I'll reuse.'

■ A towel NOT on the rack or hook means 'Please replace.'

Sweden   **Chefs for the Environment:**

This is a network of around 200 members ranging from restaurants, food manufacturers and retailers. The aim of this scheme is to enhance the environmental awareness of their members, by communicating Information on environmental issues and practice.

Green Consumerism

As the general public's awareness of the problems facing the world's natural resources increases and their understanding of green issues develops, more and more consumers are demanding improvements in the environmental performance of products and companies. There now exists a consumer group that is genuinely concerned about how lifestyles affect the environment. These consumers are known as *green consumers*. Various attempts have been made by academics, advertising agencies, and market researchers to develop typologies of green consumers, segmenting them into different shades of green. Remarkably much of the data described in the many research reports that have been published appears to be contradictory.

The public is concerned about environmental issues but there is an *attitude–behaviour gap*. Although consumers state their willingness to spend more on green products (attitude) and companies respond to these demands, these same consumers later claim that green products are too expensive (behaviour). Several reasons have been put forward to explain the attitude–behaviour gap (Robers, 1996: 218):

1. Green products are expensive.
2. Consumer priorities mainly concern price, quality, and convenience.
3. Consumers are often confused by the variety of green products.
4. Businesses hesitate to offer green products because of strict requirements imposed either by law and/or by associations and consumer groups.
5. Consumers often disagree with businesses that *'overmarket'* green products.

In 1989, British consumers were asked in a survey to indicate the most important problems facing their country. They placed concern about the environment on top of the list. By 1992, environmental concern had fallen to fourth position –

with just eleven per cent of respondents selecting the environment as top priority. By 1996, this had fallen to a mere three per cent of consumers polled (see Table 4.3). This shows that the environment is much less of a daily concern for most British adults than unemployment, health care and law and order.

Table 4.3   **The most important problems facing Britain (per cent)**

Issues	1989	1992	1996
Unemployment	24	62	44
Health Care	29	28	34
Law and Order	16	16	22
Environment	35	11	3

Source: Martin/MORI, 1997.

In the USA, a recent survey indicated that 79 per cent of the public describe themselves as environmentalists, 82 per cent participate in recycling activities and 83 per cent said that they would be prepared to change their shopping habits if it meant protecting the environment (Robers, 1996). In 1988, Eurobarometer carried out a survey on general attitudes in the European Community ('The Europeans and their Environment'), and found that in the UK, 67 per cent thought that pollution and environmental damage were urgent and immediate problems, compared with 74 per cent for the EC as a whole. Twenty-five per cent of respondents in the UK thought that environmental pollution was a problem for the future compared with 20 per cent for the EC.

In June 1992, MORI conducted a survey of businesses in Great Britain, France and Spain about their concerns for the future. 'Protecting the environment' was selected by 62 per cent of French firms, 49 per cent of British firms, and 45 per cent of Spanish firms.

The Hospitality Green Consumer

To date, little research has been conducted on green consumerism in the hospitality sector. The link between lifestyle and the environment have not been properly researched and little is known about the consumer of green hotel products. In particular, research in the 'attitude–behaviour' gap needs to be carried out. However, the few surveys concentrating on consumer attitudes towards the environment and hospitality products that have been undertaken and have revealed a demand for green products in hospitality industry (see Box 4.2) and a concern about environmental practices.

Knowles *et al.* (1998) explain that although there have been few examples of environmental good practice in the hotel sector, many hotels now recognise that environmental problems exist, and in future, hotel groups are likely to take a more proactive stance on protecting the environment.

BOX 4.2

THE HOTEL GREEN CONSUMERS IN SELECTED SURVEYS

Surveys

Le Meridien

Results

Between the months of August and October 1994, 413 hotels around the world participated in an environmental survey, each polling 100 guests who were asked the following questions:

Do you feel concerned with environmental preservation?:

- 81.3 per cent of the respondents answered positively.

Would you give a preference to hotels conducting an Environment Preservation Plan?

- Of those who answered 'yes' to the previous question, 69.8 per cent said 'yes', and of *all* respondents 56.8 per cent said 'yes'.

An additional study was targeted at Le Meridien's 200 best customers drawn from the Carte Noire (loyal Meridien guests) database:

- 83.3 per cent were concerned with environment preservation, with 58 per cent of these respondents giving preference to hotels conducting an Environment Preservation Plan;
- Of *all* respondents, 48.3 per cent would choose hotels with Environment Preservation Plans.

Lodging hospitality magazine and Virginia Polytechnic Institute and State University

In 1995, a survey of 489 travellers passing through two airports, expressed their views on hotels and the environment. The major findings were:

- 70 per cent said that they were likely or extremely likely to stay in a hotel with a proactive environmental strategy;
- 26 per cent said it didn't matter to them, while less than 3 per cent seemed to be against the idea of environmental considerations in a hotel;
- 42 per cent said the efforts to help conserve resources in a hotel can produce long-term benefits, yet most respondents believed hotels have a strong obligation to conserve resources;
- 91 per cent of respondents believed that hotels should use energy efficient lighting where possible; and
- 86 per cent felt that hotels should provide recycling bins for guest use.

TRENDS IN THE GREEN SECTOR

Trends in the green sector tend to revolve around the formulation of methodologies to measure the sustainability performance of both destinations and organisations.

Green strategies in tourism have been charged with being extremely 'tourism-centric' and ignoring the principles of sustainability. The formulation of methodologies that measure the progress towards sustainability is one of the greatest challenges. This can be achieved with the use of environmental indicators and environmental auditing at both destination and organisation level.

Environmental Indicators

Sustainability levels can be evaluated using *environmental indicators*. Environmental indicators are instrumental tools for measuring environmental performance. They provide an essential component to assess progress towards sustainability (Diamantis and Westlake, 1997; Diamantis, 1998, 1999).

Although environmental indicators are still at an early stage, there is evidence that they are core elements in the measurement of sustainability (Macnaghten *et al.*, 1997). The environmental indicators available to practitioners include:

1. *Indicators of environmental pressure* which measure the impact on the environment caused by human actions.
2. *Indicators of environmental conditions* which focus on the qualitative and quantitative aspects of natural resources as well as to the quality elements of the environment.
3. *Response indicators* which assess society's response and concern for the environment.
4. *Policy performance indicators* which are the means of providing a normative indication of the whole destination's contribution to reducing negative environmental impacts (OECD, 1994: 9).

The World Tourism Organisation (WTO) has also carried out research into sustainable tourism indicators. It concludes that there are two main types of indicators (WTO, 1995):

1. *Core indicators*: Tourism demand-driven indicators such as site protection, waste management and use intensity;
2. *Destination specific indicators*: Indicators related to different ecosystems and site-specific management issues.

Macnaghten *et al.* (1997: 152) suggest that there are three stages to achieve the desired the level of sustainability (see Figure 4.1):

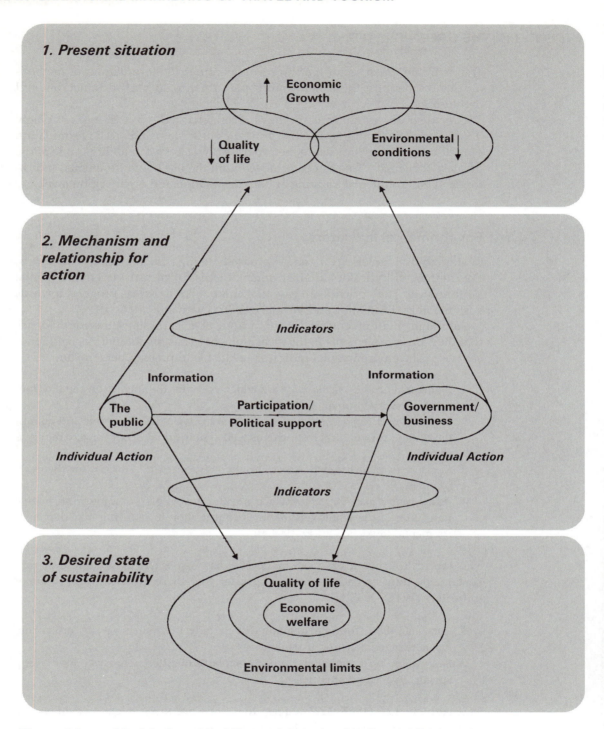

Figure 4.1   Model of sustainability and the role of indicators (Macnaghten *et al.*, 1997: 152)

1. the present situation is assessed
2. new mechanisms and relationships for action are developed based on environmental indicators to maintain the current position
3. based on further indicator studies, government and business actions are devised to achieve a desired level of sustainability.

Although the model relies on very broad principles, it summarises effectively the implications of sustainability. Using this approach, the concept of sustainability becomes more of an adaptive paradigm rather than merely focusing on issues and definitions.

Environmental Auditing

Environmental auditing is a management technique that monitors actual and potential environmental impacts of tourism organisations and destinations. It is

> A management tool comprising a systematic, documented, periodic and objective evaluation of how well environmental organisation, management and equipment are performing with an aim of helping to safeguard the environment by:
>
> 1. facilitating management control of environmental practices;
> 2. assessing compliance with the company policies, which would include meeting regulatory requirements. (UNEP/IEO, 1989: 100)

Over the last ten years, many companies have conducted environmental audits to reduce the environmental impacts of their activities. More specifically, environmental auditing provides the following benefits. It:

1. identifies areas that cause pollution and so that preventative action can be put in place
2. provides information about environmental conditions
3. targets resources and measures their progress
4. establishes environmental training programmes
5. allows management to give credit based on environmental achievement
6. increases the overall level of environmental awareness.

Environmental auditing targets resources by measuring their progress. At the strategic level, environmental auditing techniques should be incorporated into methodologies for measuring sustainability. The crucial task facing destination authorities is to continuously monitor impacts by measuring sustainability. The outcome of this process can provide strategies for the green sector based on actual results and policies rather than on short-term actions aimed at reducing specific environmental impacts. Hence, strategies can be devised to reflect the performance of environmental indicators. These can also assist the formulation of methodologies for another technique, that of environmental auditing.

Environmental auditing can be used by service firms to provide *'benchmarks'*. Benchmarking allows organisations to compare their practices with those of competitors. It requires them to compare the performance of all aspects of their operations to achieve standards of excellence.

Although environmental protection constitute a great responsibility with financial and management implications, the environment deserves strategies that will secure its long-term attractiveness, rather than strategies that merely maintain profit levels. The need to implement environmental auditing and indicator methodologies in the future is clearly a necessity.

GREEN STRATEGIES

All businesses, large and small, damage the environment and consequently they must take responsibility for protecting the earth's natural resources. Organisation and destinations need to protect the resources on which the tourism and hospitality industries rely from environmental damage by developing green strategies (see Table 4.4).

Table 4.4   **The green strategies of destinations and organisations**

Green Strategies of Organisations	Green Strategies of Destinations
■ Strategies to enhance the quality of life	■ Strategies to enhance the quality of life
■ Strategies to minimise environmental impacts, that is, pollution, waste	■ Strategies to minimise environmental impacts, that is, pollution, waste
■ Strategies to enhance consumer education	■ Strategies to enhance consumer education
■ Strategies for intangible products	■ Strategies for intangible experiences
■ Strategies to enhance portfolio growth	■ Strategies to enhance portfolio protection
■ Promotional strategies	■ Promotional strategies
■ Strategies for customer satisfaction and the interests of society	■ Strategies for customer satisfaction, the interests of society and the welfare of the natural environment
■ Strategies to increase sales	■ Strategies to increase tourist arrivals
	■ Strategies to minimise the social and ecological costs of large visitor numbers

At the Organisation Level

When green issues came to prominence, some tourism and hospitality companies adopted green strategies and made a commitment to protect the environment (see Table 4.4). However, the process an organisation undergoes to become 'green' requires a number of stages. Peattie (1995: 126) refers to Hunt and Auster (1991) who claim that there are five levels of commitment:

1. *Beginner*: organisations with a low financial commitment – lack of environmental programmes and little or no involvement by management.
2. *Fire fighter*: organisations with ad hoc project funding – no formal environmental programmes and little formal involvement by management.
3. *Concerned citizen*: organisations with a small budget – environmental programmes reflect corporate responsibility and management is involved in theory.
4. *Pragmatist*: organisations with an adequate environmental budget – policies and management are involved to minimise environmental impact.
5. *Proactivist*: organisations with an unlimited budget – policies and management are actively involved to minimise environmental impact.

Today, tourism and hospitality organisations fall into the first four categories (Beginner to Pragmatist). Few companies that are truly proactive, and those that are, are mostly large corporations such as British Airways. Knowles *et al.* (1998) found in a survey of London hotels that 94 per cent of the hotels that responded took some actions to protect the environment or pursued environmental strategies. These strategies were based on the three 'R's:

● **R**educing pollution or emissions
● **R**ecycling materials
● **R**eusing resources if possible.

However, only 19 per cent of the hotels questioned had an environmental policy and just 50 per cent of these publicised their initiatives to their guest (Knowles *et al.*, 1998). The survey concluded that hotel groups tend to be 'responsive' to environmental demands rather than 'responsible' (Knowles *et al.*, 1998).

In theory, the green strategic management process follows a number of steps, from environmental and resources analysis to strategic implementation (see Figure 4.2).

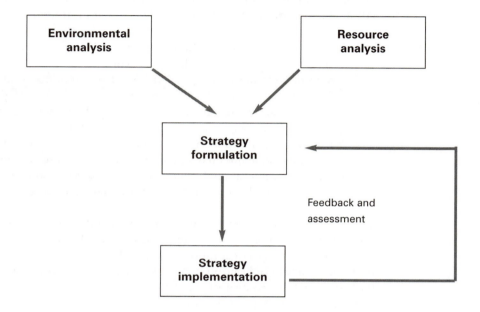

Environmental scanning
Value-chain assessment: environmental auditing
Competitor analysis: sector-wide greening
Ecological aspects of corporate environment
Regulatory assessment

Intergenerational effects
Distribution and extent of costs and benefits
Continual environmental auditing

Figure 4.2   The green strategic management process (Smith, 1992)

In practice, it seems that organisations pursue four main strategies:

1. repositioning existing products as green products
2. changing existing products so that they are less damaging to the environment
3. developing new enterprises that deal with green products and targeting green consumers
4. integrating environmental practices in every aspect of the organisation's operation.

In general, companies mostly follow the first two strategies. Tour operators reposition products, for instance by converting 'mass' tourism packages so that they are perceived as 'eco-tourism' packages. Some hotels transform their existing products by applying the three 'R's technique. Only a few companies adopt the last two approaches: developing new enterprises focused on green products or integrating environmental practices in every aspect of their organisation (see Boxes 4.3 and 4.4).

BOX 4.3

BRITISH AIRWAYS – GREEN STRATEGIES

British Airways (BA)
British Airways first published an environmental annual report in 1991. Its environmental department applies an environmental management system to all aspects of the organisation. A thorough examination of the firm's sustainable development practices is conducted through regular environmental audits. BA has pioneered environmental audits in certain destinations such as the Seychelles.

BA rewards the environmental achievement of its employees each year and it sponsors other initiatives such as the Tourism for Tomorrow award for tourism firms that have developed successful environmental projects. BA concentrates on five main areas:

■ Noise

■ Emissions to atmosphere, fuel efficiency and energy

■ Waste, water and materials

■ Congestion

■ Tourism and conservation.

BOX 4.4

GRECOTEL – GREEN STRATEGIES

Grecotel
Grecotel is the largest hotel company in Greece with 22 hotels in the four- and five-star categories. In 1992, Grecotel became the first hotel group in the Mediterranean to establish an environmental and culture department. This department deals with the following issues:

■ Creation of environmental policies

■ Staff information and training

BOX 4.4 (cont'd)

GRECOTEL – GREEN STRATEGIES

- Encouraging suppliers to produce eco-friendly products
- Regular environmental audits monitoring and documentation
- Creation of an environmental code of conduct in company purchasing policy
- Successful recycling and energy efficiency activities such as 78 per cent reduction of aluminium usage, 50 per cent reduction of glass consumption, and 30 per cent reduction of water consumption
- Creation of a computerised energy saving control system
- Since 1997, the complete discontinuation of plastic disposable glasses, cups and plates has been achieved in all Grecotels
- Promotion of Greek and local products: in 1997, 52.3 per cent of total cheese consumption in the 16 Grecotels was from various Greek producers. The balance was made up of 14 different varieties of European cheese.

Over the last few years, marketing-led strategies that boast environmental concern without taking any real action have backfired, resulting in negative publicity. Consumers have become suspicious of such products, especially those that refer to alternative forms of tourism and eco-tourism. This has deterred many firms from trading green products or from using green products as strategic tools.

Green marketing should be based on market-led strategies rather than marketing-led strategies where 'green' alliances provide the backbone of the strategic effort.

Green Marketing

Green or environmental marketing is the holistic management process responsible for identifying, anticipating and satisfying the requirements of customers and society, in a profitable and sustainable way (Peattie, 1995). There are four key ways of distinguishing green marketing from societal marketing (Peattie, 1995):

1. It has an open-ended rather than a long-term perspective
2. It places greater emphasis on the natural environment
3. It treats the environment as something that has an intrinsic value over and above its usefulness to society
4. It focuses on global concerns rather than those of individual communities.

Companies adopting the green marketing concept take advantage of the myriad opportunities presented by global concerns. Marketers are discovering that there is the potential of increasing market share, while improving the environmental performance of products and services. Furthermore, because of wide media coverage of green issues such strategies enhance corporate and brand image. They also encourage amicable community relations. The Intercontinental Hotel Group marked a public relations success by working with local school children. A competition was created whereby the children were asked to depict the importance of the environment in a drawing, and the winning entries were displayed at the different hotels in the group.

Many organisations now form 'green strategic alliances' with other organisations.

Green Alliances

Green strategic alliances represent a new strategic approach to green marketing (Peattie, 1995; Crane, 1998). Although there is no uniform definition of a green alliance, it is usually described as 'any formal or informal collaboration between two or more organisations which is aimed at developing common solutions to the collaborators' environmental problems' (Crane, 1998: 560).

Green alliances are usually formed in collaboration with organisations from other sectors such as the commercial sector, the public sector and the voluntary sector. There are several types of green alliances, ranging from licensing arrangements and sponsorship to public policy alliances. These alliances are based on the long-term objectives of the partners. Although critics suggest that most alliances are tactical in nature, overall they agree that they achieve a number of strategic objectives. Green strategic alliances have a number of benefits (Mendleson and Polonsky, 1995: 9):

1. increasing consumer reliability and confidence in green products and services
2. assisting enterprises to assess environmental information
3. developing new markets
4. creating better publicity for green products and services
5. enhancing public education about company activities.

The partnership between Green Globe and SGS International Certification Organisation is an example of a green strategic alliance. Together they validate the Green Globe Certification. This programme provides the following benefits to companies (Green Globe, 1998: 23):

- reduction in operating costs through systematic management of resources
- improved company image to the growing band of environmentally conscious customers
- maintenance and improvement in environmental quality for tourism businesses

- ensured compliance with present environmental legislation and easier integration of future legislation into management systems
- demonstration of compliance with Agenda 21 principles.

Other examples include the alliance between the Sydney 2000 Olympic committee and Greenpeace. This alliance was formed to allow the committee to re-assure residents and visitors that the Olympics would be run in an environmentally responsible manner. The alliance also enhanced Greenpeace's image by portraying it as an organisation that supports business efforts rather than continuously criticising them. The partnership contributed to Sydney's successful bid for the Olympic Games in 2000. The organisers claim that the awareness of environmental programmes will be increased during the games. Therefore, green alliances provide an important tool not only for the organisations within the service sector but also at the destination level.

At the Destination Level

A number of green strategies are applied by destinations (see Table 4.4). These strategies enhance the destination's attractiveness and competitiveness. Many tourism destinations formulate ecotourism strategies.

Eco-tourism

Since 1987, eco-tourism has represented the cutting-edge of the application of sustainability at destinations. Eco-tourism is made up of three elements. First, it is nature based in both protected and non-protected areas; second, it is educational providing interpretation programmes; third, it promotes sustainability by supporting conservation programmes. Eco-tourism strategies reflect these elements. Some countries such as Canada have extensive eco-tourism strategies (Canadian Tourism Commission, 1997). These include:

1. *Product development*: strategies aimed at improving the quality of products, increasing the number of new products, improving market suitability and diversifying off-season products.
2. *Packaging*: strategies include strategic alliances at local level and improved information for both local residents and tourists.
3. *Resource/sustainability*: strategies include the co-ordination of access to natural resources and environmental monitoring programmes.
4. *Business development/management*: strategies to improve training and to enhance risk-management skills.
5. *Marketing/promotion*: strategies to upgrade promotional materials and domestic and overseas marketing.
6. *Training/human resource development*: strategies to identify training needs and priorities, to develop standards and certification and to develop training programmes.

7.   *Industry organisations*: strategies to encourage organisations to form alliances.

Although priorities differ from region to region, these strategies are adopted throughout the whole of Canada. For example, the well-established eco-tourism region of British Columbia only focuses on improving resource protection and sustainability and on penetration of key markets. In contrast, Quebec focuses on eco-tourism product development, which it supports by pursuing diversification strategies for off-season products, and on marketing, promotion and training.

In many cases, green strategies at the tourism destination level have been seen as a short-term opportunities to attract large numbers of visitors. With a few exceptions, such as Canada as described in the earlier example and Australia where published strategies have been applied across the country, many destinations use green strategies as a marketing ploy to attract tourists. Some tourist boards and organisations emphasise their green credentials to increase visitor numbers not to eco-tourism areas but to traditional tourist areas such as mass tourism resort and urban centres.

CONCLUSIONS

The tourism and hospitality industries face many environmental challenges to ensure their future. These challenges include creating methodologies for sustainability using environmental indicators and auditing, but also ensuring that there is commitment to the process.

For many years, green issues have been well publicised and documented both in terms of agendas and actions which have enhance their effectiveness and secured the support of many tourism and hospitality organisations. In addition, green consumers are also attracted by these initiatives but they represent a smaller segment than originally thought. This is because there is a clear attitude and behaviour gap within their actions.

Companies often devise strategies based on marketing ploys rather than on the knowledge of the market and may exaggerate claims of being environmentally friendly. This deters consumers who have become suspicious and sceptical about so-called green products. Destinations may also over-emphasise their green credentials. There are only a few examples of destinations that are fully committed to a green strategic agenda. Therefore, there is a need to develop market-led strategies rather than marketing-led strategies.

Green strategies must be based on a thorough understanding of sustainability and its consequences. If sustainable tourism development is not achieved, the search for sustainability will be passed down to future generations – a scenario that will be difficult to recover from.

REFERENCES AND FURTHER READING

Berry, S. and Ladkin, A. (1997) 'Sustainable tourism: a regional perspective', *Tourism Management*, **18**(7): 433–40.

British Airways (1998) *Annual Environmental Report*, Penguin: Harmondsworth.

Butler, R.W. (1997) 'Modelling tourism development: evolution, growth and decline', in S. Wahab and J.J. Pigram (eds) *Tourism Development and Growth, The Challenge of Sustainability*, Routledge: London, 109–25.

Butler, R.W. (1998) 'Sustainable tourism-looking backwards in order to progress?', in C.M. Hall and A.A. Lew (eds) *Sustainable Tourism: A Geographical Perspective*, Longman: Harlow, 25–34.

Canadian Tourism Commission (1997) *Adventure Travel and Ecotourism: The Challenge Ahead*, Canadian Tourism Commission, Ottawa.

Crane, A. (1998) 'Exploring green alliances', *Journal of Marketing Management*, **14**(6), 559–79.

Diamantis, D. (1998) 'Environmental auditing: a tool in ecotourism development', *Eco-Management and Auditing Journal*, **5**(1), 15–21.

Diamantis, D. (1999) 'The importance of environmental auditing and environmental indicators in islands', *Eco-Management and Auditing Journal*, **6**(2).

Diamantis, D. and Westlake, J. (1997) 'Environmental auditing: an approach towards monitoring the environmental impacts in tourism destinations, with reference to the case of Molyvos', *Progress of Tourism and Hospitality Research*, **3**(1), 3–15.

Ding, P. and Pigram, J. (1995) 'Environmental audits: an emerging concept in sustainable tourism development', *Journal of Tourism Studies*, **6**(2), 2–10.

EC (1995) Green Paper on Tourism, DGXXIII, European Commission, Brussels.

Green Globe (1995) *An Invitation to Join*, WTTC: London.

Green Globe (1998) *Annual Review 1997/1998*, WTTC: London.

Green Hotelier (1997) *Magazine of the International Hotels Environmental Initiative*, **6**.

Hunter, C. (1997) 'Sustainable tourism as an adaptive paradigm', *Annals of Tourism Research*, **24**(4), 850–67.

Knowles, T. (1996) *Corporate Strategy for Hospitality*, Longman: Harlow.

Knowles, T., Macmillan, S., Palmer, J. and Hashimoto, A. (1998) 'The development of environmental initiatives in tourism: responses from London hotel sector', *Progress in Tourism and Hospitality Research*, **4**.

Macnaghten, P., Grove-White, R., Jacobs, M. and Wynne, B. (1997) 'Sustainability and indicators', in P. McDonagh and A. Prothero (eds) *In Green Management: A Reader*, Dryden Press: London, 148–53.

Martin, A./MORI (1997) Tourism, the Environment and Consumers. Paper presented in the Environment Matters Conference, Glasgow, April.

Mendleson, N. and Jay Polonsky, M. (1995) 'Using strategic alliances to develop credible green marketing', *Journal of Consumer Marketing*, **12**(2), 4–18.

Middleton, V.T.C. and Hawkins, R. (1998) *Sustainable Tourism: A Marketing Perspective*, Butterworth-Heinemann: Oxford.

Mowforth, M. and Munt, I. (1998) *Tourism and Sustainability: New Tourism in the Third World*, Routledge: London.

Murphy, P. (1994) 'Tourism and sustainable development', in W. Theobald (ed.) *Global Tourism, the Next Decade*, Butterworth-Heinemann: Oxford, 274–98.

Organisation for Economic Co-operation and Development (1994) *Environmental Indicators: OECD Core Set*, OECD: Paris.

Peattie, K. (1995) *Environmental Marketing Management, Meeting the Green Challenge*, Pitman: London.

Phillips, P.A. and Moutinho, L. (1998) *Strategic Planning Systems on Hospitality and Tourism*, CAB International: Wallingford.

Robers, J.A. (1996) 'Green consumers in the 1990s: profile and implications for advertising', *Journal of Business Research*, **36**, 217–31.

Smith, D. (1992) 'Business strategy and the environment: what lies beyond the rhetoric of greening?', *Business Strategy and the Environment*, **1**(1): 1–9.

Stabler, M.J. (1997) 'An overview of the sustainable tourism debate and the scope and content of the book', in M.J. Stabler (ed.) *Tourism and Sustainability: From Principles To Practice*, CAB International: Wallingford, 1–21.

United Nations Environmental Programme/Industry and Environment Office (1989) *Environmental Auditing.* Report of UNEP/IEO Workshop, Paris, 10–11 January, 99–102.

Welford, R. (ed.) (1997) *Corporate Environmental Management 2: Culture and Organisations*, Earthscan: London.

Westlake, J. and Diamantis, D. (1998) 'The application of environmental auditing to the management of sustainability within tourism', *Tourism and Recreation Research*, **23**(2).

World Commission on Environment and Development (1987) *Our Common Future*, Oxford University Press: Oxford.

World Tourism Organisation (1993) *Sustainable Tourism Development: Guide for Local Planners*, WTO: Madrid.

World Tourism Organisation (1995) *What Tourism Managers Need to Know: A Practical Guide to the Development and Use of Indicators of Sustainable Tourism*, WTO: Madrid.

World Tourism Organisation (1997) *Tourism 2000: Building a Sustainable Future for Asia–Pacific*, WTO: Madrid.

World Travel and Tourism Council/World Tourism Organisation/Earth Council (1995) *Agenda 21 for the Travel and Tourism Industry – Towards Environmentally Sustainable Development*, WTTC/WTO/EC: Oxford.

CHAPTER 5   The influence of human resources on tourism marketing

CONTENTS

THE INFLUENCE OF HUMAN RESOURCES ON TOURISM MARKETING

EDITH SZIVAS

INTRODUCTION

While tourism continues its growth as one of the world's largest industries, it is also experiencing major developments. Globalisation, the advances in technology, the changing nature of demand and that of competition are just a few to mention. These changes carry significant implications for tourism human resources and it is the purpose of this chapter to examine some of the arising issues.

A PORTRAIT OF TOURISM EMPLOYMENT

Tourism is traditionally seen as a labour intensive industry, which employs large numbers of labour with relatively low levels of human capital. While tourism is generally praised for its ability to create much valued employment opportunities, as an employer its image is controversial and is often tarnished by perceptions of low skills and marginality. However, despite the image problems, tourism occupations in many countries enjoy popularity and are very much sought after by prospective employees. In this chapter, the major characteristics of tourism employment will be examined.

Identification of Tourism Employment

Tourism is a 'multiproduct industry' (Diamond, 1977) where the overall tourist experience is created by a product mix. Accommodation, restaurants, attractions are just a few to mention. Arising from this fact, tourism employment encompasses employment in such diverse sectors as accommodation, catering, attractions, airlines, souvenir shops, tour operation and travel agencies, transportation and so on. The different sectors of tourism are associated with a wide range of occupations with a diversity in human capital requirements.

It has to be noted that despite this diversity, the discussion on tourism employment in the literature tends to be focused on hotel employment (Burns,

1993), neglecting a whole range of sectors which are all part of creating the 'tourist experience'. This chapter interprets tourism employment in the wider sense and incorporates all the tourism-related activities and sectors.

The discussion on tourism human resources is complicated by the fact that not all tourist facilities cater solely for the tourists. Many offer their services both for the tourists and for the local communities, making the distinction between tourism and non-tourism employment and human resources difficult. The classification by Smith (1989) is a helpful approach here. He classifies the facilities and firms serving the tourists on two levels: one tier encompasses all those establishments whose total revenue is derived from tourists; probably the best example for this first tier is the airline businesses. At a second tier are those businesses that serve both the tourists and the locals. Hotels, restaurants, attractions, taxis and so on fall into this category. The actual business mix between tourism and local usage shows great variations between countries. While in many developing countries, tourist facilities are for the exclusive use of the international tourists, in developed economies many establishments are shared between the international tourist, the domestic tourists and the local residents (Baum, 1993).

Another problem in defining the boundaries of tourism employment is the prevalence of the informal economy in tourism (Cukier-Snow and Wall, 1993; Shaw and Williams, 1994). It is not uncommon to see that in many tourist destinations certain businesses and professions operate in the grey or shadow economy. Tour guides, vendors and in many countries taxi drivers often make their living from the shadow economy.

And finally, it has to be pointed out that tourism employment spreads across a number of industries, for example agriculture, retailing, passenger transport, business services and local government (Messenger, 1991), which further enriches the diversity in employment opportunities offered by tourism.

The Characteristics of Tourism Employment

The ever-changing nature of consumer demand in tourism results in a work environment where routine plays a minor role and where improvisation and flexibility are important parts of the job. When compared to monotonous occupations such as factory work where the factory line dictates and where the work is impersonal and mechanic, tourism occupations tend to offer a more attractive alternative for many. This is supported by Riley (1986) who found a strong element of 'not factory' in the orientation of hotel workers to their industry.

A distinct characteristic of tourism work is that the boundaries between work and leisure time are often obscured. Marshall (1986 cited in Urry, 1990; Shaw and Williams, 1994) found that restaurant employees did not see their job as a real work because of the strong amalgamation of work and leisure. In hotel and restaurant work, part of the working hours constitute leisure when customers, many of whom are friends or acquaintances, are entertained. Furthermore, much of leisure time is spent at the workplace, further obscuring the boundaries between work and leisure. This suggests that businesses like restaurants might gain the loyalty of their peripheral employees from the fact that the 'symbolic boundaries between work and leisure' are weak.

The fact that a large proportion of tourism jobs involve direct contact with customers is a further possible attractive aspect of tourism work. While it has to be acknowledged that the high level of interpersonal contact involved in tourism jobs is not without negative socio-cultural consequences (Shamir, 1981; Mathieson and Wall, 1982), it is attractive for those who enjoy dealing with people. Mars *et al.* (1979, cited in Wood, 1992: 18) suggest that the hotel industry tends to attract those who 'derive satisfaction in situations in which a large number of ephemeral but jovial relationships can be made'.

Labour flexibility is at the very heart of tourism employment. Given the seasonal and periodic variations in demand in tourism, seasonal (Ball, 1989) and part-time work is common in the industry (International Labour Office, 1989b; Jafari, 1990). This inevitably has a negative effect on job security, career prospects and pay and makes tourism employment unattractive for those who are looking for permanent full-time jobs with clear career opportunities. However, there is another side of the coin that has to be considered. It can be argued that part-time and seasonal work offer a certain flexibility, which might be attractive for certain segments of the labour market. Women and students are cited most often to take up part-time work opportunities, while seasonal jobs are also thought to attract people from the periphery of the labour force (Mathieson and Wall, 1982). Shaw and Williams (1994) point out that despite the inevitable inconvenience caused by unpredictable variations in work and the insecure nature of part-time and seasonal employment, there is a certain attraction attached to such occupations. They suggest that two factors be considered. First, that often there is no better alternative job in the local labour market and second, that non-material benefits like accommodation, tips and the psychological income derived from working and sometimes living in an attractive environment provides a valuable trade-off for low wages and insecure jobs. Furthermore, the social expectation of women to have dual careers as mothers and family care-takers means that they are unavailable for full-time jobs or can only be engaged in occupations with fixed working hours.

It is often argued that, particularly in the hotel industry, the skills needed are those which women obtain naturally outside of their jobs in their role as wives and mothers, therefore women can join the industry for certain occupations without any formal training. Tasks like serving meals, working in kitchens and making beds are similar to those undertaken in the household and similar jobs in hotels are traditionally regarded as female occupations (Shaw and Williams, 1994). This view is largely capitalised on in developing countries with low levels of education and large numbers of women outside the formal labour market.

The industry offers jobs both on a full-time and part-time basis, and requires stable and casual, seasonal and migrant labour (International Labour Office, 1989a). While tourism is often condemned for offering large numbers of jobs on the periphery of the labour market, it has to be noted that it is this characteristic that often makes it a desirable employment option for many. It has to be noted that this aspect of tourism employment sheds a negative light on its image.

At the establishment level there is diversity in size, business type and in the extent of fluctuation of customer demand. What follows from this is that the establishments which vary by so many factors also show a diversity in the types and degrees of skills they require and, consequently, are characterised by organisational diversity (International Labour Office, 1989b). There are also variations in employment conditions according to organisational size. This diversity, be it sectoral, functional or organisational, is linked to a diversity in human resources in the industry.

Alpert (1986) writing about the restaurant industry, states that demand fluctuates by hours of the day, by days, weeks, seasons and is influenced by special occurrences and events. While part of the fluctuations in consumer demand is predictable to a certain extent, there is also a 'stochastic' element in demand. The predicted change in demand calls for the employment of part-time and seasonal workers (International Labour Office, 1989a) while the stochastic element in demand necessitates 'the labour insurance of standby workers' (Alpert, 1986).

There are two major consequences of this. The negative consequence from the employee point of view is that the need to employ a buffer supply of labour for peak hours forces employers to push wages down (Alpert, 1986) and that it works against full-time core jobs. However, it can be argued that the availability of part-time and seasonal jobs contributes to the accommodating nature of the industry as it provides employment opportunity to those not able to or not wanting to commit themselves to full-time jobs.

At the centre of the labour mobility and turnover issue in the tourism industry lies the notion of skills (Riley, 1996). First, the industry is characterised by seasonality and large fluctuation of consumer demand (Ball, 1989) which gives rise to the need to control the supply of labour. One way to manipulate labour supply is to capitalise on the unskilled labour force with its large external labour market (Alpert, 1986). Being able to take on unskilled labour that can be easily trained on the job means that labour does not present a constraint on the organisation's ability to adjust to the changes in consumer demand. Another way to adjust labour supply is to create a core–periphery labour situation (Guerrier and Lockwood, 1989) where the periphery (those in part-time and seasonal jobs) is used as a variable labour supply. Their, voluntarily or forced, mobility is self-evident. And finally, a third way to manipulate labour supply is through multi-skilling allowing employees to perform a variety of tasks, depending on the demand pattern.

The Image of Tourism Employment

The image of tourism employment appears to be split: on the one hand tourism jobs possess a certain image of glamour, while on the other hand, they are deemed as of low status and of low skill. A report by the National Economic Development

Council (1992) on the UK tourism market states that although there are positive characteristics attributed to tourism by career teachers such as opportunities to travel, meeting people, foreign language use and variety, the industry's traditional image of low pay, long hours and minimal training still prevails.

In the tourism literature tourism is generally described as a low-skill industry (Mathieson and Wall, 1982; Jafari, 1990). A report by the International Labour Office (1989b: 9) states that despite the improvement in the overall image of the industry in recent years, 'in some countries the sector is not yet viewed favourably as an employer owing to poor employment and working conditions and high levels of unskilled employment'. Jobs in tourism are often seen as 'menial and low level for unskilled hands' (Brachmann, 1988 cited in Sindiga, 1994) and many of them are regarded as demeaning. The tourism employee is often seen as 'uneducated, unmotivated, untrained, unskilled and unproductive' (Pizam, 1982: 5).

The international research 'Tourism as a Factor of Change: A Sociocultural Study' fostered by the Vienna Centre, which encompassed seven countries (Bulgaria, Hungary, Poland, Spain, United Kingdom, the United States and Yugoslavia) found that generally, tourism jobs did not possess a great deal of status and respect, and the most respected occupations in the industry were hotel and restaurant managers, tourist guides and mountain refuge managers. A significant finding in the study is that despite the image problem, the majority of the respondents in each country expressed a willingness to take up a job in tourism (Jafari *et al.*, 1990). Airey and Frontistis (1997) found similar findings in an Anglo-Greek comparative study on attitudes to tourism employment.

A useful analysis of the status of jobs and professions across the different sectors of tourism and across a number of countries is provided by a report by the World Tourism Organisation (1983). In broad terms, the study concluded that government organisation professions generally enjoy good status, which probably results from the entry requirements, career opportunities and conditions of employment. In the accommodation sector, managers and supervisors enjoy an improved status which is the result of growth in organisational size, higher entry requirements, development of vocational education and training, and the involvement of regulatory and voluntary bodies. Lower level jobs in the sector do not enjoy similar positive characteristics. Many occupations in the transport sector, and particularly those in the air transport segments, enjoy favourable status. Those whose work is related to tourist attractions and entertainment facilities rarely enjoy high status, the exception being those associated with the most prestigious tourist attractions. In the tour operator segment those engaged in central operations enjoy reasonable status because of the career opportunities they have, whereas the field staff suffer from low status. The status of travel agency occupations is generally relatively low. The status of tourist guides varies from country to country. They tend to be self-employed, often work only part-time or seasonally. In some countries it provides career opportunity, in others it is seen as an opportunity to travel before settling down. The status of guides is enhanced by the fact that the work usually requires considerable language skills. The status of the job is the highest in countries with strong cultural values and where the entry requirements into the profession are high.

The variation in the appraisal and image of tourism occupations is probably most apparent in the comparison of developing and developed economies. Cukier-Snow and Wall (1993) note that although most of the hotel jobs are menial, in developing countries they pay better wages than occupations in agriculture and are, therefore, appraised relatively favourably. It is well documented that in these countries the younger generation prefers tourism jobs to work in traditional industries. Diamond (1977) points out that the appraisal of the skill level of tourism jobs depends on the general skill and educational level of the country.

STRATEGIC ISSUES IN TOURISM AND THEIR EFFECTS ON HUMAN RESOURCES

Strategy, and especially a change in strategy, carries important implications for human resources. Different strategies inevitably require different skills, capabilities and attitudes from human resources, which cannot be ignored when devising new marketing approaches and strategies. In the followings four major issues and their human resource implications will be discussed.

Technology

Despite the relatively low overall skill levels in the industry, the industry is experiencing rapid technological change. This inevitably affects human resources. They are the ones who, on the one hand, have to live with the technology and who, on the other hand, can use it as a strategic tool. The Internet, smart highways, intelligent agents, on-line airline ticket reservations and electronic ticketing – just to mention some of the new developments.

While a lot has been said about the labour de-skilling effect of technological substitution, it is inevitable that the new technologies place new and often increased demand for skill development in the industry. In order to be able to capitalise on these new technologies, tourism firms will increasingly be looking for employees with skills and expertise to operate the new technology. Skills in Internet marketing, database operation will be particularly sought after. The advances of technology within the industry necessitate that employees in many tourism occupations acquire specialised skills.

The change does not occur without some resistance among tourism employees but appropriate human resource strategies can help eliminating the problems through training programmes and measures aimed at changing attitudes. Strategists within firms have to remember that visions and strategies can fail if not supported by appropriate human resources strategy and management.

Globalisation

Tourism is experiencing many aspects of globalisation, of which three will be discussed here.

The 'Shrinking World'

People are travelling to faraway places and are making use of the advances in technology. The globalisation of the media and its penetration into the everyday life, together with the use of Internet mean that today's customers are increasingly empowered with information. The advances in transportation allow them to reach places they have never dreamt of visiting before (Brown, 1998). The implications for tourism human resources are that the more experienced and knowledgeable customers demand higher quality in products and service and that they use past experience to compare the relative merits of tourism firms and tourist destinations. Competent tourism employees with the right service attitude and with commitment to the job and the industry are increasingly seen as instrumental in achieving competitive advantage.

Multinational Corporations

The growth of multinational corporations in tourism means that firms are increasingly operating transnationally (Brown, 1998). Hussey (1998) suggests that firms should give strategic consideration to cultural differences between countries, as they do affect their operations. It is not difficult to see that managers, employees, suppliers, customers and even policy-makers carry different cultural background in different countries. Hofstede's (1991) research provides a useful tool for the exploration of intercultural differences. The model uses the following five dimensions to measure cultural differences between countries:

- Power distance
- Individualism
- Masculinity
- Uncertainty avoidance
- Confucian dynamism.

Using the model, it is possible to examine the interaction of various national cultures with each other.

Apart from the cultural aspects, multinational companies cannot ignore the socio-economic conditions of the countries they operate in. In some countries there is a resistance by the locals to take up tourism jobs; in others social norms or religion restrict female employment. Companies operating in foreign countries find that to be successful in dealing with human resources in that country it is necessary to take into account the particular local employment and socio-cultural conditions.

Strategic Alliances

This is an aspect of globalisation, which is particularly common in the airline industry. The co-operative agreements between actual and potential competitors (Hill and Jones, 1995) can mean that competitors share common skills and corporate cultures. However, in many cases the alliance is formed between firms whose corporate culture and technological base is different from that of the partner companies. The success of the strategic alliance depends on the ability of the partners to harmonise their culture and management styles and cross-train their employees to be able to operate each other's technology (Faulkner, 1995; Hussey, 1998).

Changing Nature of Competition

According to Fayos-Solá (1996), the New Age of tourism is characterised by shifts from demand segmentation to demand super-segmentation, from rigid markets, distribution and distribution channels to flexible ones, from mass production to niches of integrated values and from costs minimisation to total quality.

Furthermore, competition is shifting from concentrating on the core product to that occurring in the augmented product, a phenomenon that gives an increasing role for tourism human resources. Providing high-quality service with the right attitude is vital for tourism firms thriving to gain and maintain competitive edge. In the service sector, front-line personnel with a high degree of customer contact are often more important for the marketing function and strategy than the higher ranking employees without customer contact.

The marketing strategy of an organisation determines the level of service the firm is to provide to its customers, and also how the organisation is to be perceived by the market. In the case of hotels, the role of the receptionist is instrumental in this sense; he/she is in the position to communicate and reinforce the messages the firm wants to communicate to its customers. Alternatively, he/she can 'work against' and jeopardise the carefully planned marketing strategy (Fifield, 1996).

Sustainability

Whatever view we take of the strategic position of the sustainability movement, it is an approach which has gained recognition in the industry. In many cases sustainability is used as a strategic tool to gain competitive advantage over the competitors. Tourism employees are increasingly in need to be aware of the relevant issues and techniques. Without appropriate human resources to carry out the everyday operational tasks in a manner that respects the environment, even the most carefully designed programmes and projects are likely to fail. Furthermore, without staff that understands the economic and socio-cultural aspects of tourism, equitable and sustainable tourism development can only remain a theory.

NEW APPROACHES TO HUMAN RESOURCE STRATEGY

It was argued at the previous section that human resources are playing a vital role in today's globalised and increasingly competitive tourism market. What follows now is a discussion on how human resource strategies at the organisational and destination level can assist the marketing strategies.

At the Organisational Level

Personnel management has not been left unaffected by the emergence of strategic thinking in organisations. The question that often arises is how human resource strategy fits with personnel management and whether there is a difference between the two. To put it simply, human resource strategy can be seen as a wider concept which looks in a comprehensive way at managing people at organisations, while personnel practices can be regarded as the implementing tools of the human resource strategies (Torrington and Hall, 1998). Alternatively, it can be argued that the strategic elements are only a portion of the overall human resources function within an organisation (Hussey, 1998). Whatever the relationship between the two, it must be remembered that human resource strategies do not exist in a vacuum. Human resource strategies are conditioned by the external environment and are linked to organisational strategies.

The relationship between organisational and human resource strategy shows great variations among firms. In some cases human resource strategy is seen as a mere tool to ensure the implementation of organisational strategy but it is more and more often understood that people are a vital element in achieving competitive advantage (Torrington and Hall, 1998).

The major conclusion here is that organisational and, arising from this, marketing strategies can only be successful is supported by appropriate human resource strategies and human resource management. Adopting a more customer oriented approach or applying sophisticated information technology is only possible with staff who are motivated and who possess the necessary skills or are able and willing to learn them.

For Tourist Destinations

In today's competitive environment the success of tourist destinations is strongly influenced by the quality of their human resources. An important part of the tourist experience comes from the human element; the quality of service, the attitude, responsiveness and helpfulness of the staff adds value to the core tourist product.

Attitudes towards tourism employment are not always favourable and certain cultures and religions might constrain especially the employment of women in the industry (Inskeep, 1991). Furthermore, despite the fact that the necessary numerical supply of labour for new tourism development might exist at a destination, developers and marketers have to take into account that the necessary skills or attitudes might not be readily available. And finally, occasionally the unfavourable image of tourism employment discourages people to take up tourism occupations.

Arising from this, human resources evaluation and planning at a destination should take into account not only the numerical availability of prospective tourism employees, their skill levels, geographical distribution and so on, but also the prevailing socio-cultural and socio-economic conditions. Awareness of these issues and strategies to overcome them will assist to realise the destination's vision successfully.

CONCLUSIONS

The chapter looked at the traditional view of tourism employment and human resources. It then went further to examine some of the strategic issues faced by the tourism industry and highlighted their implication for human resource management.

It was argued that the tourism industry is increasingly faced with the need to change its view on human resources. Without realising the value of human capital and the importance of strategic human resource management and without employees who possess the necessary skills and attitudes, the principles of strategic marketing will remain theories. Only competent and motivated employees can deliver high-quality service and achieve competitive advantage for their firms and tourist destinations.

REFERENCES AND FURTHER READING

Airey, D. and Frontistis, A. (1997) 'Attitudes to careers in tourism: an Anglo-Greek comparison', *Tourism Management*, **18**(3): 149–58.

Alpert, W.J. (1986) *The Minimum Wage in the Restaurant Industry*, Praeger: New York.

Ball, R. (1989) 'Some aspects of tourism, seasonality and local labour markets', *Area*, **21**(1): 35–45.

Baum, T. (1993) *Human Resource Issues in International Tourism*, Butterworth-Heinemann: Oxford.

Brown, F. (1998) *Tourism Reassessed. Blight or Blessing?*, Butterworth-Heinemann: Oxford.

Burns, P.M. (1993) 'Sustaining tourism employment', *Journal of Sustainable Tourism*, **1**(2): 81–96.

Cukier-Snow, J. and Wall, G. (1993) 'Tourism employment. Perspectives from Bali', *Tourism Management*, **14**(3): 195–201.

Diamond, J. (1977) 'Tourism's role in economic development: the case re-examined', *Economic and Cultural Change*, **25**(3): 539–53.

Faulkner, D. (1995) *International Strategic Alliances*, McGraw-Hill International: New York.

Fayos-Solá, E. (1996) Human Capital in the Tourism Industry of the 21st Century. 21–23 January 1996. Conference, Madrid.

Fifield, P. (1996) *Marketing Strategy*, Butterworth-Heinemann: Oxford.

Guerrier, Y. and Lockwood, A. (1989) 'Core and peripheral employees in hotel operations', *Personnel Review*, **18**(1): 9–15.

Hill, C.W.L. and Jones, G.R. (1995) *Strategic Management Theory: An Integrated Approach*, 3rd edn, Houghton Miffin: New York.

Hofstede, G. (1991) *Cultures and Organisation*, McGraw-Hill: Maidenhead.

Hussey, D. (1998) *Strategic Management. From Theory to Implementation*, 4th edn, Butterworth-Heinemann: Oxford.

Inskeep, E. (1991) *Tourism Planning. An Integrated and Sustainable Development Approach*, Van Nostrand Reinhold: New York.

International Labour Office, Hotel, Catering and Tourism Committee (1989a) *General Report*, International Labour Office: Geneva.

International Labour Office, Hotel, Catering and Tourism Committee (1989b) 'Productivity and training in the hotel, catering and tourism sector', International Labour Office: Geneva.

Jafari, J. (1990) 'Research and scholarship: The basis of tourism education', *Journal of Tourism Studies*, **1**(1): 33–41.

Jafari, J., Pizam, A. and Przeclawski, K. (1990) 'A sociolocultural study of tourism as a factor of change', *Annals of Tourism Research*, **17**(3), 469–72.

Mars, G., Bryant, D. and Mitchell, P. (1979) *Manpower Problems in the Hotel and Catering Industry*, Gower: Farnborough.

Mathieson, A. and Wall, G. (1982) *Tourism: Economic, Physical and Social Impacts*, Longman: Harlow.

Messenger, S. (1991) 'The UK hospitality and tourism industry: an overview of the issues affecting the supply of education and training in the 1990s', in C.P. Cooper (ed.) *Progress in Tourism, Recreation and Hospitality Management*, **3**: 247–63.

National Economic Development Council (NEDC) (1992) *UK Tourism. Competing for Growth*, National Economic Development Council: London.

Pizam, A. (1982) 'Tourism manpower: the state of the art', *Journal of Travel Research*, **21**: 5–9.

Riley, M. (1986) 'Some social and historical perspective on unionization in the UK hotel industry', *International Journal of Hospitality Management*, **14**(3): 99–104.

Riley, M. (1996) *Human Resource Management in the Hospitality and Tourism Industry*, 2nd edition, Butterworth-Heinemann: Oxford.

Shamir, B. (1981) 'The workplace as a community: the case of British hotels', *Industrial Relations Journal*, **12**(6): 45–56.

Shaw, G. and Williams, A.M. (1994) *Critical Issues in Tourism: A Geographical Perspective*, Blackwell: Oxford.

Sindiga, I. (1994) 'Employment and training in tourism in Kenya', *Journal of Tourism Studies*, **5**(2): 45–52.

Smith, S.L.J. (1989) *Tourism Analysis*, Longman: Harlow.

Torrington, D. and Hall, L. (1998) *Human Resource Management*, 4th edn. Prentice-Hall: London.

Urry, J. (1990) *The Tourist Gaze*, Sage: London.

Wood, R.C. (1992) *Working in Hotels and Catering*, Routledge: London.

World Tourism Organisation (1983) *Tourism Employment: Enhancing the Status of Tourism Professions*, WTO: Madrid.

CHAPTER 6 Managing the service encounter: consistent high-quality delivery through 'internal marketing'

CONTENTS

6

MANAGING THE SERVICE ENCOUNTER: CONSISTENT HIGH-QUALITY DELIVERY THROUGH 'INTERNAL MARKETING'

GEMMA MCGRATH

The four Ps of service marketing: people, people, people, and people.

Richard Dow (cited in Kotler, 1991)

INTRODUCTION

This chapter is about the management of the service encounter and the issue of consistent high-quality service delivery of tourism products. In an ever-growing market place, the provision of consistent high-quality service is a strategic marketing tool as competition increasingly hinges on the quality of the services provided, not only their provision. The focus of this chapter is deliberately general in order to offer a broad overview of the main issues involved in the service delivery of tourism products, although specific reference is made to examples and cases for illustration. The chapter is structured in four main sections: the aim of each section is to offer a distillation of the main operational problems the service encounter creates for management and their possible solutions.

In the first section, the nature of the tourism product and the operational implications for the management of the service encounter are discussed. The centrality of the front-line, or customer-contact employees emerges clearly in the context of service companies, as does the relative powerlessness of management given the 'live' nature of the encounter. As such, the management of power itself is analysed and the discussion centres on the search for commitment from staff by regaining a level of normative power in the employee–manager relationship. Management by consent is necessary in order to evoke commitment, and not calculation or compliance in employee motivation.

In this light, the second section discusses the need for 'internal' marketing in service industries to complement the traditional 'external' marketing efforts particular to any company, whether goods or services. In an increasingly competitive market, internal marketing turns service quality delivery into a strategic marketing tool, as service suppliers are competing on differentiating their service. Internal marketing allows management to sell the need for high-quality service to the customer-contact employees. In recent years, the use of internal marketing has tended to rely on quality working life (QWL) training programmes and empowerment strategies.

Section 3 discusses how a company's strategic marketing efforts can be affected by its organisational structure and by the company culture. If 'internal marketing' is to be successful, flatter, more flexible structures are needed in order to overcome the difficulties involved in managing the service encounter. 'Internal marketing' needs to be at the core of an organisation's structure and culture in order to be effective in communicating the message throughout a whole company that it is in the business of providing a total quality experience for the customer. Centralised governments and bureaucratic organisations, by dint of their very structure, can make the search for quality service more difficult.

Drawing together the issues in the preceding sections, Section 4 focuses on international service companies operating in less developed areas of the world and the need for adapting western training programmes to areas where the customer-contact employees may have less experience of the whole tourism phenomenon. 'High-context', area-specific training is needed in order for the industry to be made intelligible to employees in order for the service encounters to be successful. Standardisation needs to be balanced with regionalisation in order for 'internal marketing' to be able to operate in this context. The creation of affiliation, not alienation, between customer-contact employees and management's aims is central to overall operation success. The wider implications of this issue, at the destination level, are also discussed.

The chapter concludes by restating the unique nature of service marketing and how the attendant issues involved require that 'internal marketing' be central to any overall company strategy. If 'internal marketing' for the customer-contact employees is to be effective, such efforts need to be at the core of an organisation. The structure of an organisation and its culture can help or hinder the use of 'internal marketing' as a strategic marketing management tool for high service quality to be delivered consistently. In the context of international hospitality operations in less developed areas, there is a greater need for training and 'internal marketing' to be high context and area specific.

SECTION 1: THE TOURISM PRODUCT

Tourism is a growing, dynamic and interactive industry, (Cooper *et al.*, 1993; McGrath, 1994). Tourism products, by natural extension, embody these characteristics, but they also have several distinctive features of their own, further differentiating them from goods (Booms and Bitner, 1980; Gilbert, 1991). A tourism product can be defined in specific or general terms. A product can be any one component part of the industry, such as a hotel, an attraction, or more generally, the term can refer to a country's natural (or man-made) resources, such as Brazil's fauna and flora, which in turn, come to constitute its tourism products. In common with other service products, the tourism product has various characteristics, which distinguishes it from physical goods, and indeed other services. It is generally accepted that the tourism product is on the whole a service product with its own distinctive features.

OPERATIONAL IMPLICATIONS FOR THE SERVICE ENCOUNTER

Chapter 1 discusses all the features of a tourism product, but of immediate relevance to the issue of quality service are the following features of the tourism product: its inseparability, heterogeneity, intangibility and labour intensity. The main points of interest here are what these characteristics mean for the service encounter.

Inseparability

The inseparability of the product from its delivery means that the service encounter is always 'live' and never a dress rehearsal. It is not possible, for example, to simply discard a negative service experience as you might a faulty drill from the production line: the inseparable nature of the tourism product does not allow for such correction time 'behind the scenes'. Increasingly, it is the front-line, customer-contact staff that have become the focus of management's programmes in the search for delivery of excellent customer care.

As a service is delivered by a person, that person becomes an inextricable part of the service. The delivery of a service also requires that a client is present, in order for the service to be delivered, and as such there is a necessary client–staff interaction, which is feature unique to service delivery. This inseparability means that to varying degrees, both the client and the service-provider, the member of staff, will affect the service outcome.

Heterogeneity

By their very nature, services are heterogeneous in that they are highly variable simply because their quality will depend on who is providing them, how they are being provided and where they are being provided. Similar to how the tangible elements of the tourism product may differ (the beds may be more comfortable in one than the other, even within the same category hotel may), the levels of service offered may also vary between one hotel and another. The quality of service experienced, for example, in different hotels in a chain around the world will also vary, despite management efforts towards quality control, and investing in good personal selection and training: the Hilton in Rio, for example, offers more westernised service than the Hilton in Lima and the difference may be due to the different levels of development between Brazil and Peru, (*Financial Times*, 1992). This hotel directory warns a largely business market of this very variability: 'It is worth remembering that there may be differences in the standard of hotels from country to country: a hotel that is highly rated in one country may be considered inferior if compared to the same category in another country' (p. vii).

Service quality involves people and people, unlike robots, are prone to experiencing changing states of mind, which inevitably will have some bearing on the service encounter. Standardisation is used by service companies in an attempt to minimise the amount of variability involved in the service encounter. Large-scale service operators, such as fast food chains and airlines, try to standardise their services as much as possible, to reduce and control this unpredictability in order to maintain consistent high-quality service delivery levels.

Intangibility

Some tourism products have more tangible elements than intangible ones. A meal in a restaurant at a destination, for example, has more tangible elements to it, than say, a short-haul flight, at the end of which, the client will have nothing tangible to show for the money spent on the service of being flown from one part of the world to another. Whereas with the meal, the client will have eaten real, tangible food. The tangible elements of the tourism product centre more on the tourism patrimony at the destination, the infrastructure and super-structure. The intangible elements are not only more numerous, but they are crucial to overall client satisfaction. This is closely linked to the subject of the core and augmented product.

They centre much more on the subjective nature of the tourism product such as image, friendliness, perception, helpfulness, courtesy, security and general atmosphere. Even if the tangible elements of a tourism product, such as a meal, are fine (the food is tasty) but the intangible elements are lacking in good quality (the service is unhelpful, the restaurant has no atmosphere) then the experience will not be perceived as an overall satisfactory one. Therefore, image is heavily relied upon in the industry to communicate messages to potential consumers about the quality of the products. As such, trading in the realm of the imagination, hopes, expectations, wants and needs are aroused and need to be matched with the reality of what the service actually delivers. More trust is required on the part of the consumer in buying services as the quality of the service, due also to its inseparable nature, cannot be tested or evaluated until the service is already underway and occurring in the present 'live' moment.

The inverse of the above example is also relevant, as the service tangibles should always correctly project the service quality. If, on the other hand, the intangibles such as the atmosphere and appearance of the restaurant had given confidence to the potential consumer, but then the tangibles, the food had not been good, there would be a gap between the expected, the anticipated and the actual service received. It is important to keep this gap, the service gap, (Parasuraman et al., 1985) as narrow as possible as such experiences result in unsuccessful service encounters which engender disappointment, negative word-of-mouth marketing, and a likely loss of trust and a disinterest in the using the service provider again in the future. However, on the other hand, the gap between customer expectations and actual delivery can be kept narrow when the image created by a company in its advertising is matched by the service experienced during delivery. The key is to keep this gap as narrow as possible by meeting, or even exceeding the customer's expectation, therefore resulting in the virtuous circle of satisfaction, positive word-of-mouth marketing and a likely increase in trust and an interest in using the service provider again in the future.

Labour Intensity

The tourism industry, as expressed by Go (1988) is a 'people looking after people business'. A large part of the overall holiday experience, despite some of the tourism product's tangible elements, is the quality of the services that the visitor receives and the skills of the staff in tourism firms and at tourism destinations. The tourism product is therefore characterised by the high staff-to-client ratio, particularly the front-line staff – the customer-contact staff. The service encounter, as it contains much potential for the customer service to be suffered or enjoyed, emerges as central to a company's overall strategy. Indeed, excellent companies have understood that satisfied customers are synonymous with satisfied, motivated staff, which has engendered the search for quality training programmes and a proliferation of empowerment and quality working life schemes in many service companies (Peters and Waterman, 1982; Gilbert, 1991; Kotler, 1991; Riley, 1991; Hales, 1993).

COMPETING ON SERVICE QUALITY

Increasingly, since the deregulation of several major service industries, efforts at product differentiation in order to compete have intensified (Kotler, 1991). In service companies, such as airlines, such differentiation has centred not only on improving on the quality of the products, but on the quality of the service, and furthermore, to compete on the differentiation of their service quality and its delivery. This is due to the fact that the tangible elements of the product are so similar and difficult to differentiate (a hotel bed is a hotel bed and a seat on an airplane is a seat on an airplane) the competitive edge is sought on the intangibles, such as service. Differentiating service provision however cannot happen only externally. If it is to be truly effective, the message that something is truly different about a company, has to be spread inside it, and to this end, 'internal marketing', which is discussed in the subsequent sections, allows for this to occur within an organisation.

MANAGERIAL POWER RESOURCES

Managerial work, the work of a manager, involves the process of planning, allocating, motivating, co-ordinating and controlling the work of others, namely, those who work for a manager (Hales, 1993). The work of a manager has been aptly described as 'getting results through other people' (Heller, 1972). Management, then, involves a key task, which is the management, or the handling, of other people in order to influence a desired outcome: that the necessary work be undertaken in the best possible way for the best possible result. However, the types of managerial power available to most managers make the management of motivation problematic and this subject area has been well documented by various theorists (French and Raven, 1959; Salman and Thompson, 1973). Hales's analysis of this topic, centres on the following managerial power resources: physical power, economic power, knowledge power and normative power (Hales, 1993). Table 6.1 illustrates these power resources together with the different legitimacy profiles of each and crucially, the behavioural response each one creates from those being managed.

Table 6.1   Power, influence, legitimacy and response: a model

Power	Modes of influence	Legitimacy	Response	
	(overt actual/overt provisional/covert)			
Physical	Force/threat/menace	Likely to be perceived as non-legitimate		Alienative compliance
Economic	Reward/promise/implied promise	Legitimacy ambiguous and problematic	Economic calculation	Instrumental compliance
Knowledge	Rational persuasion/suggestion/ accepted practice			
1 Administrative	Rules/accepted procedures			
2 Technical	Specifications/accepted methods		Rational calculation	Cognitive commitment
Normative	Moral persuasion/moral suggestion/moral obligation	Likely to be perceived as legitimate		Moral commitment

Source: Hales, 1993.

Predictable Power Resources

During the evolution of western society over the last century, two power resources, normative power and physical power, have become less overtly applicable to the modern workplace. The physical power resource, in the context of democratic economies, has increasingly become obsolete as a way a manager can motivate a worker. However, in less developed countries, or areas in the world where working conditions do not include much employee protection, physical power may still be wielded. In the light of international tourism operations, which cut across different levels of development, this power resource may still be relevant and not as obsolete as in the more developed parts of the world.

Normative power, the power which relies upon moral persuasion and to some extent, a degree of indoctrination in order to evoke commitment, has also become less applicable to the modern workplace. As organisations have grown in size over time, new structures, such as bureaucracies, became popular in order to manage work on a large scale (Riley, 1991; Hales, 1993). Therefore, opportunities for face-to-face interaction, between manager and employee characteristic of smaller scale operations, decreased and so opportunities for normative power to be exercised have also dwindled, which, subsequently, led to an intensification of management's search for moral commitment from employees.

Although, as can be seen from Table 6.1, physical power and normative power have different legitimacy profiles, what they do have in common is that the behavioural responses they evoke are predictable. The use of physical power evokes a response of alienative compliance while normative power can evoke moral commitment. In the absence of supervision, it is predictable that normative power will endure, while it is predictable too, that once the threat of force of physical power stops, so too will the employee's effort.

Unpredictable Power Resources

From the kinds of power which most managers have been handed down, it emerges then, that economic power and knowledge power remain as modern-day management tools. Unlike the behavioural response from normative and physical power resources, the response from economic and knowledge power is unpredictable. These power resources engender a calculative or a compliance response from employees and can create negative attitudes. Both economic and knowledge power are finite in that there is a cut-off point at which offering economic rewards to an employee to work harder or longer, may no longer produce the desired effect (Riley, 1991; Hales, 1993). The unpredictability of economic power can in effect be a powerless resource. For an employee for whom pay is not a salient need will not respond to an economic 'carrot' (reward) or 'stick' (withdrawal). On the other hand, such responses cannot be relied upon to be consistent throughout a workforce or in one individual. An employee will have different salient needs according changing priorities and natural evolution through the life cycle.

Knowledge power can also fail to evoke commitment for the same reasons. There may come a point in an employee's career when he may not want to train any further, so trying to motivate such an employee using knowledge as a power resource will fail to produce the desired results. Conversely, the knowledge power most manager's hold over their subordinates, can also be degraded as employees upgrade their own, thereby making obsolete that power. It is predictable then that there will come a time when an employee will outgrow knowledge and economic power, just like parental power over children eventually diminishes and ceases. Moreover, the legitimacy profiles of these two power resources are also ambiguous and contingent on how those being managed perceive a manager's use of his or her power.

The Management of Power

The kinds of power resources to which most managers have access make managerial authority problematic. Management cannot rely on the unpredictable nature of the calculative or compliance response in order to motivate employees to in turn deliver consistently high-quality service. There is a fundamental problem for management from the relativeness of the responses from economic and knowledge power. Such employee responses place management in a powerless position, stealing management's thunder. As a result, the search for ways to regain commitment from employees has formed the bulk of management strategies over the last two decades.

The search for commitment from employees requires that a level of normative power be regained in the employee–manager relationship. In order to evoke commitment from employees, and not calculation or compliance as motivation responses, managers need to manage by consent. Managerial authority hinges on the level of legitimacy perceived by those motivated or 'managed', since it is people who are managed, people who do the managing and people who are being served as customers and it is the feelings, perceptions and evaluations of all these people which are of interest for our purposes here. Therefore, it is the very management of power that requires reviewing. Service managers, because of the unique nature of the service encounter, discussed in the following section, need not only to manage by consent, but also to build their authority upon it. Implicit in this need is a shift in emphasis for management from the control element of their roles to the co-ordinating one. As such, 'power over' employees (domination and control) has given way to the understanding that 'power to' (facilitation, enabling) styles of management are required (Hales, 1993; McGrath, 1994) in order to empower the employees to own and even love their jobs, and in turn serve successfully.

MANAGING THE SERVICE ENCOUNTER

Given the nature of the tourism product, there are important operational implications for the management of the service encounter. Due to the highly interactive nature of service delivery, its inseparability, heterogeneity and intangibility, two key issues emerge. First, that the service encounter is central to the overall customer experience, and second, as discussed in the preceding sections, that it has inherent problems for management.

Essentially it is the interaction between customer and front-line staff which 'runs the show' of a service company, while management, particularly of a large-scale organisation, are relegated to 'back stage' as they cannot intervene to prompt, control and check the quality of each and every encounter running live 'on stage'. Indeed, managing the service encounter engenders a sense of relative helplessness (Lewes and Entwistle, 1990) as, given its nature, there is so little room for manoeuvre and input from the manager at the time when it counts, in the present tense. As Jones, Taylor and Nickson have expressed, 'the manner in which managers can intervene to ensure a successful outcome has always been extremely narrow' (1997: 541).

Figure 6.1 illustrates this point by inverting the standard labour triangle and showing the distance between management and the customer and how in fact the customer-contact employees are the ones who take centre stage during service encounters and as such are a key component in the marketing of services, even if managers choose to manage by walking around (MBWA). The customer-contact employees emerge at the centre of the service encounter, together with the customers themselves, and by dint of this interaction, both parties act as the 'stars' of the whole service performance.

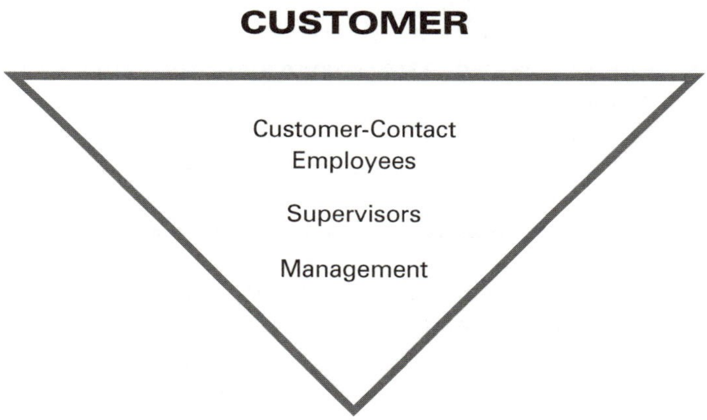

CUSTOMER

Customer-Contact
Employees

Supervisors

Management

Figure 6.1   Inverting the labour triangle: customer-contact employees and customers are centre stage while management are behind the scenes (adapted from Mahesh, 1998)

Therefore, customer-contact staff hold the power, ultimately to 'make or break' management marketing strategies since they are in a position to deliver the service which has been marketed to the external client. Moreover, management then is in essence at the mercy of the unpredictable nature of people and the 'live' nature of service delivery. This highlights the need for an internal marketing strategy, which should to be developed in order to train and motivate its 'internal' customers, namely its customer-contact employees, in the delivery of consistently high-quality service levels.

SECTION 2: INTERNAL AND INTERACTIVE MARKETING: TWO STEPS CLOSER TO MOTIVATION

The term 'external marketing' describes the planning process within a company's overall strategic marketing of its products. External marketing therefore refers to all the normal work undertaken by a company in order to prepare, price, promote and distribute the products to its customers. Gronroos (1984) understood the extra complexities involved in service delivery and argued that service marketing required more than traditional 'external' marketing. Gronroos developed a model (Figure 6.2) to represent how different the dynamics of service marketing are and how it involved two other features, namely 'internal' and 'interactive' marketing.

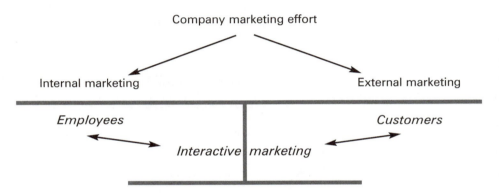

Figure 6.2   Marketing in service industries: balance in the marketing effort (adapted from Gronroos, 1984 and Kotler, 1991)

Interactive marketing refers to the skill of the customer-contact employees in handling every single 'live' service encounter. Interactive marketing needs to be planned for through the training of customer-contact employees by management, but most importantly, the employees need to be sold the importance of excellent service, in order for them to endeavour to deliver it, whether supervised or not, and this is internal marketing. For internal marketing to function successfully, a level of normative power needs to be regained in the employee–manager relationship. Internal marketing describes the work that needs to be undertaken by the company to train and motivate its *internal clients*, namely its customer-contact employees in order to solicit their participation and adherence to the company's overall strategic mission statement to provide the *external clients* with high-quality service delivery. Moreover, as is discussed in Section 4 of the chapter, there also needs to be a supportive work environment for the employees, if they are to give their very best service (Riley, 1986).

Gronroos' model has been one of the most helpful contributions to service market strategy (Kotler, 1991). Both internal and external marketing emanate from management, represented as the weight coming down from the top onto the scale, which should in turn exert equal pressure and both internal and external efforts need to have equal weight in a service company's overall vision. Although interactive marketing is about the relationship between customer-contact employees and the customers, this relationship needs to be planned by management through the training of customer-contact employees, in order to motivate them to want to give the best possible service during their interaction with customers.

For a service company's external marketing to be truly effective, internal marketing needs to be central to its overall strategy as otherwise, the gap between the expected service (due to the company's advertising eliciting expectations in the customer) and the perceived service quality can become wide. As discussed earlier, the intangible nature of the tourism product means that, at the very least, expectations created about levels of service need to be met, but better still, they should be exceeded: such levels of service are likely to encourage repeat visits from the consumer and positive word-of-mouth marketing, which in turn will reinforce the external marketing efforts. In the same way that strategic marketing needs to permeate an organisation's operation, internal marketing needs to be at its core in order for service quality to be a priority.

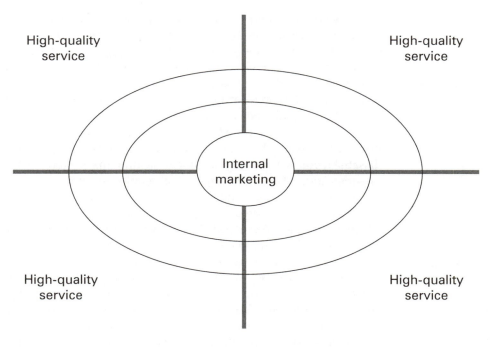

Figure 6.3   Internal marketing as a strategic marketing tool for high service quality

The quality and consistency of a company's interactive marketing will be directly measurable against the quality and consistency of its internal marketing. In other words, the interactive marketing is the practice, or the results of the theory of the internal marketing. Interactive marketing, the part of the process where customer meets employee, where demand meets supply, is the litmus test of a company's internal marketing. Interactive marketing is about the 'moments of truth' that will distinguish a service encounter for a customer, be it a positive or negative experience, it is what sticks in the mind of the customer, what he or she takes away with her, what he or she will remember.

Jan Carlson, ex-President of SAS airlines, coined the term 'moments of truth' when discussing the importance of having customer-contact employees who are equipped with training which allows them to respond to each problem as it occurs, in an empowered way. Precisely because of the distance between management and the customer-contact employees, in the majority of large-scale companies, an apt analogy can be made of a football player and his manager. It is not possible for the football player to stop playing and ask his manager whether he ought to score a goal or not: in the same way, there is no time for such negotiations in 'live' service delivery.

SECTION 3: ORGANISATIONAL STRUCTURE AND CULTURE

Both the structure and culture of an organisation influence the level of normative power that it is possible to regain in the employee–management relationship. Seaton and Bennett (1996) consider organisational structure to be one of the five most important factors for successful strategic marketing. In the context of service industries, the search for increased customer-contact employee satisfaction led to a search for greater flexibility in organisational structure (Hales, 1993). Bureaucratic and centralised structures, resulting in rationalised, piecemeal work, were identified as problematic for management as although they provided a greater level of control, there were two major problems: employee dissatisfaction with work and, since few humans are motivated by boredom or dissatisfaction, the subsequent lack of employee commitment.

The 1980s witnessed a general understanding that the search for commitment from employees required changes in organisational structure, to allow for some job redesign and greater employee ownership of their work and roles (Peters and Waterman, 1982; Hales, 1993). As discussed earlier, full decentralisation, although understood to be instrumental, is still a rarity, largely because it requires old forms of management, of 'power over' to be relinquished for a 'power to' attitude and this needs a greater degree of long-term trust to exist between employees and managers. Partial decentralisation, more companies found, offered a two-fold solution. Restructuring created flatter structures, which enabled management to reach customer-contact employees, and also provided considerable economic gains as supervisory and middle-management roles were made redundant.

However, regaining a level of normative power in the work place of large-scale organisations required more than changes to a company's structure. The importance of a large-scale moral commitment search, through training schemes and quality of working life programmes, was needed in order to reach all the 'internal customers', the employees of an organisation. The fomenting of a company culture is key to the overall success of the delivery of consistent high-quality service delivery, (Gilbert, 1991; Cooper, 1993; Hales, 1993). Culture is strongly linked to 'internal marketing' efforts to sell the employee, the 'internal client' the idea that the company they work for is the best possible one with which to be employed.

British Rail and British Airways provide good examples of the need for changes in organisational structure to be reinforced by a strong company culture of commitment. In the late 1980s, British Rail launched an advertising campaign announcing 'We're getting there' promising the consumer improvements in their overall service delivery. However, this was launched prior to finding out whether the consumers of British Rail had, in fact, noticed any improvements. British Rail's efforts to improve service had centred on a short-term employee training programme designed to deliver better, friendlier, more smiley service, as well as to provide the employees with a brighter uniform. There had been no changes to the company's structure, but more importantly, the training offered had not provided a corporate culture to pass on the norms and values of customer-care from top management then to permeate the whole organisation. As such, the results of the training efforts were short term, and furthermore, the service gap widened, providing further disparity between the customer expectations and actual service experienced, and therefore creating eventual disappointment. Moreover, the quality of the core product, in this case, the arrival of trains on time at their destination had not been addressed with equal effort as the augmented product of better quality snack facilities, cleaner trains and friendly staff.

British Airways, however made changes both on a structural level and also provided a strong company culture. Change at BA started with the appointment of Colin Marshall, who had successful previous experience of service marketing. BA was suffering from financial difficulties due to overmanning and from slow rates of growth. By restructuring the organisation and shedding over 60 senior management positions, and by creating a strong company culture of customer care and the importance of high-quality service delivery, the company created the fastest and largest turnarounds from loss to profit ever experienced.

The need for 'internal marketing' to be as strong as 'external marketing' in service companies is crucial. If external marketing is pursued aggressively without thought for the importance of internal marketing, no real change in service quality can occur. Changes in company structure need to also be accompanied with a strong internal company culture. Similarly, by promoting a company culture without any structural changes, change and improvements are difficult to achieve. An analogy can be made with a house in need of repair: either deep structural changes can be made in order to remove 'dead wood' to improve its overall construction or simple surface decoration to make it look better on the outside, while the major problems still lie unaddressed beneath the paint and wallpaper.

In Costa Rica, a highly centralised economy, tourism has been developed and actively promoted and thriving over the last fifteen years, (McGrath, 1994). However, its future development is constrained by its organisational structure and the lack consistent high-quality service from those working in tourism, due largely to negative social impacts. It is also due to the fact that most of the destination's carrying capacities have been exceeded. It is a country rich in natural resources and which boasts a high concentration of unique bio-diversity in a relatively small landmass. Over the last twenty years, tourism has been developed by the government, with a strong reliance on the well-established National Park Service (Servicio de Parques Nacionales) and the natural resources have been packed and sold as eco-tourism products.

Over time, however, over-reliance on the promotion of these products by the National Tourism Board (Instituto Costarricense de Turismo) has lead to negative impacts, largely environmental and socio-cultural, deteriorating their value, especially in the more popular parks with exponential arrival figures. Costa Rica's intensification of its tourism development in the mid-1980s coincided with a poor balance of payments, falling export prices for traditional raw materials, and the country's first real and serious unemployment problem. Such a scenario is common to many less developed countries. As is the problem of the public sector, in general, placing much more emphasis on the promotion element of the strategic-marketing process than on the evaluation and monitoring parts of the process (Cooper, 1997). Costa Rica's National Tourist Board was aggressively marketing its products overseas, but without any real strategy as to where the destination was, where it wanted to be in the medium to longer term, and how it was going to get into such a position.

One of main causes of this problem, however, has been Costa Rica's highly centralised government. With no local representation of either the National Park Service or the National Tourism Board at each park, who are empowered to make relevant decisions which can be implemented on time, a more sustainable type of tourism development cannot be worked towards, let alone achieved. Seaton and Bennett (1986) have identified the importance of the right organisational structure as one of the most important keys to a company achieving its goals and overall strategy.

In this case, it is clear that the 'external' marketing efforts were very strong, yet there was no 'internal' marketing present within the National Park Service or the National Park Service. Indeed, one of the main recommendations emerging from the research undertaken was that much more dialogue be planned between these two public sector bodies to allow for integrated tourism development to be co-ordinated. With no 'internal' marketing as part of the overall marketing strategy, the 'external' marketing undertaken became out of balance, but also, this had implications for the motivation of the staff, the quality of the service, and the overall visitor satisfaction with the products and their delivery (McGrath, 1994). Without the right structure in place, it is not possible to have a culture, which will enhance employee satisfaction, which in turn will enhance visitor satisfaction: organisational culture and structure are closely bound together and complement one another.

The use of 'internal marketing' in excellent companies, such as Disney, Marriott and Scott hotels embraces the need for employee autonomy, recognition and reward. Therefore, these companies, have not only partially decentralised the structure of their operations, but they also have strong company cultures which increases employee affiliation, creating a virtuous circle of high employee job satisfaction, high commitment and high service delivery.

SECTION 4: INTERNATIONAL HOSPITALITY OPERATIONS IN LESS DEVELOPED AREAS

The management of the service encounter in the context of less developed areas carries its own specific problems. Traditionally, tourism training and education has been supplied by the direct importation of western models, to areas with different socio-economic structures (Go, 1988). Where international hospitality companies choose to operate in these areas, area-specific training should be implemented for the consumer-contact employees (Blanton, 1981). While 'internal marketing' can also work as a strategic marketing tool for such operations, prior to such training taking place, there needs to be a thorough consideration of the characteristics of the local area.

On the subject of service quality available across different world regions, the *World Hotel Directory*, (*Financial Times*, 1992: vii) warns its largely business market of the variability involved: 'It is worth remembering that there may be differences in the standard of hotels from country to country: a hotel that is highly rated in one country may be considered inferior if compared to the same category in another country.' While companies may make every effort to standardise service by importing foreign labour, particularly in managerial roles, there is still the problem of how to motivate customer-contact employees who may have been recruited from the local host community. Moreover, in the attempt to control unpredictability, and provide a globalised service of uniform quality across the world, there is the risk of squashing out local, regional colour, which may be precisely what attracted tourists to the area in the first place. While predictability may be a pre-requisite of the business market, in the leisure market, there are two inherent risks with standardisation.

First, as the leisure market is increasingly segmenting and demand is becoming more customised, there is a need to balance globalisation with regionalism, and this, on demand-side, is particularly relevant for the independent travel market while from a supply point of view, it is important for safeguarding the uniqueness of the world's different regions. Second, and from the customer-contact employee's perspective, especially less developed areas, there is a need to develop more appropriate training programmes. Training for these areas needs to be 'high context', area specific, and not a 'one-fit-all' basis. Training programmes need to be integrated into an area being developed for tourism and not just superimposed upon them.

One such example is MAPATO, a cross-cultural training programme run at tourism college in Kenya and organised by David Blanton (1981), devised with the specific aim to counter the 'conversion courses' of international training programmes. One main aim of the programme is to iron out misconceptions that staff may carry about the tourists arriving in their country. Tourist motivations are discussed and videos of the crowded, industrialised tourism-generating regions in cities in northern Europe and the USA are used in order to give the hosts a sense of the 'push' factor involved to get away from bad weather, in order for them to understand more fully the 'push' factor and the appeal of spending time in a spacious, warm and relaxing country. This is vital in order to give the phenomenon of tourism some context as most traditional societies have no cultural frame of reference for tourism, and such explanations are crucial if resentment and negative socio-cultural impacts are to be minimised.

Also the use of interviews with tourists on the videotape explaining what their occupations are back home, gives the hosts, who are training to work in tourism, and who are soon to serve tourists as their new job, a sense of perspective. The interviews show how there is effort involved in saving for a trip to Kenya and how for the rest of the year, when not on holiday, tourists have to go back to work and their normal everyday lives. This preparatory work is important in correcting the notion that all tourists are rich and idle, happy to sunbathe all day and be waited on. Such training allows for the gaps between hosts and guests to be closed, so minimising conflicts and maximising understanding.

Implications for Destination

There is a knock-on effect from experiencing consistently high quality service in the wider context of the tourism destination as a whole. Good and high-quality service creates good word-of-mouth marketing about a country, an area or an attraction. It is likely, then, that quality service will motivate more people to visit there, as those hearing of the place will naturally be inclined to trust their family's or friends' reported experience. The strategic importance of good-quality service, therefore, is not limited to the service encounter within one specific company. On a broader level, a destination which is planned strategically will have taken account of the socio-cultural impacts of the service encounter: attempts to improve the quality of the service encounter demonstrate a clear understanding of the wider issues at stake, such as the destination's social carrying capacity.

Moreover, such planning helps narrow any gaps between the host and the guest, as customer-contact employees, out of their working hours of course, form part of and indeed make up the larger host community. This gap, like the gap between expected and perceived service, needs to be as narrow as possible for a successful service encounter. On the subject of the mismanagement of local labour in the Caribbean, McAffee (1991) discusses the importance of fair working conditions for employees. Where already there are wide economic gaps between the host and the guest, as is common when the destination is in a less developed area, and the host is working in a customer-contact role, there is a real need for careful management if social tensions are not going to grow and manifest themselves in poor quality service. McAffee (1991:173) states that 'a tourism industry based upon exploitation, servility and hypocrisy is bound to foster hostility among those required to serve and smile for poverty-level wages'. There is a human and economic argument for appropriate training. If the smiles of the employees are to be real, and come from within, they need to have a reason to smile: satisfied, protected employees make satisfied customers.

Figure 6.4 is a pictorial representation of the wider picture involved in the importance of the delivery of high-quality service, in the general context of any given destination. The fine dotted line surrounding the service encounter represents how closely linked this is to the overall impression a tourist will form of the destination: the two are not separated by a thicker line to indicate how the impact of service quality spills over into overall visitor satisfaction and how, conversely, the customer-contact employees are also affected by the types of tourists they encounter on a daily basis. Often, and certainly in the case of mass tourism, opportunities for interaction between host and guest are limited to the guests meeting the host population through the customer-contact staff (Doxey, 1978; Mathieson and Wall, 1982). Unlike the independent traveller, who is free of the 'tour bubble' to explore further into a host community, the mass tourist will form an impression of the country or area largely from the quality of his interactions with the customer-contact employees.

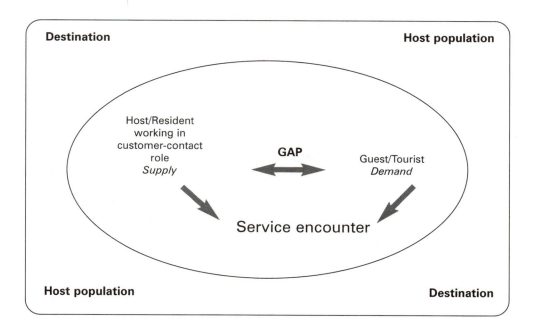

Figure 6.4   The wider implications for a destination of successful service

CONCLUSIONS

The unique nature of service marketing and how the attendant issues involved requires that 'internal marketing' be central to any overall company strategy. If 'internal marketing' for the customer-contact employees is to be effective, such efforts need to be at the core of an organisation. Internal marketing needs to be given equal importance and weight as external marketing. The structure of an organisation and its culture can help or hinder the use of 'internal marketing' as a strategic marketing management tool for high service quality to be delivered consistently. In the context of international hospitality operations in less developed areas, there is a greater need for training and 'internal marketing' to be high context and area specific.

ACKNOWLEDGEMENT

I wish to thank Dr Colin Hales for his insightful and stimulating management lectures. I would also like to acknowledge the influence of his ideas in creating and developing this chapter.

REFERENCES AND FURTHER READING

Blanton, D. (1981) 'Tourism training in developing countries: the social and cultural dimension', *Annals of Tourism Research*, **8**(1): 116–33.

Blau, P.M. and Schoenherr, R.A (1973) 'New forms of power', in G. Salaman and K. Thompson (eds) *People and Organisations*, Longman/Open University Press: London, 13–24.

Booms, B. and Bitner, M. (1980) 'New management tools for the successful tourism manager', *Annals of Tourism Research*, **7**(3): 337–51.

Cooper, C. (1997) Strategic Perspectives on the Planning and Evolution of Destinations: Lessons from the Mediterranean? Paper presented at conference, University of Westminster, December.

Cooper, C., Fletcher, J., Gibert, D. and Wanhill, S. (1993) *Tourism: Principles and Practice*, Pitman: London.

Dow, R. (1991) in Kotler, P. *Marketing Management: Analysis, Planning, Implementation and Control*, 6th edn, Prentice-Hall: New Jersey.

Financial Times (1992) *World Hotel Directory*, Pitman: London.

French, J.P.R. Jnr and Raven, B. (1959) 'The bases in social power', in D. Cartwright (ed.) *Studies in Social Power*, Institute for Social Research: Ann Arbor.

Gilbert, D.C. (1991) 'Tourism marketing – its emergence and establishment', *Tourism Marketing*, **1**: 77–90.

Go, F. (1988) 'Co-operative education and tourism training', *Annals of Tourism Research*, **8**(1): 139–40.

Gronroos, C. (1984) 'A service quality model and its marketing implications', *European Journal of Marketing*, **18**(4): 36–44.

Hales, C. (1993) *Managing through Organisation*, Routledge: London.

Heller, R. (1972) *The Naked Manager*, Barrie and Jenkins: London.

Jenkins, C.L. (1980) 'Education for tourism policy makers in developing countries', *International Journal of Tourism Management*, **1**(4): 238–42.

Jones, C., Taylor, G. and Nickson, D. (1997) 'Whatever it takes? Managing "empowered" employees and the service encounter in an international hotel chain', *Work, Employment and Society*, **11**(3): 541–54.

Kotler, P. (1991) *Marketing Management: Analysis, Planning, Implementation and Control*, Prentice-Hall: New Jersey.

Lewes, B.R. and Entwistle, T.W. (1990) 'Managing the service encounter; a focus on the employee', *International Journal of Service Industry Management*, **1**(3): 41–52.

McAffee, K. (1991) *Storm Signals: Structural Adjustment and Development Alternatives for the Caribbean*, Zed Books: London.

McGrath, G. (1994) Destination Resource Management: Integrating Ecotourism in Costa Rica. MSc dissertation, University of Surrey.

Mahesh, V.S. (1988) 'Effective human resource managment: key to excellence in service organisations', *Vikalpa*, **13**(4): 9–15.

Mathieson, A. and Wall, G. (1982) *Tourism: Economic, Physical and Social Impacts*, Longman: London.

Parasuraman, A., Zeithaml, V. and Berry, L. (1985) 'A conceptual model of service quality and its implications for future research', *Journal of Marketing*, pp. 41–50, Fall.

Peters, T. and Waterman, D. (1982) *In Search of Excellence: Lessons from America's Best-run Companies*, Harper & Row: New York.

Riley, M. (1986) *Customer-service Training – A Social-Psychological Framework*, Butterworth-Heinemann: London.

Riley, M. (1991) 'Human resource management', *Tourism Management*, June.

Salman, G. and Thompson, K. (eds) (1973) *People and Organisations*, Longman/Open University Press: London.

Seaton, A.V. and Bennett, M.M. (1996) *The Marketing of Tourism Products: Concepts, Issues and Cases*, International Thomson Business Press: London.

PART 3

STRATEGIC MARKETING IN THE TOURISM SECTORS

Part 3 presents marketing strategies in the different sub-sectors of the tourism industry. The emphasis is on marketing strategies rather than on describing the nuts and bolts of operational marketing. Therefore, the 4Ps framework is not adopted in this section as this would lead down the route of describing how to market a tourism product rather than considering why a sector is changing and how practitioners are responding.

Each chapter presents an overview of the different sectors, the trends that are provoking changes and the strategic responses by tourism marketers.

CHAPTER 7   Strategic marketing of tourism destinations

CONTENTS

7

STRATEGIC MARKETING OF TOURISM DESTINATIONS

RICHARD BATCHELOR

DESTINATION DEFINED

The original 'Mrs Beeton' household management and cookery book had a recipe for jugged hare. This commenced, 'First catch your hare'. When considering the development of destination marketing strategies, one must determine at the outset what a destination is. The spectrum of definitions is extremely broad.

At one end are compact product complexes such as theme parks, country club hotels and holiday villages. These may be destinations for a day trip, short break or longer holiday. They are often owned and operated by a single commercial concern, although certain services may be provided by tenant operators – beauty salon, burger bar, golf shop and so on.

At the other end of the spectrum whole continents can be considered and marketed as destinations. The European Travel Commission (ETC) and Pacific Area Travel Association (PATA), for example, seek to market Europe and the Pacific. Here there is no question of absolute ownership of the destination product. The destinations are represented or 'run' for marketing purposes by co-operatives.

In between there are many types of destination, defined by the tourist and/or by administrative bodies that assume responsibility for them, including:

- self-contained resorts – country club hotels, holiday villages
- villages, towns, cities
- areas which extend beyond administrative boundaries but have a cohesive identity with a specific theme, such as national parks (for example Snowdonia, Shakespeare Country)
- regions defined by administrative boundaries (for example Norfolk, Tuscany) or brand names (the Highlands, the Riviera)
- countries
- groups of countries (for example Southern Africa, the Caribbean) and continents.

DESTINATION MARKETERS

Generally speaking the larger the geographic area encompassed, the more potentially complex the marketing of it. Not necessarily because of the complexity of the destination's components, but because of the nature of organisation charged with its marketing. Except in small-scale destinations, rarely does the responsible marketing organisation have full control of all elements of the product and service. One exception was to be found in the former USSR, where Intourist effectively owned, operated and marketed the full range of tourism products in a vast country.

Like destinations, the organisations that have assumed or been charged with the responsibility of marketing them vary enormously. There are:

- single and multiple owner private sector operators
- public sector bodies ranging from small local authorities to government agencies
- public/private sector partnerships (for example many local tourism associations)
- co-operatives of destination marketing agencies (for example ETC, RETOSA, Scandinavia, Caribbean).

It is important to recognise this complex range of destination marketing agencies, as, in developing its marketing strategy, each has to consider its partners' and owners' objectives as well as its own operational limits.

WHO IS THE DESTINATION'S CUSTOMER?

The Chartered Institute of Marketing's definition of marketing is 'the management process whereby customer needs are anticipated, identified and satisfied profitably'. A clear-cut definition, but one which is interpreted in a variety of ways by destination marketers.

The wholly owned destination will certainly interpret marketing 'profitably' as a contribution to the bottom line of the balance sheet. But what of a tourist board, which operates no tourism products or services? What is its definition of profit? Is it altruistic in seeking solely to increase the profit of commercial suppliers at the destination, or does self-justification and preservation affect the strategies it adopts? Impressing its paymasters with its own performance may well enter into the equation.

At the end of the 1980s the marketing objectives defined in the British Tourist Authority's (BTA) 'Strategy for Growth' were simply:

- to earn for Britain as much foreign currency as possible by competing successfully in international tourism
- to spread tourism throughout Britain
- to spread tourism throughout the year.

Quite standard objectives related to earnings, seasonal and regional spread.

By the beginning of the 1990s BTA was stating an additional marketing objective explicitly:

- to achieve non-government funding of 67 per cent of total marketing spend.

The rationale for this was three-fold. First, the BTA needed to boost its marketing budget in order to be able to fund worthwhile campaigns. Second, it recognised the benefits of public/private sector partnership marketing to create greater market impact. Third, the trade 'financial contributions' were strong evidence to government that BTA was meeting industry needs and warranted continued grant funding.

This is one small example of how the strategies of destination marketers can vary because of internal pressures. In short, the potential tourist is just one of the customers the destination marketer has to satisfy.

Just as the type of destination can vary widely, so can the types of customers or clients the destination marketing body seeks to satisfy. A National Tourist Office (NTO) naturally counts potential visitors as its prime clients. But it will also seek to satisfy the needs of many intermediaries in its selected markets, such as tour operators, retailers and the media. Additionally it must satisfy stakeholders in its destination, namely:

- the providers of tourism product and services, who, through financial and in-kind contributions, are its direct partners
- other providers, who, by dint of being taxpayers, have a right to the NTO's services
- its primary funding agency or government.

It must also satisfy its destination's residents in so far as tourism impacts on their way of life and environment.

In a local authority, officers have to satisfy the needs of their often rapidly changing elected members as well as the ongoing demands of local residents and business tax payers.

In co-operative destination agencies such as the ETC and RETOSA, these internal clients' needs can run the risk of assuming greater importance than those of its tourist target markets. Satisfying disparate 'member' needs can become a major challenge, keeping the small vocal members happy, as well as the powerful large ones.

THE DESTINATION'S STRATEGIC VISION

Because of the complexity of its client base the vision or mission statement of a destination can be fairly complex. The mission statement of the Bass leisure corporation quoted in Chapter 2 is really a motherhood statement:

Our mission is to deliver excellent value by achieving a unique breadth of hospitality, leisure and drinks business which brings increasing numbers of people together across the world to share great leisure moments.

No one can disagree with it. It omits, however, reference to the needs of its stakeholders, or rather shareholders, to see a good return on investment. Destinations' mission statements tend to be more all-embracing and complex (*viz.* Hawaii's in Chapter 2). One succinct example was developed by Poland's State Sports and Tourism Administration in 1996:

Competing internationally through focused partnership activity.

This summarises a number of key issues for Poland's tourism:

- recognition that tourism growth could not be taken for granted and that being competitive in attitude and quality of product was necessary as the country adopted a market economy
- the need to select markets and segments due to lack of resources and to achieve a good return on investment
- the need for all sectors of the Polish tourism industry, national, regional, private and public, to work together.

It is far more of a rallying cry and demonstrates the imperative that a marketing strategy's vision must be capable of being shared by all of the destination's stakeholders. They must be willing to accept it and subscribe to its implementation.

The concept of partnerships is a recurring theme in many destination marketing strategies and is indicative that destination marketers have to recognise their own limitations.

DEFINING THE DESTINATION'S MARKETING REMIT

Destination marketing agencies of all sorts could be tempted to claim they alone are responsible for the promotion of their destination. In reality they should recognise their function is not to take on total responsibility for all aspects of the destination's marketing. Their responsibility is to provide the strategic marketing framework for the destination's tourism industry and to perform certain key roles, which the often small-scale stakeholders cannot perform themselves.

At the national level the diversity of mostly small tourism suppliers in the destination cannot be expected to fulfil certain key marketing tasks. It falls to the NTO to:

- research current and emerging markets and identify segments with best potential

- project the appropriate destination image in target markets and to defend that image against negative publicity
- develop market intelligence – market structure, key influencers and contacts, distribution channels and so on for the use of suppliers
- provide destination information, both general and specific, to consumers, trade and media
- provide promotional opportunities for suppliers to deal with consumers and trade intermediaries cost effectively
- monitor visitor satisfaction and advise on product development, improvement and presentation requirements.

Supplier involvement is necessary, indeed essential, in some of these areas of activity, hence the recurrent emphasis on partnership marketing. Indeed a measure of many destination marketing agencies' effectiveness is related to the degree of involvement and support they achieve from their stakeholders. For example in the early 1990s the BTA had a stated marketing objective of attracting two thirds of its total international marketing budget from what it termed 'non-Government funds'. This was co-operative funding raised from the private and voluntary tourism sectors as well as from other public funded agencies such as local authorities.

DESTINATION IMAGE

A key element of the situational analysis, which destination marketing agencies need to undertake, relates to the market's image or perception of the destination. As custodian of the destination's image the marketing body must evaluate how this is perceived in the marketplace and determine how and by what means it can be enhanced.

The communications life cycle is a useful guideline in this respect. It encourages the marketer to identify the stage at which market segments stand in the transition from product ignorance to commitment to purchase. This allows the selection of the appropriate marketing tools and techniques to communicate with potential customers and bring them to the point of purchase.

Akin to the product life cycle, the communications life cycle has five stages:

- Unaware
- Aware
- Understanding
- Conviction
- Response.

Some years ago the island of Aruba identified the North East of the USA as its prime target market and that the relevant market segments were almost entirely unaware of the island and its appeals. Whereas many destinations would have adopted a PR approach to address this communications gap and image problem, Aruba was able to afford large-scale consumer and trade advertising. By outspending most other Caribbean destinations, indeed many US states and major foreign tourism destinations, it almost literally 'put Aruba on the map' and greatly advanced the island's position on the communications life cycle.

The marketing tools used to influence segments at stages along the communications life cycle can vary considerably. Typically advertising or mass media coverage are needed to reach the unaware, whereas direct marketing with concrete travel offers are most suited to those at the response stage.

The state of Awareness can, in tourism terms, sometimes be a double-edged sword. After the ravages of hurricane Mitch there was certainly world-wide awareness of Honduras and Nicaragua. But from the tourism destination marketing viewpoint it was publicity one could well do without. Glasgow did not suffer the ravages of a hurricane, but suffered tremendously from the decline of its industrial base. The city's 'Glasgow's Miles Better' campaign is a good example of how negative destination images can be turned around.

The market was certainly aware of Glasgow, but the image was almost entirely negative. At least the city was on the map, but it took major development initiatives with surrounding publicity – designation as European City of Culture, the opening of the Scottish Exhibition and Convention Centre and the Burrell Collection of Art and so on – to change the awareness from bad to good and on to a positive understanding of the destination. The major development and event strategy adopted was also supported by a 'domestic' campaign seeking to encourage Glaswegians to believe in their city's renaissance and be proud of it.

Palestine is currently suffering from even higher profile image problems. Almost constantly in the news, awareness is high. Creating an understanding of the reality of the tourism appeals and relative security of the destination are enormous tasks for the Palestinian Ministry of Tourism and Antiquities. However, even in this difficult situation there are opportunities to enhance Palestine's position on the communications life cycle.

First, the very presence of many of the world's prime media in Jerusalem offers the opportunity to divert them to see and report on the cultural, archaeological and religious attractions in the West Bank and Gaza. This should go someway to redress the negative balance generated by the political scenario.

Second, word-of-mouth publicity through religious channels and specialist tour operators has managed to maintain significant flows of 'pilgrim' tourists to sites such as Jericho and Bethlehem with visits exceeding one million annually. So one can appreciate that religious group segments are much further along the communications life cycle than the public at large. A useful ploy to improve understanding further might be to harness the 'pilgrim' resource by supplying them with 'Having a wonderful time in Palestine' stamped postcards to send to their friends and relatives.

DESTINATION MARKETING OBJECTIVES AND TARGETS

The marketing objectives destinations set themselves are usually focussed on increasing visits and expenditure. The Wales Tourist Board's 1997–2000 UK Holiday Tourism Marketing Strategy simple states:

Objectives
- 1.5 per cent growth in trips per annum
- 5 per cent growth in spend per annum.

Poland's International Tourism Marketing Objectives are more extensive, but quite typical:

- project a positive image of Poland as a tourism destination
- optimise foreign currency earnings from tourism
- improve the regional and seasonal spread of traffic
- generate increased employment
- only develop tourism which is environmentally friendly while identifying urgent product improvements needed to meet immediate market potential.

Some of these objectives can (and do) have quantifiable targets set against them. However, the image- and environment-related objectives are almost impossible to measure. Their purpose is, along with the measurable objectives, to remind the destination marketers to ensure no activity is undertaken which does not contribute to one or more of the objectives. They are leitmotifs in the marketing planning process.

There are many more types of objective that can be included. None should, of course, be mutually exclusive and, like the following set from the BTA's 1989–1993 strategy, should have easily monitorable targets:

- increase visits to Britain from abroad by an average 5 per cent per annum
- generate an average increase in overseas visitor spend of 10 per cent per annum at current prices over the period
- maintain a good spread of markets with 30 per cent from North America, 40 per cent from Europe and 30 per cent from the rest of the world
- maintain out-of-London overseas visitor nights at a minimum of 60 per cent of total nights
- achieve non-government funding of 67 per cent of total marketing by the last financial year in the period.

What the BTA was reluctant to do in this instance, and is the case in the vast majority of destination strategies, was to add a caveat such as 'provided funding from our sponsoring agency is maintained at the same level in real terms over the period'.

In this 1989–1993 strategy BTA gives its so-called 'Forecasts of Potential'. In clarification it states:

> Although BTA forecasts indicate potential tourism growth, expansion cannot be taken for granted. It will depend – in the first instance – on external factors, which may change to the disadvantage of the trade. The UK has many strengths in tourism but international competition is fierce. Prospects for growth also depend on Government helping to create the conditions suitable for expansion and the free movement of tourists internationally. Much will also depend on the co-operation of the trade, local authorities and other tourism interests. They will need to pursue aggressive marketing, enterprise and investment campaigns to develop facilities which will meet the changing market requirements and rising international standards.

Provoked perhaps by reluctance to antagonise its government sponsoring department, there is no hint made here that the potential would not be realised if government financial support to BTA were not maintained.

Rarely are destinations bold enough to spell out the direct linkage between their activities and their funding sources.

Poland's 1996–2000 International Marketing Strategy is more pragmatic about what it terms 'achievable targets', saying:

> The targets are forecasts of growth potential assuming a number of factors, in particular:
>
> ● economic and political stability of Poland's priority markets
> ● political stability in Poland and its neighbouring countries
> ● *continued government support for the State Sports and Tourism Administration's international marketing activity*
> ● improving co-operation between Polish tourism interests – public and private sectors – in destination marketing and joint promotions
> ● development of tourism facilities and services to meet market requirements and rising international standards.

This might seem a rather defensive or pessimistic stance, but it is, in effect, realistic. Uncontrollable external factors are the bane of the destination marketer's life. But the caveats mentioned earlier also highlight the crucial need for co-operation from all supplier sectors.

BRANDING THE DESTINATION

The destination marketer rarely has the opportunity to select the name for his destination, it is usually inherited along with a wealth of perceptions and associations (both good and bad) in the consumer's mind. Venice, Vietnam,

Timbuktu, Sellafield, Blackpool, Palestine all conjure up different images, some positive, some negative. The marketer usually has to adapt and mould the inherited brand name to project as positive a message as possible.

One exception to this norm was the creation of EuroDisney, where a whole new destination was created and branded. Ironically the operators got their initial branding wrong and had to engage in a lengthy and expensive re-branding and relaunch as Disneyland Europe.

Where the destination branding is inherited, the positive tourism slant to it is often achieved by the addition of a slogan or strap line. Hence Robin Hood's Nottingham and Dickens' Broadstairs are used to emphasise a particularly strong and emotive facet of the destination in tourism terms.

This can be restrictive. Nottingham recently felt it was over-dependent on its Robin Hood image and wanted to emphasise more of its modernity, design culture and other heritage links such as the lace industry, Byron and D.H. Lawrence associations. But research showed that they would lose credibility and consumer confidence if the Robin Hood association were dropped altogether. The final decision was for a slogan 'Nottingham – our style is legendary' complemented by an archer logo. Time will tell if the decision was right.

Occasionally the powers that be in destinations make life difficult for the destination marketer by insisting on the use of the district or local authority name – for example Woodspring, Kesteven, and so on – which mean little or nothing to the customer. Although the marketer employed by Woodspring District Council may have to market considerable territory outside the town boundaries of Weston-Super-Mare, expansion of the town's famous brand name to embrace this hinterland is far more acceptable to the potential visitor than having to learn to recognise a whole new brand name.

Torbay, which combines the three towns of Torquay, Brixham and Paignton, has successfully developed its branding. The three distinctly different towns keep their identity as a sub-title to Torbay. This has pertinence for the cognoscenti, who know the three distinct aspects of the resort. Torbay then proclaims the bold slogan 'The English Riviera', which positions the resort as sophisticated and blessed with good weather. This last point is emphasised by the use of a palm tree as a logo. A surprising, attention-grabbing image to those who do not know Torbay, but a positive affirmation of reality.

Torbay has subtly developed this branding over the years. For instance, to help extend its season, it portrays its palm tree logo decked out in Christmas lights.

Destination boundaries are rarely meaningful for the visitor, but other associations are far more motivating. Many destinations use literary connections (often enhanced by film or TV exposure) to brand themselves – Herriott Country, Hardy's Wessex, Burns' Country and so on. Apart from highlighting places with associations, this type of ploy evokes a whole atmosphere for a larger geographic area.

With most destinations having a diversity of appeals, this type of single theme branding can be restrictive. On the other hand brandings can be so all-embracing as to have little relevance. 'Coke, it's the real thing' underlines the product differentiation *vis-à-vis* its competitors. But does 'Zambia, the Real

Africa' have the same impact? Perhaps it would if this African destination had some of Coca-Cola's advertising power!

Care has to be taken with the way brandings do, or do not, translate. Poland circumvented a potential problem here. The name 'Poland' is rarely the same in two languages, so it was decided to stick with the Polish name 'Polska'. A slogan in English, 'the natural choice', was attached. In English this has a subtle double meaning. Such subtleties do not always translate easily, but language adaptations are used to suit each target market and particularly to emphasise Poland's key attractions for that market.

MARKET SEGMENTATION AND PRIORITISATION

Market segmentation has rightly been adopted by tourism marketers as a fundamental means of achieving cost effective marketing. By identifying key market segments with high propensity to purchase one's product and clearly defined characteristics and profile, it is possible to design and implement highly targeted marketing strategies. It is no longer acceptable to admit that 'Only 50 per cent of my advertising works – the trouble is I don't know which 50 per cent.' With increasing pressure on budgets, the scattergun approach has to be replaced with the rifle shot.

By segmenting markets one is able to identify where one will get best returns on marketing investment. The process entails the selection of a few prime segments in each market and concentration on them to the exclusion of others.

This sort of approach is well suited to compact destinations such as theme parks and holiday villages, where market segments can be clearly defined through visitor analysis and then targeted precisely. The same is true of destinations with special interest products, such as riding or bird watching. In the case of special interests, the segments are often clearly delineated by the distribution channels one selects to reach these customers – typically specialist media.

However, regional or national destinations can have difficulty in defining small, compact segments to target due to the range of appeals and attractions they offer. The destination marketer may risk alienating a niche product sector within the destination by concentrating on segments with limited potential for certain products. Although seeking to meet marker needs and be market driven, the destination marketer often has to bow to product supplier demands.

The Wales Tourist Board has segmented its domestic markets quite precisely. This has resulted in the definition of target groups (by demographics, motivation, holiday type preference, and so on) within priority areas. This permits the use of highly targeted direct marketing to be undertaken with measurable results. However, WTB has recognised that it must also undertake more generalised promotional work, albeit concentrated in its prime target geographic areas. This consists primarily of poster advertising and public relations activity. It ensures generic publicity for the full range of the Board's clients' products.

While undertaking precision marketing to key segments, larger destination marketing agencies, such as national tourist offices, have to bear in mind the needs of their 'internal' clients, the wide gamut of product suppliers. Given the fragmented nature of the product in most regional or national destinations, suppliers are reliant on the destination marketer to supply certain vital services over and above any targeted segment campaigns.

First, market intelligence and qualified trade/media contacts are often best researched and collected by the destination marketer and then passed on in appropriate ways to product suppliers.

Second, co-ordination of promotional activities for the small supplier's benefit in the form of exhibition stands, roadshows, workshops, joint advertising and other promotions is a vital function of the destination marketing agency. Without this type of co-ordination and support many suppliers would not be able to penetrate markets effectively.

Third, agencies such as national tourist offices have a role as information provider both to the trade and consumer in the marketplace, which is vitally important to all suppliers and is not target segment specific. The creation of destination web sites, with hyperlinks to suppliers' own sites, is one developing aspect of this information provider role.

These types of function must remain a priority of the destination marketer even though selective marketing is practised through segmentation.

Again, the fragmented product supply sector looks to the destination marketer to identify new markets and undertake pioneering, missionary work well before specific segments can be identified. So it can be seen that, while segmentation has a significant place in the destination marketer's armoury, many other weapons and techniques must be maintained if both customer and internal clients are to be satisfied.

MONITORING AND EVALUATION

Destinations that make direct financial transactions with tourists are best equipped to monitor and evaluate the effectiveness of their publicity. Not only can cost of enquiries be monitored, but resultant bookings and the value of the business generated can be determined. This permits an appraisal of the relative values of promotional media and techniques.

Destinations, such as those represented by national tourist offices, that have no physical product or service to sell, have a much harder time demonstrating their effectiveness. Traditionally national tourist offices have laid some claim to the increases in visits to, and expenditure in, their destinations. However, hard data is usually available only many months after the event, and the marketing agencies also have to admit they are not alone in extolling the virtues of their destination. So tourist statistics are often not highly regarded as a reliable measure of effectiveness.

The level of coupon response and cost per coupon from consumer advertising is no real yardstick either. Advertisements can be designed to maximise response, but may alternatively have a significant motivational impact without prompting a coupon to be clipped. Research into recall of advertisements, focus groups to identify the advertisements with the greatest impact and surveys of whether coupon respondents actually travelled, are all helpful, although costly, monitoring techniques.

Media exposure obtained through public relations activity is often analysed in terms of circulation/readership data and the cost of an equivalent amount of advertising space. This typically shows how cost efficient public relations work can be. However, the 'value' of exposure is rarely adjusted according to the degree of positiveness of the article or coverage, or whether it includes a point of contact for bookings or further information.

The evaluation of effectiveness of exhibitions is particularly difficult, whether a trade or public show. The numbers of contacts made or sales leads generated are not a particularly reliable measure, as typically several encounters with a contact are needed before a decision and purchase are made. One cannot tell how crucial the exhibition encounter was in this process. Exhibitions are certainly an efficient method of renewing existing contacts, but again the value of this is probably impossible to quantify. Research has been undertaken at consumer travel shows to estimate the additional business destination exhibitors generated, but the results are far from convincing. Often a consensus opinion of standholders and the fact they decide to exhibit again is the best measure.

The British Tourist Authority has run a number of product marketing campaigns in recent years – Movie Map of Britain, Gardens, Golf, and so on. Some of these have generated databases of enquirers, which have been used to undertake formal research. Even after 6–9 months, high percentages of respondents typically recall receiving the publicity material and in many cases still have it. Many affirm they made one or several trips as a result of the information and plan more in the future. By extrapolation and by applying average visitor expenditure figures, BTA has been able to estimate the additional tourism flows and expenditure generated by at least part of these product marketing campaigns. The ratios of tourist spend to the campaign costs are usually quite impressive.

On a small scale such evaluation is effective and worth the not insignificant research survey and analysis costs. Unfortunately, precise monitoring techniques are not possible for many areas of destination marketing activity. Both the Australian Tourist Commission and the British Tourist Authority have gone a long way down this path. This has enabled BTA to claim that, for every £1 of its marketing spend, £29 additional expenditure has been made by overseas tourists in Britain. Much of this £29 will find its way into the Treasury's coffers via VAT, excise and other taxes. So the inference BTA is now making is that more should be invested by government in its operations for the government's own benefit. Whether this more forthright approach for recognition of the vital role of destination marketing will be successful remains to be seen.

As we have seen, destination marketing, particularly for large areas, can be much more complex than initially apparent. The 'product' is largely intangible and remote from the end user, which poses particular presentation and communications problems. Not least, the destination marketer has to address his customers' perceptions of the destination, whether they are accurate or prejudices. At the same time as appealing to the tourist customer, the destination marketer often has to satisfy internal clients and his funding sources. While Janus-like, he has to direct his attention two ways, he has the satisfaction of knowing that his scene-setting work is often a critical factor in enabling small tourism suppliers access their customers effectively.

REFERENCES AND FURTHER READING

Davidson, R. and Maitland, R. (1997) *Tourism Destinations*, Hodder & Stoughton: London.

Goodall, B. and Ashworth, G. (eds) (1988) *Marketing in the Tourism Industry: The Promotion of Destination Regions*, International Thomson Business Press: London.

Heath, E. and Wall, G. (1992) *Marketing Tourism Destinations: A Strategic Planning Approach*, Wiley: New York.

Laws, E. (1995) *Tourist Destination Management: Issues, Analysis and Policies*, International Thomson Business Press: London.

Lickorish, L.J. with Jefferson, A., Bodlender, J. and Jenkins, C.L. (1991) *Developing Tourism Destinations: Policies and Perspectives*, FT Management: London.

Middleton, V.T.C. (1994) *Marketing in Travel and Tourism*, Butterworth-Heinemann: London.

Montanari, A. and Williams, A.M. (eds) (1995) *European Tourism: Regions, Spaces and Restructuring*, Wiley: London.

Pompl, W. and Lavery, P. (eds) (1995) *Tourism in Europe: Structures and Developments*, CAB International: Wallingford.

Ringer, G. (ed.) (1998) *Destinations: Cultural Landscapes of Tourism*, Routledge, London.

Sinclair, M.T. and Stabler, M.J. (eds) (1991) *The Tourism Industry: An International Analysis*, CAB International: Wallingford.

CHAPTER 8 Strategic marketing in the hospitality sector

CONTENTS

8 STRATEGIC MARKETING IN THE HOSPITALITY SECTOR

TIM KNOWLES

HOTEL SECTOR OVERVIEW

The hotel industry is becoming more international in nature, a process started in the late 1940s by American groups such as Hilton and InterContinental. Both groups were, in those days, tied to airlines by equity holdings; the location of foreign-owned hotels was therefore associated with the growth of air traffic. This process of internationalisation was in turn, largely geared to the needs of the American business traveller. At the same time international investment within the hotel industry was also growing rapidly.

Hotel groups in Europe were more tourist orientated and, for the most part, did not develop to any great extent until the late 1950s and the early 60s when economic prosperity in Europe encouraged the growth of mass international tourism.

Prior to the 1960s the international operations of hotel chains were more or less confined to Europe and North America, and during that decade domestic hotel agreements became common in the United States. Expansion by European concerns accelerated in the 1980s, when American operators began selling off their international divisions. This gave the large American operators experience of contractual arrangements. On the basis of this experience they turned their attention to the developing countries where new business centres have emerged and where, as a whole, the tourist growth rate has been higher than in the industrialised countries. Key targets for the hotel groups have been the oil-exporting countries of the Middle East and North Africa and the newly industrialised countries in Latin America, South-East Asia and the Pacific basin. The expansion of multinational hotel companies into the third world, where the risks of capital investment are regarded as high, has consolidated the importance of contractual methods of undertaking business like franchising, management contracts and licensing within the overall growth strategy of these companies. The international chain hotel companies were and are still expanding, at the expense of the small, mid-priced independent hotels.

Key indicators suggest that the US hospitality industry has reached the mature stage of its life cycle. This is evidenced by declining occupancy levels, growth in supply outpacing growth in demand, and increasing levels of price competition. In contrast comparable indicators for Europe reveal that the industry has by no means progressed as far along its life cycle.

The European hospitality industry is still very fragmented with a yet unrealised potential for significant economies of scale and a higher degree of product differentiation. As a result, from a supply point of view, Europe appears a favourable location for corporate expansion. Expansion also has been given a further boost by the completion of the Single European Market, 1 January 1993, the Maastricht Treaty and the introduction of the Euro as currency. The opening of frontiers and the removal of physical, technical and fiscal barriers is expected to promote further trade between member states. This will require increased communication and arguably a greater number of actual contacts between business people around Europe. This growth in business travel will be accompanied by increased demand for hotel accommodation.

The same is true for non-business travel. At a practical level the easing of border controls and visa requirements will reduce the inconvenience usually associated with travelling abroad. These trends have been reinforced by the Union's steps in the liberalisation of transport and above all its deregulatory approach to air transport. Growth in passenger numbers will also have a positive effect on the hospitality industry. In the context of a growth strategy, the approach of Accor has involved the establishment of a Europe-wide presence through the expansion of its segmented product line and the consolidation of its leading position in France and Europe as a whole, mainly through leasing/management contracts and franchises. Similarly, Ladbroke plc's growth strategy aims at achieving a major pan-European presence in capital/major cities, besides continuing to consolidate its UK portfolio. In addition to European hotel companies, companies from the rest of the world are also looking to expand into Europe. The growth strategy of New World/Ramada aims at an aggressive expansion into Europe's primary and secondary cities.

In summary it can be shown that the late 1990s has seen an increased degree of consolidation and globalisation in the hospitality industry.

Over the past 10 years there has been a significant change in the ownership of hotels world-wide, with the tendency to construct and operate larger properties, which require larger investments. The hotel owner is usually a financial institution, insurance company or a number of joint equity-owning companies, which typically employs an industry expert to help control and monitor the hotel investment. Independent hotels by their very nature tend to be smaller in size, and are increasingly surviving mainly in the higher market segments of the hotel industry. Although these may seem difficult times for independents, a select number will continue to have a privileged place in the market because they can make decisions on their own without recourse to institutional investors, be flexible and offer personalised services to a specific market segment. With this exception, however, the hotel industry is experiencing a gradual but steady switch from independently owned and operated hotels, to hotel chain affiliation. In the immediate post-war period 50 years ago, less than one hotel in ten had any chain affiliation. Today, more than 60 per cent of all hotels in for instance the USA belong to chains. This rapid growth of hotel chains can be attributed to three factors:

1.   The emergence of franchising systems.
2.   Hotel management contracts.
3.   The need for corporate growth.

The expansion of hotel chain companies can also be explained by the desire for and availability of economies of scale. It is through this that the advantages provided by national and international reservation networks, staff training and marketing programmes can be recognised. In the United States, Canada and Europe combined, there are an estimated 3,000 hotel groups with more than 10 hotels each. The 200 largest companies account for the operation of at least 20 per cent of all bedrooms.

A number of trends in geographical terms among the worlds hotel chains can be identified. In North America, hotel companies have a continuing interest in Mexico, the Caribbean and Europe, and in particular the growth of the budget hotel sector. Mexico continues to draw interest from international and domestic companies. Days Inn and the HFS company has opened hotels in Monterrey, Mexico. Spain's Sol group has significant interests in the Caribbean as does France's Accor. In South America Hyatt International has opened hotels in Buenos Aires, Argentina and Santiago, Chile and is looking at more suitable locations in South American cities.

In the UK, the recession in the hotel industry ended in 1994. This was evidenced by the London-based BDO Hospitality Consulting Group, reporting up-market London hotels showing an increase in occupancy in 1994 compared with the previous year. However, on the European mainland, economic conditions worsened during 1994 in France and Germany, unaccustomed to a recessionary climate. Growth returned to these countries in 1997.

In Asia, Japan's corporate, economic and political problems have influenced not only the Japanese economy but the regional economy too. Hong Kong continues to be an economic focal point for the region despite the region's economic problems. Mainland China has drawn interest because of its economic swing toward a free market economy post-1979, the easing of political tensions, plus the sheer size (and buying potential) of its population.

The strategy of being geographically diverse in terms of guest mix and location seems ever more beneficial. As economists worried about the mainland European recession in 1994 and analysts warned of an impeding overbuilt Asian market, the United States was just starting to see its hotel supply and demand equation swing back into balance.

The evidence from this discussion is that the advice to keep a balanced portfolio and look beyond domestic markets holds true for hotel companies as well as for individual investors.

SECTOR TRENDS

Macro-economic Environment

Relating the earlier discussion of strategic management in this book to the world-wide hotel industry, the first half of the 1990s was a difficult time for hoteliers. After several years of expansion in the 1980s, some of the leading hotel groups were left with financial problems as supply outstripped demand. Companies suffered as both the UK, US and mainland Europe slipped deeper into recession. It was clear that changes in the macro-economic situation effected demand variations from the business and leisure segments, which in turn affected demand for hotel accommodation. The application of a PEST analysis to this industry has over the past 10–15 years illustrated the cyclical nature of the hotel sector. Taking the example of London and the key financial ratio of occupancy, the peaking of occupancy during 1987–1989 was followed by substantial drops during the period 1991–1993. Post-1993, a rise was recorded to a level in some cases over 80 per cent in 1997 and a levelling off in 1998. As the London hotel market enters the next millennium with projected percentage falls in the UK's GDP growth, it is expected that occupancy will also fall along with average achieved room rate (Knowles, 1998). These political and economic factors are applied in Box 8.1, a case study of the Middle East and African hotel industry.

Setting the Scene

Setting this all in context, the strategic implementation of a hospitality firm's expansion, particularly growth, is a complex process involving the understanding and utilisation of many factors. Primarily, the growth of hotel groups can be explained by the potential advantages of size. These advantages more accurately defined as economies of scale take several different forms:

- Financial economies enable the group to raise finance internally and borrow on better terms.
- Managerial economies derive from the fact that administration costs do not necessarily increase in line with the volume of business, for example, centralised room bookings.
- Technical economies are also associated with the benefits of centralisation, for example, the provision of services for example, laundry and maintenance from the centre to individual units.

Moreover, significant economies of scale can be derived from risk spreading which enables groups to offset losses in some areas against profits in another – a very important consideration in an industry characterised by uncertainty, seasonality and multiple target markets. Moreover there are purchasing economies to be achieved from the ability of groups to buy supplies in bulk and negotiate favourable terms. Finally, groups can benefit from marketing economies that offer the opportunity to create a recognisable group image in the market and promote it jointly thereby increasing consumer awareness as well as reducing costs (Knowles, 1996).

BOX 8.1

ANALYSIS OF THE MIDDLE EAST AND AFRICAN HOTEL INDUSTRY 1996–98

This region presents an example of how both political and economic factors have affected performance in the hotel industry. For instance, the political impetus of a co-ordinated policy of tourism promotion saw Manama in Bahrain post a 14.5 per cent increase in occupancy and a 26.7 per cent rise in rooms yield during 1997, a stark contrast to the violence that marred performance in that country during 1996. In contrast the state of Israel saw the resort of Eilat (above 80 per cent occupancy) cocooned from the political uncertainties which effected performance in Tel Aviv and Jerusalem. Occupancy in the latter two cities fell in the wake of a renewal of terrorist activity. The Jordan capital of Amman suffered from the knock-on effects not only of increased tensions in Israel but also in neighbouring Iraq. Egypt and its capital Cairo which had otherwise enjoyed a prosperous year in 1997 was severely affected by the attack on tourists in Luxor. Turning to East Africa, the Kenyan capital of Nairobi saw the benefits of strong demand during the first half of 1997 negated by later violence. This time the catalyst was the presidential election, eventually won by Moi. In contrast Karachi in Pakistan enjoyed a favourable political and economic climate during 1997 with good occupancy and average rate results. The economic crisis that engulfed the country in the wake of sanctions being imposed after nuclear tests has had a damaging effect on the 1998 performance of the country's hotels (Pannell Kerr Forster, 1998a).

Economies of scale coupled with the need to expand into key markets around the world have been, in part, the cause of recent mergers and acquisitions of hotel companies. As a result of that, the international hospitality sector is evolving towards a new pattern of industrial concentration in which the global market is dominated by a small group of large hotel companies.

Determinants

The choice of region to expand into reflects the individual objectives of the hotel company, by either:

● locating to a region with an established demand, or
● by locating in an area which will in the future experience growth in demand.

Another determinant of global expansion is the ability of a company either to raise the appropriate capital, which is difficult in recession, or to select an appropriate growth medium, that is acquisition, management contracts or franchising, topics that are considered later in this chapter with detailed discussions on the US company, Hilton Hotels Corporation.

The major hotel corporations have been looking increasingly to Europe and North America (which between them receive three-quarters of all international tourist arrivals), and the Asia/Pacific region which despite its recent economic problems may represent a buying opportunity for firms. This process originated with the takeover of InterContinental by Grand Metropolitan in 1981 (subsequently sold to the Japanese company Siebu Saison and then finally to Bass in 1997), and Hilton International by Ladbroke plc in 1987. Such mergers over recent years have increased in frequency and magnitude. The international hotel industry as far as chains and brands are concerned has typically been dominated by the USA. However, in recent years two changes have occurred:

1. European, and especially British and French hotel interests have been playing an ever more important part and now control some of the best known chains and brands in the world.
2. The emergent Asia Pacific region is beginning to influence the international hotel scene, with its recent economic problems representing a short-term setback.

Additionally, the geographic distribution of the major corporate hotel chains is very concentrated. The US, UK and France together account for 75 per cent of the total number of rooms controlled by the top 200 corporate chains around the world.

Motivations

Hotel companies have traditionally been keen to expand overseas for a number of reasons. In addition to the obvious search for new markets as a prime route for growth, there is a need to expand profitability in areas that promise high revenue, and the perceived need to exploit differences in the business cycle in different areas of the world as an *insurance policy* against recession in the major markets – the cyclical nature of the industry has already been referred to in this chapter. At present, the prevailing attitude among international hotel companies is that a hotel company in order to become successful has three basic options:

1. To become global through greater market coverage both geographically and by segment.
2. To create a focused approach to a particular national or regional market.
3. To fill a well-defined niche in the marketplace.

These three approaches are not mutually exclusive. It is perfectly possible for a company like France's Accor to seek to develop a global network of budget hotels, a strategy which simultaneously meets at least two of these criteria. On the other hand, the Canadian-based company, Four Seasons Hotels, aims for just one segment, the up-market business traveller. Primarily located in North America, Four Seasons Hotels limits its geographic dispersion to major cities and specialises in the operation of medium-sized properties from 200–400 rooms. The premise of this strategy is to serve this particular target market better or more efficiently than its more broadly positioned competitors.

Consolidation

For many hotel companies the key to prosperity in the current industry environment revolves around consolidation. With the location specific nature of the hotel industry, consolidation translates into greater market coverage, increased visibility, and greater opportunities for cross-destination marketing in addition to the benefits of economies of scale and scope. Therefore, hotel companies are continuingly seeking new ways to increase their market share. The pattern of consolidation of hotel firms is a major determinant both of chain size and of prospects for further expansion. There are three basic forms through which a hotel company can develop:

- acquisition
- management contracts
- franchising.

But as groups expand, so the patterns of consolidation become more complex causing the emergence of combinations of these forms as well as new ones such as sale and leaseback, joint ventures and alliances. A combination of affiliations will increase organisational complexity but at the same time allowing for more rapid expansion.

Global expansion, however, relies not just on the need to achieve international growth but the examination of other criteria. Failure to understand these factors will result in expansion which will have risks that outweigh the possible rewards. Thus in order to assess the feasibility of expansion, the hotel chain has to find a receptive region in which to locate and then find a suitable growth medium which will achieve the growth objectives and maximise financial return.

Turning to the hotel environment of the USA, this mature market has had the largest involvement in global expansion. An examination of the environment within which hospitality firms operate, coupled with trading patterns within the US gives an insight into the pressures on hotel chains to go for global growth. It is these pressures that are the main determinants of global expansion.

STRATEGIC RESPONSES

Consolidation

The key response by hotel firms during the 1990s is the continuing consolidation of the world-wide hotel industry. While this industry response is nothing new, its dynamics have been driven for years by companies seeking to maximise market share and enhance shareholder value. In a past era, it was the railroads, then the automobile industry, airlines, the cable business, and in today's world we see so-called 'mega-mergers' in such industries as technology and entertainment. In the United States there is a rapidly consolidating casino-gaming industry (a sector of hospitality) as the emergence of new gaming jurisdictions diminishes, and the barriers to entry and success in the business become ever greater, those companies with limited access to reasonably priced capital become logical candidates for acquisition. For instance, Hilton Hotels Corporation has actively led this consolidation, as illustrated by the acquisition of Bally Entertainment Corporation. This merger made Hilton the world's largest gaming company in a business where it is important to be big. But as rapidly as the gaming business is consolidating, it has paled in comparison to the speed at which merger and acquisition activity has occurred in the hotel industry. In a three-year period there has been Marriott-Renaissance, Stakis' purchase of Metropole from Lohnro, Accor agreeing to a joint venture with N.H. Hotels in Spain, Doubletree and Red Lion, which preceded Doubletree's merger with Promus, Marriott and Ritz-Carlton, the sale of Inter-Continental to Bass. There has also been the advent of the Real Estate Investment Trusts (REITs) – Patriot American's acquisition of Wyndham, Meditrust buying LaQuinta, and Starwood's purchases of both Westin and ITT Sheraton. The availability of capital, the ability to effect cost-savings and operational efficiencies, the increasing importance of branding, and the growing trend towards world-wide travel will bring even more consolidation in the hospitality business. This is building even further on tourism's current status as the world's largest industry.

Drivers

One key driver in this consolidation process within the US is the availability of low-cost public capital. Abundant public capital has fuelled a major increase in acquisition activity, both in terms of company acquisitions as well as acquisitions of single hotel assets. In the US the amount of public equity raised by the hotel industry has mushroomed during the post-1991 recovery period. In 1993 $563 million was raised. That number nearly doubled to $1 billion in 1994. It doubled again in 1995 when $2 billion was raised and in 1996 over $5 billion was raised. When one adds in debt offerings, public lodging companies in the US raised nearly $6.5 billion in capital. There are however a number of inherent difficulties making it unlikely that US companies will make major capital investments in other parts of the world.

The primary barrier to international investment is the divergent views on the value of real estate outside the US. What is an acceptable return on investment for shareholders of non-US assets is typically not acceptable to shareholders of American companies. For instance, during 1996, Hilton Corporation sold its 30 per cent equity interest in the Conrad Hong Kong. The reason for the sale was not the economic problems in Asia or the uncertainty surrounding Hong Kong's reverting to Chinese rule. The sale was because the new owners' return will likely be in the low single digits, which in Asia is considered acceptable. But for US shareholders, when faced with the choice of continued low single digit returns or selling equity at a substantial profit, the latter option was adopted. A comparison can be made with another acquisition which occurred at about the same time. In January 1997 Hilton Corporation purchased the Anchorage, Alaska, Hilton. This is a 600-room hotel that had been managed by the company for 10 years. It was bought for $70 million, with an expected return on this purchase close to 15 per cent. The implementation of a growth strategy or strategic response is illustrated with a case study of Hilton Hotels Corporation in Box 8.2.

BOX 8.2

IMPLEMENTING A GROWTH STRATEGY

At Hilton Hotels Corporation, three objectives of its growth strategies are:

1. To make effective use of the capital markets
2. To acquire full-service hotels
3. To lead the consolidation of the gaming industry.

The company's recent pursuit of ITT Sheraton was simply an execution of that strategy. By using Hilton shares in the proposed deal it was a use of the capital markets. Acquiring the company would have brought a number of good full-service hotel properties, and ITT's gaming properties, which operate primarily under the Caesars brand name, would have strengthened Hilton's existing leadership position in the world's two largest gaming markets, Las Vegas and Atlantic City of the US. Needless to say, the transaction would have created enormous value for the shareholders of both companies. For Hilton, had it been successful, it would have represented a couple of giant steps on the road to achieving its stated growth strategies. However, in the end Hilton was outbid by Starwood.

Acquisition, Alliances, Management Contracts or Franchising?

In developing this theme of world-wide consolidation, especially as it relates to US companies investing in foreign hotel assets, the direction being taken appears headed more toward management contracts and franchising agreements, and perhaps less towards outright acquisition. For instance Goldman Sachs have reported that:

> Given the trend towards globalization, increasing scale and branding, outright ownership is much more capital intensive and has prompted a move towards management contracts and/or franchises. Such an approach is more commonplace in the US, but it may represent one of the easier ways of expanding in Europe as it becomes more difficult to find suitable sites.

It is argued in this chapter that while those hotel companies participating in global consolidation will emphasise management contracts and franchising, there is a need for caution. First, the firm must establish the infrastructure to manage hotels all over the world. Second, local marketing, operational facilities and systems must be created and supervised. Finally, the appropriate local political and cultural connections must be maintained. In summary, management contracts and franchising represent a huge undertaking and companies must weigh the human and financial resource costs against the value of a particular management contract in some distant corner of the world. In may be that the costs will outweigh the benefits, particularly when viewed against good ownership or franchising opportunities. These views are developed in relationship to the hostile takeover bid for ITT Sheraton (see Box 8.3).

Economies of Scales

It is therefore emerging from this discussion that there is value in consolidation and in both hotels and gaming – bigger is, in fact, better. Primarily, consolidation eliminates the smaller, less well-capitalised firms. With their limited access to capital and constraints on tapping into such operational necessities as reservations systems and guest loyalty programmes, these smaller companies will have little choice but to become sellers because they cannot grow. In capital-intensive businesses like hospitality the simple fact is that the bigger firms produce the greatest performance.

Having developed the argument for consolidation it is important to note that there is room for niche operators in both the gaming and hotels. However, for those interested in growth, being acquired, merging or establishing an alliance is the most appropriate strategic choice. Consolidation, in most cases, also results in the creation of cost-savings, operational efficiencies and synergies. The elimination of duplicative overheads, combining reservations systems and sales efforts, economies of scale in purchasing, and sharing of customer databases, all bring value to shareholders. Using Hilton's acquisition of Bally

---

BOX 8.3

THE BATTLE FOR ITT SHERATON

Hilton's effort to acquire ITT Sheraton was an interest in the 72 owned hotels which account for 75 per cent of their cash flow. However, of these 72 properties, only about half fitted the company's criterion for ownership that is, large, full-service properties in primarily US markets where little new supply is being built. With some exceptions the plan with regard to the international properties in ITT's own portfolio was to sell these assets to buyers who would be likely to pay a premium for these hotels. Specifically, it did not fit in with Hilton's growth strategy to own Sheraton's CIGA properties, spectacular as they are. These deluxe CIGA hotels would be tough to justify owning them when shareholders demand double-digit returns. However, there are buyers – wealthy individuals, financial owners – who would have made logical owners for these properties. Therefore, the ITT Sheraton transaction, for Hilton, was a unique opportunity to acquire a number of big, city-centre, full-service hotels in domestic US markets seeing limited new supply.

Entertainment Corporation as an example, when the merger was announced in 1996, anticipated cost-savings and synergies of about $35 million annually were expected. The annual rate in 1997 was closer to $70 million. Putting a reasonable multiple of 10 times on these cost-savings and synergies Hilton is creating about $700 million a year in real value for shareholders. Where there is consolidation in the hotel business, industry analysis also finds bigger, more prevalent and powerful brands.

The Importance of Branding

The importance of branding has been well known in the hotel industry since a man named Kemmon Wilson started franchising Holiday Inns in the US during the 1950s. From that time forward, hotel owners and operators have required three things for success: a good location, a quality product, and a well-known, well-respected brand name. To be a major firm in today's hotel industry, a good brand – or collection of brands – is a necessity. However, as of 1998, branding is largely an American phenomenon. About 70 per cent of the hotels in the United States are branded, while the rest of the world averages below 20 per cent. In Europe about 20 per cent of the hotels in the UK are branded, while the remainder of western Europe averages only around 10 per cent. The fact that relatively few hotel properties in Europe, Asia, the Middle East and Latin America carry brand names provides significant potential for the major hotel brands to expand from regional bases. As with consolidation in general, the benefits of branding include the ability to market cost-effectively, the efficient use of reservation systems, and the creation of purchasing benefits which can significantly reduce costs. In developing this subject of branding it is important to differentiate between the hotel and casino-gaming businesses, the latter being an important element of hospitality. In hotels branding is extremely important. In the gaming business, however, the industry is probably some years away from seeing any kind of true branding advantage. Customers go to particular casino properties drawn by the experience, the entertainment and the value, not by the brand name. In Las Vegas few customers know that the Mirage and Treasure Island are both owned by Mirage Resorts Incorporated or that the Flamingo and Bally's are both owned by Hilton Hotels Corporation. A customer at a Harrah's casino in Mississippi does not immediately seek out the Harrah's property when arriving in Las Vegas. To gaming customers, branding is not important.

The importance of branding in the hotel business also played a role in Hilton's pursuit of Sheraton and its brand. Hilton wanted the hotel properties, but not the Sheraton brand name. The plan was to license the brand, logo, franchise system and other items to a third party. Hiltons view was that the Sheraton brand name is a high-quality, well-known and valuable asset but would have been more valuable to another owner than to Hilton. Hilton has its own high-quality, well-known and valuable brand name, with the name being the most recognised and esteemed brand in the hotel business. These twin themes of marketing and branding are related to the alliance of Hilton Hotels Corporation and Hilton International in Box 8.4.

Technology

Another important strand in marketing is the appropriate use of technology as a strategic response. For years, the guest loyalty programme Hilton Honours has been an industry leader, but members could not receive points at Hilton International Hotels. In other words, a customer of the New York Hilton, presenting his Honours Card at the London Hilton, would succeed only in having the card rejected. Just like the previously competing sales offices, this situation also had the company at a clear competitive disadvantage, and only reinforced in the customer's mind the notion of two Hiltons. Therefore, one of the first initiatives of the strategic alliance was to launch Hilton Honours World-wide, the result being that a Hilton customer is a Hilton customer – whether he or she is in San Francisco, Tokyo, Chicago or Berlin. Since it was started, the Honours World-wide programme has signed up 700,000 new brand loyal members. The two companies through the alliance are also co-operating on franchise and management agreements around the world. This has had an immediate benefit to the companies in that they are now able to franchise the Hilton name in Canada and Mexico. Recently, Chartwell Leisure agreed to develop 20 Garden Inn Hotels throughout Mexico. While the two companies have been working hard on creating sales and marketing initiatives to promote the concept of a single Hilton brand, they are also working on bringing this concept to life in a visual manner.

To that end, in May 1997, they unveiled a new Hilton Identity Programme, including a world-wide logo. This, it is expected, will communicate to travellers everywhere that the Hilton brand is united once again (Bollenbach, 1997).

BOX 8.4

HILTON CORPORATION AND HILTON INTERNATIONAL: A STRATEGIC ALLIANCE

Using the Hilton brand effectively can be considered from two perspectives. On a domestic US basis the company is expanding the Hilton brand through aggressive franchising of full-service hotels and its new mid-market Hilton Garden Inns. The second way – and perhaps even more important from a long-term strategic perspective – is maximising the brand throughout the world, which meant Hilton Hotels Corporation had to build a relationship with Ladbroke plc (the owners of Hilton International). To understand the issue fully it was not very long ago that the two companies – Hilton Hotels Corporation and Ladbroke – were not co-operating, but were also suing each other. It was agreed by the respective companies that there was tremendous benefit to each (and their shareholders) if they could bring the Hilton brand together on a world-wide basis. After working through a series of details in 1996 the re-unification of the Hilton brand name was announced. Technically speaking, the new relationship with Ladbroke is termed a 'strategic alliance'. The alliance with Ladbroke has resulted in some very specific and tremendous programmes and initiatives that are proving highly successful for both companies and customers. The primary benefit is that the travelling public is increasingly seeing a seamless, global Hilton Hotel network, one that encompasses 400 hotels in 49 countries around the world. In fact, Hilton is now the world's largest operator of four- and five-star hotels under a single brand. The newly created Hilton Marketing World-wide organisation combines a joint sales force with that of Hilton International, giving more than 275 professionals selling a single 'Hilton' network around the world. This co-operation is a far cry from the past, when the two would have sales offices in a particular city and would be competing with each other for business!

SUMMARY

It has been shown in this chapter that there are many differing factors that influence the global expansion of hospitality firms, all of which impact on the company's decision for international growth.

Analysing these factors is difficult due to the complexity of the hospitality industry and the unique aims, objectives and trading environments of each company within the industry.

However, through examining the trading environment of the past decade there can be understanding of the pressures affecting a company's future and an insight into the options available to the strategist as he or she tries to progress the company as far as possible.

When one considers the hotel industry, a majority of companies are being forced into global expansion through the exhaustion of growth opportunities in their domestic economy and the desire to reduce the cyclical influence of a single economy on the hotel chain's performance. These factors, considered as the wider environment, are the key motivation behind global expansion.

Hotel chains will only expand internationally if they can do so feasibly. Once a decision to expand has been taken the company must locate in the best location available. There are a number of options available here: expansion can occur in places of existing demand, but relatively low hotel concentration. An alternative is to expand in places of expected hotel demand growth like Continental Europe or finally to expand into key global gateway cities and face the challenge of achieving co-ordination among a dispersed hotel portfolio. Whichever choice is made, the hotel strategist must accurately forecast the potential of a region, if there is no mechanism for doing this, expansion will be risky and may not be viable.

Another aspect discussed in this chapter is that expansion must be achieved through the most suitable growth medium. This could be franchising, management contracts or strategic alliances. Each of these choices has its advantages but also disadvantages which if not understood and avoided could make global expansion a less feasible strategy.

The factors generating global expansion of hotel chains fall into these three categories: why expand, where to expand to and how to expand. If hotel chains can formulate their strategies around these criteria then they will have the opportunity to compete in the competitive global market.

REFERENCES AND FURTHER READING

Bollenbach, S. (1997) Keynote Speech. International Hotel Investment Conference, InterContinental Berlin, Germany.

Jones , P. and Pizam, A. (1993) *The International Hospitality Industry: Organisational and Operational Issues*, Addison Wesley Longman: London.

Knowles, T. (1996) *Corporate Strategy for Hospitality*, Addison Wesley Longman: London.

Knowles, T. (1998) *Hospitality Management: An Introduction*, 2nd edn, Addison Wesley Longman: London.

Pannell Kerr Forster (1998a) *Middle East and Africa City Survey 1998*, Pannell Kerr Forster Associates: London.

Pannell Kerr Forster (1998b) *Euro City Survey 1998*, Pannell Kerr Forster Associates: London.

Teare, R. and Boer, A. (1991) *Strategic Hospitality Management*, Cassell: London.

Teare, R. and Olsen, M. (1992) *International Hospitality Management*, Addison Wesley Longman: London.

CHAPTER 9

Strategic marketing in the air transport sector

CONTENTS

9 STRATEGIC MARKETING IN THE AIR TRANSPORT SECTOR

FRANÇOIS VELLAS

Air transport marketing is a prominent element of tourism marketing policies. Many destinations with potential tourism resources cannot develop their tourism industry because they lack the necessary access facilities, in particular for air transport.

Air access is therefore an essential condition for tourism development and tourism marketing strategies. The problem facing destinations that want to develop their tourism industry is selecting the investment priorities.

- Should investment first be made to develop infrastructure for air transport, thus opening air links with the main generating countries and setting up marketing campaigns in these countries?

Or

- Should tourism infrastructure such as accommodation be developed before creating air transport links?

To a great extent, the future of air transport and tourism marketing strategies depends on how these issues are tackled. Therefore to understand the relationship between air transport and sustainable tourism development, it is important to analyse airline marketing trends and strategies. This chapter presents:

- an overview of the sector
- trends in the air transport sector
- strategies in the air transport sector.

OVERVIEW OF THE SECTOR

Traditionally, marketing was not a major preoccupation of airline companies. They enjoyed virtual monopolies both on domestic and international routes. For this reason, most countries had a national airline, even if it was very small. To collaborate, they entered inter-line agreements with other airlines but kept their independence.

The aim of airline marketing was to increase demand rather than to increase market share. However, since deregulation of the air transport industry, the operating environment has completely changed. The objective of marketing now is to contribute to the global strategic effort of the airline. Indeed, 'Open Sky' allows free entry to the market and the possibility of increasing market share.

The international marketing of airlines is based on strategy, internationalisation and the use of new technology. Liberalisation and deregulation have opened the market to international competition. New operating conditions exist and airline marketing strategies, which before were hampered by the rigid constrictions imposed by the Chicago Convention in 1944, have been revolutionised. Initially, airlines reacted by concentrating their marketing efforts on price competition. The subsequent price wars forced out many new companies that had entered the deregulated markets. This was the case, for instance, of Laker Airways.

Internationalisation and new technologies have transformed the corporate and marketing strategies of airlines. The focus now is on creating barriers to dissuade and to prevent other companies from entering the market:

- Because of internationalisation, airlines now develop alliances with other airlines and international hub and spoke networks.
- Computers reservation systems (CRSs) – now called global distribution systems (GDSs) – link airlines together in computerised systems and this has encouraged new operational practices such as code sharing.
- Deregulation now allows airlines to adopt marketing techniques such as pricing strategies, segmentation, diversification and yield management.

Today, marketing strategies are the focus of airline business strategy and will determine future trends in the sector. These new strategies are transforming the sector as they are mainly based on mergers and acquisitions and on segmentation of both supply and demand. These include:

- the strategy of 'mega-carriers' which bring together major airlines in commercial and marketing alliances
- those of 'low-cost' companies
- those of niche market airlines
- those of charter airlines linked to tour operators.

TRENDS IN THE AIR TRANSPORT SECTOR

Current and projected trends reflect the link between tourism and air transport. However, this link is changing. Indeed, tourism and air transport are not growing independently any more because their strategies are increasingly inter-dependent.

Furthermore, future trends will not mirror past trends because, despite the crisis at the end of the 1990s, the Tiger economies will continue to show strong growth. Air transport marketing will therefore by affected by three factors:

- continued growth
- changes in market share in favour of Asian countries
- joint use for marketing tools by airlines and tourism firms.

The Impact of Continued Growth

An economic analysis of air transport demand shows that the exceptional growth in passenger traffic depends on price elasticity. However, prices are much more elastic for leisure air transport demand than for business air transport demand.

Therefore, the marketing strategies of airline companies are based on pricing differential in different market segment. As a result, the growth of air transport has mirrored the growth in tourism flows. ICAO statistics show that between 1986 and 1996, the growth rate of passenger traffic was 5 per cent a year (see Table 9.1).

Table 9.1   **World demand for air transport (1986–96)**

Year	Passenger Traffic*	Percentage Variation
1986	1452	–
1987	1589	9.4
1988	1705	7.3
1989	1774	4.0
1990	1894	6.7
1991	1844	–2.6
1992	1926	4.4
1993	1949	1.2
1994	2098	7.6
1995	2230	6.3
1996	2411	8.1

* Revenue passenger miles in billions (the number of passengers multiplied by the number of miles flown)
Source: ICAO, 1996–97.

North America still dominates air transport with 40 per cent of global market share. However, in terms of international air transport, North America is in third position after Europe and Asia Pacific (see Table 9.2).

Table 9.2 **Distribution of scheduled passenger transport by region, 1996 (percentage of total world)**

Region	International Traffic	Total Traffic
North America	21.0	40.3
Europe	34.8	24.5
Asia Pacific	30.6	25.1
Latin America/Caribbean	5.7	4.8
Middle East	4.5	3.0
Africa	3.4	2.3
World	100	100

Source: ICAO, 1996–97.

In 1996 Europe and North America represented more than half the world's air traffic – 64.8 per cent. However, in terms of international traffic, together they account for 55.8 per cent. Air transport demand is very concentrated in a small number of countries: the United States, the Russian Federation, France, Germany, Canada, Australia, the Netherlands and Singapore. These countries account for 75 per cent of total passenger kilometres, both international and domestic. The United States tops the ranking with 38 per cent of passenger traffic.

Forecasts show that despite the crisis, Asian countries will have the largest share of the world's air passenger market.

Changes in Market Share in Favour of Asian Countries

According to an IATA Aviation Information and Research Department 1997 survey (IATA, 1997):

● Demand for air travel in the Asia/Pacific region is growing faster than in any other world region. It grew at an average annual rate of 10.1 per cent between 1985 and 1996. It will grow by an average of 7.4 per cent per annum between 1995 and 2010, more than the rate forecasted for the rest of the world.
● By 2010, there will be 1.1 billion passengers travelling to, from and within Asia/Pacific. This is almost equivalent to the total world-wide passenger traffic for 1995.
● The region's share of world-wide scheduled passenger traffic (domestic and international combined) increased from 16.5 per cent in 1985 to 29.9 per cent in 1995, and will grow to 42.9 per cent of world total by 2010.
● The region's share of domestic scheduled traffic grew from 13.7 per cent in 1985 to 27.4 per cent in 1995 and is forecast to reach 39.9 per cent of world total by 2010.

● The region's share of international scheduled traffic increased from 26.2 per cent in 1985 to 36.2 per cent in 1995 and is forecast to reach almost 50 per cent of world total by 2010 (IATA, 1997).

Therefore, the Asia Pacific's share of world international scheduled passengers is forecasted to reach 49.8 per cent of world total in 2010 as shown in Figure 9.1.

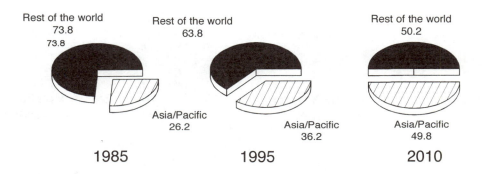

Figure 9.1   Asia/Pacific share of world traffic (per cent) (adapted from IATA, 1997)

Because of transPacific traffic, the United States will also benefit. Figure 9.2 shows that although with 89 per cent of traffic the United States dominated the transPacific market in 1985, by 1995 its share declined to 85 per cent and by 2010 this will have fallen to just above 84 per cent.

Inter-regional traffic in Asia Pacific is one of the main reasons for the growth on air traffic, particularly from the eight main airports: Tokyo, Hong Kong, Taipei, Bangkok, Singapore, Seoul, Kuala Lumpur and Jakarta.

This growth in Asian traffic will affect the strategies of North American and European companies. For instance, according to IATA's Asia-Pacific Air Transport Forecast 1980–2010 (1997), on routes between western Europe and Asia/Pacific, airlines will have to increase the number of flights from 78,400 in 1995 to over 184,500 in 2010 to cope with travel demand.

The availability of slots will cause problems in the future and will also affect the strategy of airlines. Slot availability is determined by three factors: the runways, the apron and the terminal. This will limit possibilities for airline companies.

Finally, air space congestion will further constrain strategic possibilities. This will mainly affect the Europe–South East Asia route over India, particularly between Karachi and Calcutta.

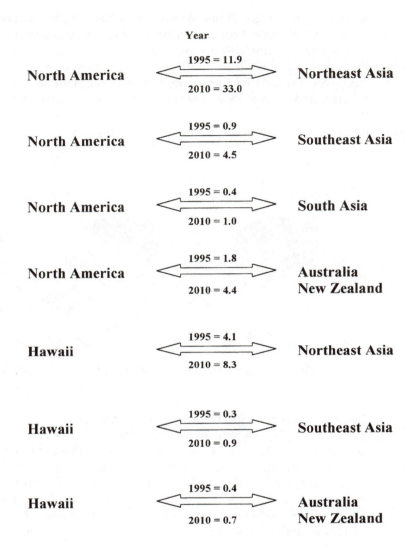

Figure 9.2   Traffic from North America on selected transPacific routes (annual passengers in millions) (adapted from IATA, 1997)

Deregulation and Air Transport Liberalisation

Deregulation and air transport liberalisation mark a turning point in the transformation of airline corporate and marketing strategies. It is mainly the North American and European air transport markets that have been deregulated. However, other regions are also affected as they trade directly with both North

America and Europe. Between them, these two regions account for two-thirds of the world's air traffic and have most of the world's largest airlines. Deregulation of air transport first occurred in the United States at the end of the 1970s and transformed the policies and strategies of US airline companies.

Liberalisation, fifth freedom rights and cabotage are the basis of deregulation. Fifth freedom rights allow commercial transport between two states other than the airline's own country. This has been the key condition for the growth of international air transport competition and liberalisation based on internationalisation and market access. Cabotage allows an airline of one country to embark passengers in another country and carry them to another point in the same country for a fee or a leasing contract. It introduces competition between domestic and international carriers and is one of the cornerstones of the new marketing strategy of airlines.

Deregulation 'internationalised' North American airlines, first towards Europe in 1978. Today there are seven American companies operating to Europe: American Airlines, United, Delta, Continental, NorthWest, US Airways and TWA.

European companies have on their side considerably reinforced their regional markets by constituting strong groups such as the British Airways–Air Liberty–Deutsche BA group. These companies have been able to develop market concentration strategies because their domestic and regional markets have been protected. Furthermore, companies like British Airway have been able to agree favourable conditions on US routes, which are very lucrative. The North American routes represent a greater proportion of international activities for European companies than for American companies – double on average.

The long-term future of airline companies depends on the strategies they adopt in the deregulated market. However, the objectives of the strategies followed by US carriers are different from those followed by European airlines.

On the one hand, US companies operate in a domestic market that accounts for a quarter of world domestic and international air traffic. To better utilise their fleets, they need to internationalise and capture new markets. Since deregulation they are able to develop market penetration strategies, particularly in European countries.

On the other, most airlines from other regions on the world (Europe, Asia and so on) do not have large enough fleets to adopt penetration strategies. In particular, they cannot enter the North American domestic market directly, which is dominated by the hub system. However, certain financially strong European companies such as British Airways, Lufthansa and KLM could acquire US carriers if they were legally able to do so. Currently, US law only allows foreign investors to acquire a maximum 25 per cent equity participation in US carriers.

For this reason, deregulation and liberalisation are vital for the future strategies of airline companies. Therefore, Open Sky agreements are very important for airline companies.

Fifth Freedom Rights and Cabotage

The aim of the Chicago Convention was to facilitate international operation and avoid real competition by fixing bilateral air service agreements between countries and sometimes even at a regional level.

The principles are based on the five freedoms of the air established to control air transport relations:

- The first freedom concerns the right of an airline of one state to fly over the territory of another state.
- The second freedom concerns the right of an airline of one state to land on the territory of another state for non-commercial relations.
- The third freedom relates to the right of an airline to carry passengers, mail and goods from its own state to another state
- The fourth freedom concerns the right of an airline of one state to embark passengers, mail and goods in another state and carry them to its own state.
- The fifth freedom relates to commercial transport between two states other than the airline's own country. This is a key condition for the growth of international air transport competition and new marketing policies.

Although fifth freedom rights were agreed at the Chicago Convention, to date they have never really come into force. The liberalisation of air transport is largely dependent on fifth freedom agreements.

Cabotage allows an airline of one country to embark passengers in another country and carry them to another point in the same country for a fee or a leasing contract. It introduces competition between domestic and international carriers and it is one of the cornerstones of the new marketing strategy pursued by airlines because passengers can decide to use other airlines that also have free access to the market.

US Deregulation

Deregulation of air transport was first introduced in 1978 in North America. US deregulation became known as the Open Sky Policy and has five main clauses:

1. *Free access to all routes* – This is the keystone of all liberalisation and deregulation air transport policies. It allows airlines to operate freely between different airports with the only limitation involving issues of security, financial guarantees and the availability of slots at airports. Airline can pursue strategies that will introduce new services to satisfy demand (that is, the opening of new routes), close down routes or change prices and schedules.

2. *No restriction on capacity and frequency on any route* – This clause allows airlines to establish 'hubs' without restrictions. The strategy rests on the freedom to greatly increase frequencies so that both transit and direct-route passengers can be accommodated. Since deregulation in the United States,

hubs have been established by the main US airline companies for domestic as well as international routes leaving the US, notably in Dallas, Atlanta, Chicago, New York, Miami and Denver.

3. *No restriction on operation in all international markets* – This reinforces the strategy based on creating hubs by allowing airlines to service intermediate points and to use an unlimited number of smaller aircraft to and from international gateways. The clause particularly favours airline companies with large fleets which can establish themselves quickly in new markets.

4. *Flexibility of tariffs* – Airlines are able to fix their own tariffs and this is one of the most important conditions for the liberalisation of air transport. The best performing airlines can service new routes and increase their market share. However, dumping must be prohibited to guarantee the long-term interests of the customer. Flexibility of tariffs has been mainly implemented by US airlines on North Atlantic routes.

5. *Liberalisation of charter rules and elimination of restrictions on charters* – Non-scheduled air transport plays a very important role in the development of tourism in certain regions of the world such as the Mediterranean basin. It allows companies to address traffic problems during peak periods and to maintain pressure on keeping air fares competitive. Hence, Open Sky also concerns charter companies, which must also have the same access to the market.

EU Deregulation

In April 1997, European deregulation moved one step closer to coming into existence when the fifteen EU countries agreed to drop restrictions on air transport within the EU. Airlines can now set their own prices and use cabotage rights. These measures should eliminate protectionist barriers within the EU.

Deregulation of air transport in Europe covers three main areas:

1. Airlines companies can set tariffs freely. However, the civil authorities of the countries concerned can oppose these, particularly, if tariffs do not relate to the real cost of flying a particular route. This regulation is to avoid the air fare price wars which followed deregulation in the USA. Furthermore, certain European governments like the United Kingdom's also want to avoid extreme variations in prices.

2. The second area relates to the standardisation of operating conditions for all airlines companies in Europe. All carriers in the EU can trade from any country within the EU if they conform to three conditions:

    ● at least 51 per cent of the company's capital should be owned by citizens of European Union member countries
    ● a minimum capital investment of 100,000 ECU
    ● the aircraft should be registered in the country that issued its certificate of airworthiness.

3. The third area concerns cabotage rights that is, the right to operate domestic flights in other EU countries and to operate flights originating from other EU countries. The cabotage right is a fundamental step in Europe deregulation as it places European airline companies in a similar competitive environment to that of the United States.

STRATEGIES IN THE AIR TRANSPORT SECTOR

Marketing Tools Used by Both Airlines and Tourism Firms

Future changes will not only concern changes in market share but also in the approach to commercialising air transport and tourism products. Airlines and tourism firms are already using new tools such as GDSs to commercialise their products. There are an increasing number of Internet sites on which flights, hotels, car rental and excursions can be booked directly without having to consult a travel agent. These websites include Travelocity (www.travelocity.com), Travelweb (www.travelweb.com), Expedia (www.expedia.com), Tiss (www.tiss.com), Enquest (www.enquest.com), Vizion (www.vizion.com) and Yahoo! (www.yahoo.co.uk/business_and_Economy/Campanies/Travel).

For example, Expedia is backed by Microsoft and linked to the travel agent system Worldspan, offering flights, hotels, tours, car hire and so on.

These new strategies emerge from the globalisation process and the deregulation of the international air transport market.

Routes and Airports: Hubs and Spokes

Hubs are essential to present-day airline marketing strategies. Using an airport called a 'hub' to re-organise their flight network allows airlines to take advantage of opportunities offered by liberalisation to restructure their system. This system allows them to increase the number of flights through the hub and reduce direct flights to cities outside the hub system.

Figure 9.3 shows the advantage of establishing a hub at an airport. It allows airline companies to deploy their fleets better and to increase frequencies and load factors. The marketing strategy for developing hubs aims at creating barriers to stop competitors entering the market. These are now commercial barriers rather than political barriers as they were in the past. Indeed, a company entering the market cannot offer the same number of flights as can an established airline using a hub system.

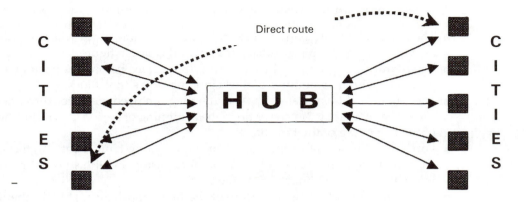

Figure 9.3   The hub and spoke system

However, a hub will only be efficient if the transit time through it is kept to a minimum. Companies must reorganise their schedules in a series of time blocks. Figure 9.4 shows how an airline would organise it arrivals and departures around a 2 hour 30 minute time block.

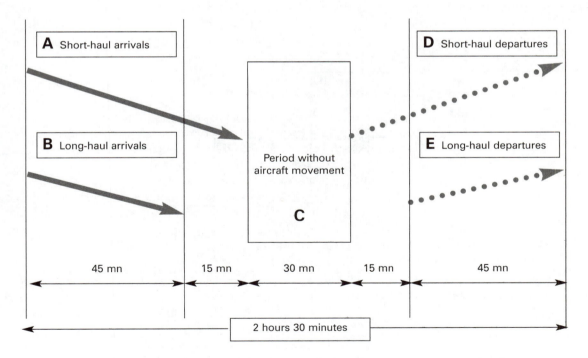

Figure 9.4   Pattern of arrivals and departures of long- and short-haul flights during a 2 hour 30 minute time block

Arrivals and departures are made within a 2 hour 30 minute time block:

- There is a 30-minute period in the middle of the time block where no flight arrives or departs. This is indicated as period C in the figure.
- Long-haul flights indicated by A arrive 15 minutes before the beginning of period C, within 45 minutes of the beginning of the time block.
- Short-haul flights indicated by A on the diagram need a shorter turnaround time. Therefore they can arrive up to the beginning of period C, within 1 hour of the beginning of the time block.
- Forty-five minutes after the arrival of the last long-haul flight (B), the first short-haul flight (D) takes off. Short-haul departures will take off at regular intervals for the last hour of the time block.
- Fifteen minutes after the departure of the first short-haul flight (D), the first long-haul flight (E) can take off. Long-haul departures will take off at regular intervals for the last 45 minutes of the time block.

Therefore, the minimum transit time between two short-hauls fights is 30 minutes; between a short-haul flight and a long-haul flight 45 minutes; and between two long-haul flights 60 minutes. At the end of period C, a new time block starts. During a day, at least five time blocks can be operated, if not more (see Figure 9.5).

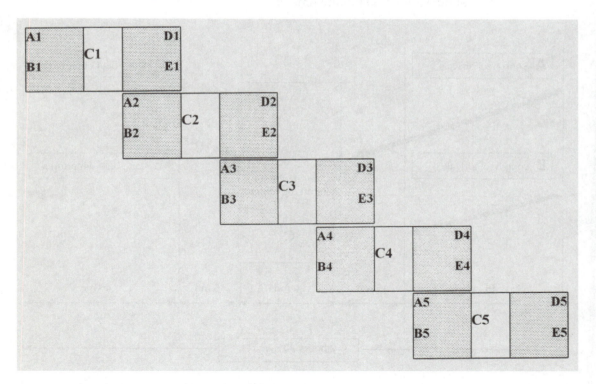

Figure 9.5   Example of time blocks during a day

This strategy greatly increases the number of flights that an airline can offer. For example, since Air France introduced this system at its hub in Paris (Roissy), it has succeeded in tripling the number of flights and doubling the potential number of markets it can exploit.

The hub and spoke system was developed at the larger airports in the United States. These provided airlines with a number of facilities to install their system, particularly time slots to allow them to restructure their networks. Delta developed its system at Atlanta airport, American Airlines at Dallas, United at Chicago and Denver and TWA at St Louis.

Hub strategies can be facilitated or impeded by the way airports are constructed. Certain airports develop their own strategies to fit in with those of the airlines that want to install a hub. Figure 9.6 shows how a hub strategy can be facilitated by the way the airport is organised. All planes from the same company arrive at gates in the same terminal. Aircraft are positioned nose to nose rather than side by side which reduces the distance for travellers to walk from one aircraft to another, thus reducing transit time. A further benefit to the airline is that customer are less likely to want to go to other terminals and will choose to continue their journey with the same company. This example of airport organisation exists at Atlanta airport, where Delta has established its hub.

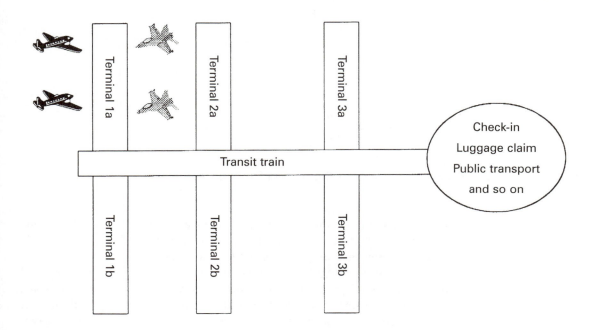

Figure 9.6   Airport organisation strategy linked with airline hub and spoke strategy

Figure 9.7 shows how gates at airports that have not been designed for the hub and spoke system may be positioned. The gates at the terminals are situated in such a way that planes must park side by side, thus reducing the number of aircraft that can use the terminal. Airlines are required to use several terminals for the arrival and departures of their flights obliging their passengers to walk long distances to board connecting flights.

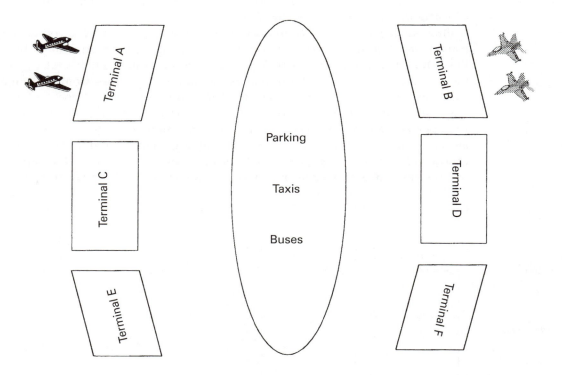

Figure 9.7   Airport not organised for the hub and spoke system

In such situations, fewer connecting flights can be accommodated in the 2 hour 30 minute time block, thus reducing the competitiveness of the airline. This is the case, for instance, at Roissy Charles de Gaulle airport in Paris.

By adopting a hub strategy and increasing the number of flights landing and departing from the airport, an airline occupies a greater number of slots, reducing availability for its competitors and therefore protecting its dominant position. This creates another barrier for entry to the market, even when it is deregulated.

Segmentation and Diversification

Since liberation and deregulation of air transport, airline companies have had to rethink their development and marketing strategies. One option is to abandon vertical integration strategies to concentrate on the core business of transporting passengers and goods.

The End of Traditional Diversification Strategies

Following the example of North American airlines, most European companies have abandoned the strategy of acquiring firms from other sub-sectors of the tourism industry. They have divested or reduced their interest in hotel chains, travel agencies and tour operators. For example, Air France has sold the Meridien hotel chain and the tour operators Jet Tour and Go Voyage.

They are also withdrawing their charter subsidiaries, which were aimed at servicing the holiday market. Swissair has integrated the fleet of its charter airline Balair into its scheduled fleet and ACI (Air Charter International), Air France's charter subsidiary, ceased its activities in 1998.

Nowadays, it is the large tour operators that are adopting vertical integration strategies. For instance, the French tour operator Nouvelle Frontière owns the Charter Company Corsair and the hotel chain Paladins. The British tour operator Thomson own the largest charter airline in the world – Britannia – and the travel agency chain Lunn Poly.

This change in strategic direction has great implications for the marketing strategy of airline companies. They have refocused what they sell to the holiday market and now only offer air travel.

Strategy of Refocusing on Air Transport Activity

New commercial conditions brought by liberalisation and deregulation are forcing airlines to invest in their core product – air transport – in order to compete. The equity released by the sell-off of other tourism concerns (hotel chains, tour operators and so on) are re-invested in purchasing new aircraft and refurbishing existing ones, creating hubs and developing GDSs. These investments allow airlines to develop and consolidate marketing strategies to build customer loyalty.

A new strategy adopted by major airlines to refocus their air transport activity is to create low-cost carriers. British Airways set up GO at London Stansted and Lufthansa and KLM have also studied options for low-cost services. Fewer than 10 millions European passengers travelled on low-cost carriers in 1997, representing a modest 5 per cent of the region's traffic. This compares with close to 30 per cent in America, where the no-frills experiment began and which has provided the inspiration for the new European airline entrepreneurs. Their goal has been to emulate the startling success of Southwest Airlines, which has grown from a small regional operator into a $4 billion dollar concern with the best profits record in the North American industry. However, European followers have to contend not only with the strength of the national flag carriers, but also with higher costs. It costs on average twice as much to turn an aircraft around at a European airport as it does at a US airport. This is partly due to lingering monopolies. As the low-cost airlines expand to develop new routes and pay for new aircraft, the fear is that costs will spiral while fares will come under pressure from intense competition from the larger companies.

The stakes continue to rise for Europe's low-cost carriers. EasyJet signed up for more than $1 billion of new aircraft in 1998, purchasing 15 new generation Boeing 737s, on top of an existing order for 12 conventional 737s. Ryanair, the largest of the European low-cost airlines, purchased 25 new 737s in 1998 with the option of another 20.

Table 9.3   European low-cost carriers

Airline	Start-up date	Fleet	Base	Passengers 1997
Ryanair	May 1985	21xBoeing 737	Dublin	4m
Virgin Express*	May 1996	18xBoeing 737	Brussels	1.8m
EasyJet	October 1995	6xBoeing 737	Luton	1.5m
Debonair	June 1996	6xBAe146	Luton	0.6m
Go	May 1998	3xBoeing 737	London Stansted	n/a

*Virgin Express took over from EuroBelgium Airlines founded in November 1991
Source: *Air and Cosmos*, No. 1635, 1997.

Frequent Flyer Programmes

Airlines are investing in relationship marketing by introducing frequent flyer programmes. This is one of their most dynamic marketing actions. It allows them to understand their clientele better and target more precisely the message they want to convey to each client. Loyalty programmes, known as 'Frequent Flyer Programmes' (FFPs), were first launched by American Airlines. Today, most airlines offer a loyalty programme and the world-wide membership to these programmes totals over 85 million as shown in Table 9.4.

The strategy is to make the schemes easily available to all passengers to ensure that the loyalty system becomes established. Members collect points, which can be exchanged for free flights, hotel nights or car hire. The greater the number of points they collect the greater the benefits they enjoy. Elite status benefits generally include improved baggage allowance, upgraded check-in, preferred seat allocation, priority handling, priority wait listing as well as special offer and gifts.

Frequent flyer programmes (FFPs) offer a method for reinforcing monopolies. This is particularly important in Europe since deregulation has eliminated legal monopolies. Another advantage of FFPs for airline companies is that they help counter the hub domination of airlines such as British Airways at Heathrow and Air France at Paris. United, Lufthansa, Air Canada and SAS have merged their FFPs for precisely this reason.

Table 9.4   **Frequent flyer programme partnerships**

Airline	Programme	Number of members	Partners		
			Airlines	Car Hire	Hotels
Aer Lingus	Travel Award Bonus	160,000	Delta, City Jet	Avis Europecar Hertz	Jurys Hotel Group
Air Canada	Aeroplan	1,000,000	Air Creebec Air Schefferville Bearskin Airlines British Midland Continental Finnair Lufthansa Swissair United	Avis Hertz Budget	Hilton Holiday Inn Marriot Radisson Sheraton Westin
Air France	Frequence Plus	1,300,000	Aero Mexico JAL Continental Delta	Avis Hertz	Meridien Sheraton Concord
American Airlines	AAdvantage	28,000,000	British Airways American Eagle Canadian Airlines Cathay Pacific Hawaiian JAL Qantas Singapore South African Airways	Avis Hertz Alamo Dollar National	Forte Forum Hilton Holiday Inn Hyatt Intercontinental Sheraton Meridien Marriot Loews Radisson Red Lion Sandal resorts Vista, Westin Wyndham
British Airways	Executive Club	1,000,000	American Airlines Aero Mexico Alaska America West ANA, Braathens Canadian Cathay Pacific Malaysia, Quantas SIA, Deutsche BA Air Liberty, Maersk Loganair, Brymon	Avis Hertz Alamo	Savoy Group Mandarin Oriental Hilton Intercontinental Marriot New Otani Radisson Ritz-Carton Taj Group
British Midland	Diamond Club	–	Air Canada Air New Zealand Luthansa, SAS South African United and Virgin Atlantic	Avis Hertz Budget	Best Western Doyle Group Hilton Radisson SAS Edwardian

Table 9.4 *(cont'd)*

Airline	Programme	Number of members	Partners		
			Airlines	*Car Hire*	*Hotels*
Japan Airline	Mileage Bank	2,000,000	Air France American Airlines	–	Intercontinental Mandarin Oriental New Otani Pan Pacific Prince, Sol Melia Summit International Westin
Lufthansa	Miles & More	2,000,000	United, Adria Air, Dolomite British Midland Air Canada Finnair, Lauda Air Luxair, SAS SIA, SAA	Avis Hertz Budget	Hilton Kempinksi Holiday Inn Intercontinental Sheraton Marriot Ramada Renaissance Shangri La, Vista
Qantas	Frequent Flier	1,000,000	Air Pacific American British Airways Canadian, SAS	Hertz Thrifty	Carlton Hilton, Forum Holiday Inn Ibis, Intercon- tinental, Sheraton Mandarin, Marriot, Mercure, Novotel, Quality, Radisson, Regent, Softel
United Airlines	Mileage Plus	–	Lufthansa Air Canada Aloha, Ansett British Midland SAS, SIA, Thai	Alamo Avis Budget Dollar Hertz National	Hilton Holiday Inn Hyatt Intercontinental
Virgin Atlantic Airways	Freeway	250,000	Air New Zealand Austrian British Midland Malaysia Midwest Express SAS	–	Holiday Inn Intercontinental Radisson, SAS Virgin Hotels Marco Polo Hotels Summit International Westin Mandarin Oriental

Source: Chetwynd, 1997.

These strategies create new barriers for competition in the deregulated market. Smaller airlines or new market entrants accuse airlines with large FFPs of contravening EU anti-competition rules. The impact of FFPs may constitute a barrier for start-up airlines with small route networks. Potential passengers already members of established FFPs are less likely to use the new entrant's services on routes overlapping the network of the existing carrier.

It is important to remember that FFPs were originally based on the hub and spoke system. But now, with the new Open Sky agreement between the United States and Europe, FFPs are one of the major components of strategic alliances. FFPs and alliances facilitate the penetration by US airlines in EU markets. Therefore, it is difficult to predict whether airline companies will be allowed to integrate FFPs into their strategic alliances as freely as they would want to in the future.

FFPs are very powerful commercial management tools. For this reason, the European Commission has paid great attention to their development, but has not yet intervened to limit them. However, action may be taken to control future alliances and mergers where FFP strategies would restrict access to certain markets.

The importance of FFPs in airline marketing strategies is increasing. FFPs are now linked to loyalty programmes operated in other sectors. For instance British Airways' FFP is connected to the Air Miles Awards programme. Other participating partners come from a variety of sectors such as:

- the retail sector – Sainsbury's Homebase
- utilities – Scottish Hydro-Electric, Amerada gas
- the telecommunication sector – British Telecom, Vodaphone
- the financial sector – Diners' Club card, NatWest credit card
- selected restaurants.

Therefore, FFPs have become inter-sectoral.

Pricing Strategies

Airline pricing strategies are important in airline marketing strategies. Once airlines have successfully established hub and spoke systems and differentiation strategies, they can increase their prices. This is the case in North America where tariffs rose from 104 on an index of 100 in 1996 to 116 in 1997. Tariffs for business and first class rose from 100 to 110 over the same period.

On the other hand, tariffs in western Europe between 1996 and 1997 only rose from 102 to 107 on an index of 100. Excursion tariffs in high season fell from 100 to 83 because of high competition.

However, according to Boeing Current Market Outlook (1997), the average world price of air travel as measured by fares has declined about 1 per cent a year over the last two decades. This is a result of greater productivity in both the equipment used and human resources. Competitive pressures on high-cost operators have also brought down fares. Advances in pricing, distribution and yield management have helped greatly. Low relative prices have increased the demand for travel.

Figure 9.8 uses US data to portray the long-run decline of yields, which has been a world-wide phenomenon. Yet more of the decline has resulted from the faster growth of demand for leisure trips, which are priced lower.

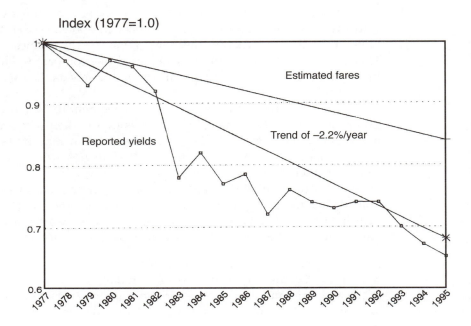

Figure 9.8   Price declines (Boeing current market outlook, 1992)

In addition to lower prices, airlines also offer greater value to travellers through increased services by:

1. opening new routes between airports
2. increasing frequency on existing routes; that is, daily services instead of weekly services on intercontinental routes and hourly services instead of twice-daily services on domestic and regional routes.

There are therefore more non-stop flights and a wider choice of departure and arrival times for the convenience of travellers.

It is estimated that the value added of the new service is more than 1 per cent a year, which compounds with the 1 per cent decline in prices to increase competitiveness.

STRUCTURAL CHANGES IN INTERNATIONAL MARKETING STRATEGIES OF AIRLINE COMPANIES

To compete, airlines must complement their marketing strategy with structural changes. These often require important investment to enhance company image and allow airlines to adapt their marketing strategy.

Renewing the Fleet

This is a highly competitive strategy pursued by some Asian airline companies, notably Singapore Airlines. Its policy is to buy new aircraft on a regular basis. In this way it replaces its fleet and sells its older planes (which are still virtually new) at a very high price. This is a very efficient method of ensuring high quality.

The strategy also reduces vulnerability to fuel price fluctuations because newer aircraft such as the Boeing 777 and the Airbus A340 are generally more fuel efficient.

Another way of refurbishing the fleet and strengthening the marketing effort is to repaint the aircraft. This is a differentiation strategy. Competing airlines use virtually identical metal tubes, offering very similar services. By decorating the tube with distinctive paintings, characters and designs the airline tries to change the way people think about the company. Several companies have experimented by painting original concepts on some of their aircraft:

- Austrian Airlines has a special livery on one of its airlines depicting famous Austrian opera stars
- Qantas has painted several planes in an Aboriginal style
- JAL has decorated aircraft with Disney and Peter Pan characters
- Crossair advertises *The Phantom of the Opera* and McDonald's
- All Nippon Airways has characters for the cartoon strip Peanuts
- Air France carries the winning 1998 World Cup soccer team.

The public identifies with this marketing technique; for example in Japan, many passengers ask to fly on 'the Disney 747'.

On a greater scale, British Airways has decorated its different aircraft with specific designs. BA's new look is designed to reflect a more global image. A selection of 50 different and individually painted tailplanes adorn the airline's fleet of more than 300 aircraft, and the same designs appear on all BA products from ticket wallets to baggage tags. The different designs include pottery from England; a wall hanging from Egypt; Chinese calligraphy from Hong Kong; a traditional painting from Japan; and a ceramic panel from Germany. However, this marketing strategy has been controversial with professionals, experts from the industry and with the public.

EasyJet has adopted another strategy and has its phone number for reservations in large numbers on the sides of its aircraft. This advertises its low-cost status as well as providing a direct sales distribution channel.

Privatisation

The privatisation of airline companies is a radical marketing strategy. Deregulation in the air transport industry has encouraged privatisation around the world. National flag-carrying companies have been unable to follow the trend towards concentration and mergers because these are incompatible with the traditional public service role that there have to carry out.

The objective behind privatisation strategies is to design marketing plans and diversification programmes to compete in the global market. For privatisation to be successful certain economic and profitability conditions must exist and appropriate actions must be taken. The United States want to see the Open Sky policy extended to all markets in the world and this is accelerating the trend towards privatisation.

The majority of airline in the EU and in central and eastern Europe are following policies of total or partial privatisation. British Airways in the United Kingdom and Lufthansa in Germany have been successfully privatised and, by internal growth and acquisition of other airlines, can now be counted among the world's largest carriers.

International Alliances

Since air transport routes have been open to competition, airlines have preferred to form alliances with their competitors rather than take equity shares in smaller airlines. Although partners still keep their autonomy, these alliances are more than just simple commercial agreements.

The objective of creating an alliance is to share means and resources to increase market share and to create barriers to the market for their competition. The strategy is to acquire repeat customers by building loyalty and limiting their options on key routes in order to control global air traffic.

In the past, commercial agreements mainly concerned joint management agreements to set up ground handling at airports, commercial representation agreements and joint-investment and operating expenditure agreements.

Strategic international alliances have introduced two new elements, which have transformed conditions in the air transport market and therefore, the way airlines market: code sharing and frequent flyer programme partnerships.

Code-Sharing Strategy and Alliances

According to ICAO, code sharing is defined as one carrier allowing another to use its identification codes or two carriers sharing the same identification code for a flight. In practice, passengers are carried by an airline other than the one indicated on the ticket.

Airlines benefit from much greater advantages when code sharing is integrated in a broad strategic alliance, than when code sharing is simply sharing identification codes. Broad strategic alliance may include co-operation in the following areas:

- joint management
- joint commercialisation
- joint purchasing of major resources such as fuel, insurance and equipment
- co-ordination of ground handling services
- joint reservation facilities.

Co-operation will generally result in extra traffic and increased revenues for the partners in the alliance.

Frequent Flyer Programme Partnerships

Sharing frequent flyer programmes increases the client base of the partners, as customers are encouraged to choose alliances rather than individual companies. This creates another barrier preventing competitors from entering the market. The STAR Alliance has adopted this marketing strategy.

Of all the alliances in existence in 1998, two will play a determining role in the future. They each boast a membership of over 170 million passengers:

- The ONEWORLD Alliance between British Airways (38 million passengers), American Airlines (81 million passengers) and Iberia (23 millions passengers) is enlarged by the companies already in the British Airways Group: Air Liberté and Deutsche BA in Europe; Qantas in Australia; Canadian Airlines; and Cathay Pacific.
- The STAR Alliance groups United (82 million passengers), Lufthansa (42 million passengers) as well as Air Canada, Singapore Airlines, Thai Airways, SAS and Varig.

Two alliances account for more than 100 million passengers each:

- QUALITY EXCELLENCE which groups Delta Airlines (103 million passengers) and Swissair with its partners Sabena, Austrian Airlilnes, Lauda Air, AOM and TAP Air Portugal.
- NorthWest Airlines (50 million passengers) and KLM (12 million passengers) have also created an alliance and have recently been joined by Continental and Alitalia.

Therefore, partners in these alliances benefit from powerful marketing advantages which airlines operating individually cannot enjoy.

In their marketing communication, alliance partners promise passengers seamless travel, unified FFPs and high standards of comfort and service guaranteed across the combined fleet.

British Airways' alliance strategy is not just based on partnership but also on equity participation and control of capital. It has acquired shares in Air Liberté, Deutsche BA, Air Russia and Qantas. In addition, it has a wide variety of franchised airlines in the UK such as Manx Europe, Cityflyer Express, Maersk UK, Loganair and Brymon. BA also has alliances of one kind or another with a further 11 airlines. It has recently entered the low-cost market and has launched GO, which serves several European destinations.

This strategy means that it is serves all tourism segments including the business travel segment.

Global Distribution Systems (GDSs) and Computerised Systems

Computerised reservation and distribution systems are essential components of airline marketing strategy. They disseminate and process information more efficiently than the traditional systems used by individual companies or printed timetables and price lists.

Each airline has its own CRS (computer reservation system). However, they are interconnected through GDSs (global distribution systems) which can be accessed by travel agents to find information on all airline companies and service providers in the system.

GDSs differ from simple information systems because they are far more comprehensive. They provide information, allow reservations to be registered and sales to be processed.

All three functions must be interconnected to ensure the effectiveness of the system. A single GDS terminal provides immediate access to all the service companies that have opted to market their products through the network.

Businesses (air carriers or independent commercial companies) that have developed GDSs and own them either completely or in partnership are known as 'vendors'. They make their system available to third parties like travel agents so that they can provide information to the public (see Figure 9.9).

Today, the services that GDSs mainly provide are:

- bookings and ticketing for air transport
- hotel reservation
- car hire bookings.

They are also starting to sell many other tourism services such as:

- reservation service for small hotels
- rural tourism products
- sports activities
- cultural activities (shows, entertainment and so on)
- local transport
- ancillary services such as insurance, financial services and so on.

However, tourism firms not only face the problem of ensuring they can be found easily on a GDS but also of knowing how to derive marketing benefit from it. Airlines are more advanced in using GDSs in their marketing as they were first to develop the technology.

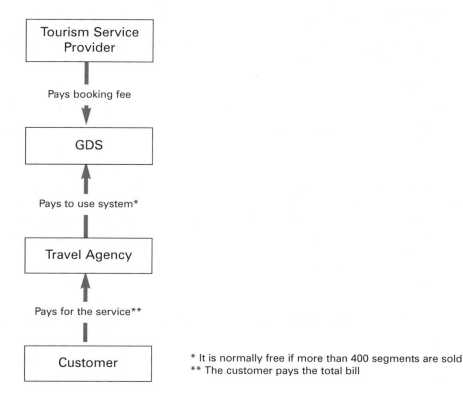

Figure 9.9   GDS and commercialisation of tourism products

The Main GDSs in the World

The main tourism distribution networks are highly concentrated and, to a great extent, dominated by American and European airlines. The four main GDSs are:

- Galileo International created by United Airlines, British Airways, Alitalia, Swissair, KLM and Olympic Airways
- Sabre established by American Airlines
- Worldspan created by Delta, TWA and NorthWest in association with the Asian carriers GDS, Abacus
- Amadeus/System One set up by the European airlines Air France, Lufthansa, Iberia and SAS.

One hundred and fifty thousand travel agencies world-wide are connected to GDSs (see Table 9.5).

Table 9.5   **Utilisation of GDSs by travel agencies in 1997**

GDS	1997	Percentage
AMADEUS/SYSTEM ONE	42,328	33
GALILEO/APOLLO	36,614	28
SABRE	33,453	26
WORLDSPAN	17,325	13

Source: Amadeus, 1998.

The geographical location and concentration of GDSs determine their importance for airlines. For example, Table 9.5 shows that Amadeus/System One GDS is well represented around the world with over 42,000 travel agencies using its services and a market share of 33 per cent. Nevertheless, in terms of number of reservations, Amadeus is in fourth position, because it is the least used system the US and Canada (see Table 9.6).

Table 9.6   **Use of GDSs by number of reservation in USA and Canada in 1997 (%)**

SABRE	31.3
WORLDSPAN	27.6
GALILEO	21.6
AMADEUS	19.5
TOTAL	100

Source: Amadeus, 1998.

Therefore, choosing the right GDS is a critical factor for tourism marketing. A 1995 survey shows that travel agents choose GDSs according to the following criteria in order of importance:

- accuracy of information
- ease of use
- rapidity of responses
- telephone support
- training
- price.

This shows that price is less important than other features of the GDS because most travel agents do not actually pay for the system if they sell enough segments.

According to travel agencies surveyed by Echo Touristique (see Table 9.7), Galileo and Sabre are considered to be the most efficient GDSs for hotel reservations and Amadeus for ease of use.

Table 9.7   GDSs compared

Criteria	Amadeus	Galileo	Sabre	Worldspan
Screen	Windows environment	Windows environment	Windows environment	Windows environment
Product: Air transport	Yes	Yes	Yes	Yes
Hotels	Yes	Yes	Yes	Yes
Car hire	Yes	Yes	Yes	Yes
Rail	Yes	Yes	Yes	Yes
Ferries	Yes	Yes	Yes	Yes
Tour Operators	Yes	Yes	Yes	Yes
Average transaction time	4.7 seconds	3.1 seconds	3.7 seconds	2.4 seconds
Material provided	Compulsory hire	Optional hire of terminals and printers	Possible to adapt the agencies' equipment	Optional hire of terminals and printers
On-site repair	4 hours max.	4 to 6 hours max.	4 to 6 hours max.	4 hours max.
Management – Accounting	Yes	Yes	Yes	Yes
Price	Monthly hire by screen: approx $200	Free equipment after 300 reservations a month	Free equipment after 300 reservations a month	Free equipment after 300 reservations a month

Source: Echo Touristique, (2320) 15 March 1996.

GDSs and Tourism Commercialisation

World information and distribution networks play a decisive role in the international tourism sector since they bring buyers and producers of tourism products into contacts. However, it is mainly North American and European tourism firms that use GDSs in tourism marketing. Two-third of agencies connected to GDSs in the world are located in North America and Europe (see Figure 9.10).

GDSs process information and bookings more efficiently than single-access systems. However, the strategic importance of GDSs has decreased since US and European authorities and the ICAO have introduced stringent regulations to prevent airlines that own the GDSs from benefiting from unfair advantages by distorting the way information is presented. Neutrality has mostly been achieved now.

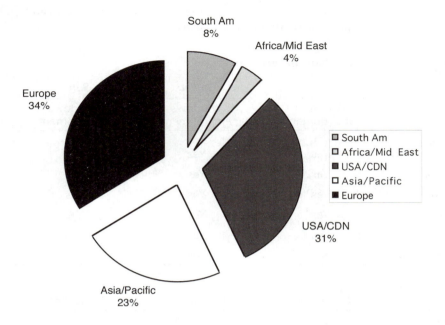

Figure 9.10   Geographical distribution of GDSs (Amadeus, 1998)

Therefore, in principle, GDSs cannot be used to gain market share to the detriment of competing companies. On the other hand, they provide an important source of income for the companies that own them.

Nevertheless, in certain circumstances GDSs are still being used unfairly. These include:

- unfair rights of access, mainly in terms of the breakdown of costs between system vendors, carriers and suppliers of tourism services
- the monopolistic market aspect of world-wide information systems, which make it almost impossible for competitors to develop new complementary system
- restrictions on displaying information and fares of certain small service suppliers.

In these conditions, there are two priority measures that must be ensured to guarantee equitable access to global information and reservation networks:

1. Making the systems neutral.
2. Improving the use of networks with the better use of Back Office Systems.

GDSs and the Internet

The greatest advance in GDS being used in tourism marketing has been their inclusion on the Internet. This integration allows the system to be accessed from anywhere 24 hours a day, 365 days a year and therefore increases sales and turnover. Indeed, because GDSs can now be accessed via the Internet, the customer can find all the relevant information to make his or her choices and reservations directly. The products that are available include:

● information on tourism products
● search for bargain offers
● automatic calculation of fares
● automatic access to fight availability
● booking facilities.

Figure 9.11 shows the three phases in the commercialisation of the tourism product via a GDS on the Internet

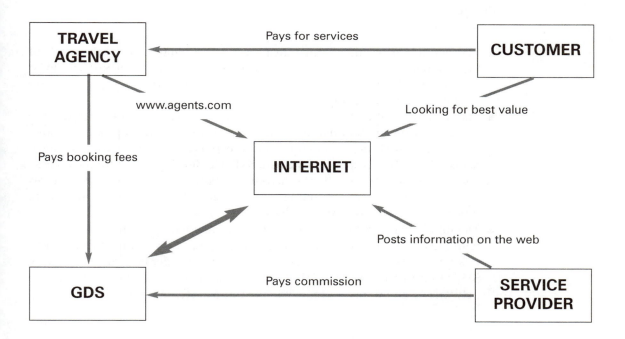

Figure 9.11   Three phases in the commercialisation of the tourism product via a GDS on the Internet

Stage 1: the customer searches for information on a trip on the internet and makes a booking through the GDS booking facility.

Stage 2: the travel agency retrieves the reservation on the GDS and prepares the paperwork necessary to process for the booking

Stage 3: the travel agent sends the relevant documents to the customer.

The commercialisation of tourism products in the future will rely more and more on the interactivity between GDSs and the Internet. Amadeus forecasts that direct sales of flights will progress from 0.45 per cent of total sales in 1996 to 8.2 per cent by the year 2002. As Terry Jones from Sabre says: 'We must find a way to convince the customer to use the web rather than pick up the telephone to call.'

CONCLUSION

The close co-operation between airline companies and firms in the other tourism sub-sectors is an essential ingredient of success, especially for new tourism destination.

In conclusion:

- International marketing of air transport must take into account the needs of the destination's tourism development. The supply of air transport should be adapted to the needs of tourism companies in terms of capacity, flight frequency and price competitiveness.
- The development of air transport marketing strategies must encompass the process of deregulation that is occurring world-wide. Appropriate air transport marketing strategies should contribute to the marketing of tourism destinations to enable airlines and tourism SMEs to develop their activities. These will be focused on negotiating favourable participation in global alliances and global systems and on setting up tourism and air travel hubs, which are fundamental to the future of airlines.
- The link between air transport and tourism marketing has been established with the developments in communication, distribution and reservation technologies. GDSs and the Internet which allow tour operators and hospitality SMEs to gain direct access to the main generating markets through the airline networks used by travel agents will continue to strengthen this link.

REFERENCES AND FURTHER READING

Airline Business (1998) *Economic Indicators, 1996–1998*, Reed Business Publications: East Grinstead.

Amadeus (1998) Paper presented by Felipe Gonzales Abad, General Director, at the Experts Meeting on Strengthening the Capacity for Expanding the Tourism Sector in Developing Countries, UNCTAD.

Beller, W., d'Ayala, P. Hein, P. (1990) *Sustainable Development and Environmental Management of Small Island*s, MAB UNESCO: Paris.

Carre, A. (1990) *Aéroport et Stratégies d'Entreprise*, Presses de l'ITA: Paris.

CCE International (1998) *Transport Aérien 2010, Un Horizon en Pointillés*, CCEI, Paris.

Chetwynd, C. (1997) 'Counting the cost of loyalty', *Executive Traveller*, **19**(2): 31–6.

OECD (1997) *L'Avenir du Transport Aérien International. Quelle Politique Face aux Mutations Mondiales?* OECD, Paris.

Rapp, L. and Vellas, F. (1992) *Airline Privatisation in Europe*, ITA Institute of Air Transport: Toulouse.

UNCTAD (1998) *International Trade in Tourism – Related Services: Issues and Options for Developing Countries*, Geneva.

Vellas, F. (1995) *Le Transport Aérien*, Economica: Paris.

Vellas, F. and Bécherel, L. (1995) *International Tourism – an Economic Perspective*, Macmillan: Basingstoke.

Wheatcroft, S. (1994) *Aviation and Tourism Policies, Balancing the Benefits*, WTO: Madrid.

WTO (1997) *International Tourism Statistics*, WTO: Madrid.

STRATEGIC MARKETING IN THE TOUR OPERATOR SECTOR

TIM KNOWLES AND PETER GRABOWSKI

Background

Tourism is a business which has become increasingly multi-national in structure and organisation over the past 30 years. An important element of this business in developed countries is the channel relationship between the providers of tourism services, wholesalers and retailers. For instance, the British tourism market, with its wide range of different types of interconnections between travel/tourism product suppliers (principals), tour operators and travel agents is a very good example of a market in which the distribution channels are well developed and diverse. Each type of channel organisational structure (including conventional, contractual, vertical, horizontal and hybrid distribution systems) operate in this market (Laws, 1997).

The focus in this chapter is on tour operators as a provider of a wide range of travel services. Their relationship with travel agents creates one of the several links within the channels of distribution of tourism products. These interlinkages can be illustrated by the UK travel and tourism industry which, in the view of some commentators, is considered to have three distinct components:

1. the UK travel industry
2. the UK tourism industry
3. the UK passenger transport industry.

The UK travel industry consists of UK-based tour operators and travel agents and serves the needs of UK residents travelling both at home and abroad. The role of this sector is to meet the needs of such clients at their point of origin and to act as wholesalers of services provided by transport operators, parts of the domestic and foreign tourism industries; notably hotel and other accommodation services. The UK tourism industry consists of UK hotels and other providers of accommodation as well as restaurants, stately homes, heritage suites and a host of other leisure and entertainment facilities utilised by tourists visiting or travelling within the UK – both domestic and foreign residents. The role of this sector is to meet the needs of people at their destination. The UK passenger transport industry comprises organisations such as UK-based airlines, ferry and cruise line operators, bus and coach companies and railways.

The role of this sector is to meet the needs of people travelling between their point of origin and their destination.

These three sectors are not entirely separate, in the sense that there is an overlap between them in the markets they serve.

Structure

Tour operators emerged on the market in order to provide services that benefit some societal groups. The travelling public uses the expertise of operators and thus saves itself time, effort and money. In return, industry principals and suppliers gain access to a widespread network of outlets, the business community gains appropriate advice regarding travel, hotel reservation and ancillary services.

From a historical perspective, the traditional tourism distribution channel has consisted of small, independent retailers whose objectives were to maximise their own profits. As time passed, these retailers started to specialise and a group of tour operators also emerged. As this specialisation developed different groups of intermediaries became prevalent in the tourism market, other processes took place which changed the pattern of tourism channels. These processes included both vertical and horizontal integration. Today, some of the most familiar travel retailers are owned by large tour operators, with the result that the organisation is in effect an integrated business system (Laws, 1997: 120).

The key to understanding the European travel business is the trend towards concentration over recent years. The industry is increasingly dominated by a few groups each with fairly defined spheres of influence based on sole ownership or strategic alliances. The emerging multi-nationals in Europe include the following:

- Wagonlits
- Airtours
- Borgtornet AB
- Club Méditerranée
- DER
- Franctour
- Grupo Viajes Iberia
- Havas Voyages
- Hotelplan
- ITS/Holland International
- Jet tours and Visit France
- Kuoni
- LTU International Airways
- Neckermann NUR
- Nouvelles Frontières
- Owners Abroad
- Thomas Cook
- Thomson Travel Group
- TUI
- Viajes El Corte Ingles

The central issue with all these firms is the move towards consolidation in a desire to achieve economies of scale and synergies through the integration of several sectors rather than achieving size in one aspect of the business alone. What has divided these businesses in recent years is a different view of which business combinations best achieve growth and is determined by six issues.

1. Domestic market size.
2. Different legal systems.
3. Relationships between industry and financial institutions and the need for local partners when investing in airlines or developing countries.
4. The relative importance of banks and stock markets.
5. The group's own history.
6. Investment opportunity.

Some of the earliest leaders in the field, for example Thomson of the UK, have been overtaken in this European consolidation process. Other firms have been more successful at generating organic growth. For example, Nouvelles Frontières has adopted a totally integrated approach with the acquisition of its own airline and expansion into other European countries. Frantour has developed through strong non-French tour operating operations, particularly in France but unsuccessfully in Italy, and additionally growth of its hotel and restaurant businesses which have synergies with its parent company SNCF, the French Railways.

Of the top 20 companies listed here, 19 are in the travel agency business and 19 are outward tour operators. The exceptions are Thomas Cook and LTU, but through their strategic alliance the former is effectively the latter's travel agency arm in Germany. Most of the 20 firms are involved in inbound tourism both in the countries in which they sell outbound travel and at their main destinations. The majority are predominantly in the leisure travel business, but for some, business and incentive travel are major elements as well. Eleven have hotel divisions within their travel firms, six have airlines and most have a strategic alliance with an airline.

It is clear from this discussion that distinguishing retailers and wholesalers is problematic as they can both be regarded as intermediaries with a high degree of cross ownership. Travel retailers make their services easily accessible to clients through either the traditional full-service travel agents (selling all travel, accommodation and related services such as travel insurance, enabling clients to create independent packages) or holiday shops (catalogue sales outlets for the tour operators who have already pre-selected and packaged a range of holidays). These two categories are however, not mutually exclusive. Most full-service retailers sell routine packages and most holiday shops offer some degree of individual product tailoring for their customers.

Despite the fact that travel agents and tour operators are distinctive in the British market, this is not the case in other markets, although they will be discussed separately in this and the following chapter. However, answering the question as to what is a travel business is not becoming easier as this integration process evolves. On a Europe-wide basis the figures in Table 10.1 illustrate the dominance of the majors.

Table 10.1   Major European tour operators by market share

Country	Tour Operators	Market Share %
Austria	Touropa/ITAS/Ruefa/Kuoni – NUR	45
Belgium	NUR	50
France	Nouvelles Frontières/Club Med	25
Germany	TUI/NUR/LTT	37
Netherlands	TUI	30
Ireland	Budget/JWT/(First Choice)	40
Scandinavia	Airtours	43
UK	Thomson	58

Table 10.2   UK travel agents and tourism associations

UK travel agents (1997)	Number of outlets	% of company's outlets to all outlets	Number of outlets in groups (in %)	Groups of travel agents
Lunn Poly	794	8.6		
Thomas Cook	388	4.2		
Going Places	702	7.6	27.4	Multiples
AT Mays	416	4.5		
Co-op Travelcare	231	2.5		
Miniples	840	9.1	9.1	Miniples
NAITA	674	7.3		
ARTAC	619	6.7		
Non-ABTA Global	203	2.2		
Non-ABTA TTA	314	3.4	63.5	Independents
Other non-ABTA	1875	20.3		
Other ABTA	2179	23.6		
All UK agents	9235	100	100	

Source: Beaver A. (1997) Summer Holidays Abroad (this report states the highest numbers, in others – Mintel, 1996, 1998 – the total number of travel agents reaches from 7500 up to 8000 outlets).

In developing these points a breakdown of UK travel agents and tourism associations is listed in Table 10.2 above, thus illustrating the dominance of the multiples and the fragmented independent sector.

Further investigation of these figures and this integration process illustrates that market share of holidays, sold by different retailer categories by sales and profit are:

- 80 per cent of holiday sales are made through travel agents, of which:
  - 61 per cent are accounted by the major multiples
  - 19 per cent through independent and regional chains
- 20 per cent (remaining) are achieved either direct with the tour operator, or by other means:
  - 11 per cent – direct via tour operator
  - 6 per cent – via Teletext
  - 3 per cent – via Internet (Mintel Report, 1996, 1998).

In analysing tour operators, this sector consists of around 1000 companies; the exact number is not known (MMC Report, 1997), although the *Travel and Tourism Gazette Directory* quotes 1346 tour operators in the British market. Around 50 of them are really big and well known, while the remaining belong to a group of small, specialised or so-called niche markets tour operators. The process of horizontal integration has grown in the late 1990s and the numbers of remaining independent operators continues to fall. The case study in Box 10.1 discusses the emerging market of Poland.

BOX 10.1

OVERVIEW OF THE TRAVEL INDUSTRY IN POLAND

'Tourism in Eastern Europe has been the subject of considerable change since the political events of 1988/89 propelled the region towards a market economy. Tourism seems to be a good example of the process of change as it cuts across a variety of economic sectors and primarily comprises small and medium-sized enterprises' (Cooper *et al*., 1998: 478).

Between 1950 and 1988 only ten big travel agencies existed in Poland. They were state owned and dealt with both tour operation and travel agency activities. These big travel firms had their branches in the major cities, their way of conducting business in a branch was highly centralised. All important decisions came from the head office, which usually was located in Warsaw.

Since 1989, private enterprise has resulted in a flood of new privately owned travel companies. There is no comprehensive documentation in terms of numbers, although estimates suggest 3000 companies.

Statistical data on numbers of tourists travelling abroad and visiting Poland over the past few years confirms that the Polish tourism industry, both outbound and inbound, is developing fast. Nevertheless there is no firm, at present, in the Polish tourism market which would be able to compete with the world's major companies; there is less clarity in the definition of channels of distribution and the tourist product is not uniformly available throughout the country. The structure of the Polish travel market, having changed from the monolithic pre-1989 situation to a highly fragmented pattern of both suppliers, wholesalers and

---

BOX 10.1 (cont'd)

retailers, is beginning to produce some organisations which are moving towards UK practices in terms of size, vertical and horizontal integration and channel management practices.

Most of the processes such as channel management and integration that are taking place in the Polish market are similar to many western countries, although the pace and the scale of the former is much slower. After 1989 the sector comprising travel firms developed very fast (probably the pace there was much faster than in any other activity), although a lot fewer treat tourism as its main activity. Most of the companies that co-operate with the Polish and foreign organisers are small. At the same time (quite often) tourism is being organised by the transport companies, hotels and businesses which manage guest houses and other accommodation establishments previously owned by industrial companies. This trend in the development of new travel companies is similar in most of previously socialist countries. Russia is another example, where two major travel companies multiplied to some 10,000 after 'perestroika', which are operating in a chaotic 'free' market.

The threats for small Polish tourist companies are coming from big (usually German) tour operators, which have already started to operate in the Polish market. As a small tour operator cannot compete with either TUI or Neckermann Reisen (even the biggest Polish tourism businesses are still very small in comparison with the big, international firms), the first strategic alliances have taken place on the Polish market. Polskie Biuro Podrozy S.A., created by Orbis, Gromada and Airtours, Korporacja Urlop or Konsorcjum Biur Podrozy are examples of alliances. Also, joint venture types of companies have established their position in the Polish market. Examples are: Scan Holidays, Fly Away Travel, American Express, Carlson Wagonlit. This year (1988) Airtours, the second British tour operator, commenced selling its products in Poland and aims to obtain 30 per cent share of the package holiday market share by the end of the year. The same share is the target for Neckermann, which means that the competition within the market will be tough for the Polish-origin companies. Although there is a group of new Polish tour organisers emerging, they act mainly as intermediaries for western tour operators.

SECTOR TRENDS

Channel Management

Central to this discussion on tour operators is the topic of channel management. Some writers state that 'channels should be viewed as an orchestrated network that creates value for end-users by generating form, possession, time and place utilities'. This organised network (system) of agencies refers to the needs of channel players to co-operate in an integrated and co-ordinated manner. This co-operation between different members in turn can be regarded as a joint striving towards individual and mutual objectives and the effort required to maintain the relationship.

The interdependency between channel members is connected with the fact that each member of a distribution channel is dependent upon the behaviour of other channel members. If any member changes their behaviour at any point in the channel, change will be caused throughout the whole channel. This mutual dependency among components of the channel implies that the whole membership of the channel must operate effectively if the desires of any individual member are to be realised.

Turning specifically to tourism, this industry combines transportation services, accommodation, attractions, food services, travel distributors and tourism promoters. Each sector of the tourism industry has a unique history but is dependent on the others for success. Authors from the tourism field define channels in a variety of ways. Middleton (1994) emphasises that channels are 'organised and serviced systems, created to provide convenient access to consumers, away from the location of production and consumption and paid for out of marketing budgets'. Others refer to two main issues: accessibility and availability, thus expanding the element of 'Place' within the marketing mix to cover not just location. It is location at point of sale that provides customers with access to tourist products. Some define a tourism distribution channel as 'an operating structure, system or linkage of various combinations of travel organisations through which a producer of travel products describes and confirms travel arrangements to the buyer'. Medlik (1996: 84) generally outlines ways in which channels might be organised:

> In travel and tourism providers of tourism attractions, facilities and services may sell direct to consumers (at their place of operation or through their own retail outlets) or use one or more intermediaries (such as tour operators and travel agents). Most large producers use a combination of distribution channels for their products and this combination is described as the distribution mix.

Intermediation

Considered from a different perspective, at the heart of this discussion on tour operators is the process of intermediation which involves selecting and packaging holiday elements, promoting and distributing them and providing information about destinations. The essence of the tour operators' job is to ensure affordable access to the package. Additionally they are involved in setting and monitoring quality standards in resorts, organising excursions and entertainments. In short, they manage relations with suppliers and distributors. Taking an historical viewpoint, the importance of distribution as an element of the marketing mix has shifted in the past four decades from last to first. For instance, it has been proposed that the 1970s was the era of 'product' followed by 'promotion' and 'price' in the 1980s, with distribution spotlighted during the 1990s.

This emphasis on distribution has led to the emergence of the topic relationship marketing during this decade, with its focus on the relationship between companies and customers which, in turn, covers the links between companies within the channels of distribution. This is essentially because channels evolved to serve customer needs. Initially, such distribution concepts were established in order to optimise the physical movement of commodities, which at the end of the process should reach the customer at the appropriate time, place and on the right terms. Then strategically oriented organisations realised that a key to sustainable long-term profitability is the fostering of a productive and mutually beneficial channel relationship.

As is the case for other industries, the main question remains the same in the context of tour operators:

> Is it always the case that bigger companies on the market, richer in financial assets, are more powerful in their relationships with others and can therefore gain competitive advantage within a new market, despite the cultural, environmental and legal differences between the national markets?

In order to address this issue, the concept of dependence of the target firm on the source firm and the reciprocal actions that take place in channel relations need to be examined. Dependence is usually defined as the target's need to maintain the channel relationship in order to achieve desired goals and reciprocal actions are the actions taken by one firm in response to actions taken by the other. Four different approaches can be used to assess dependence levels in tourism channel relationships:

1. The *sales and profit* approach which postulates that the greater percentage of sales and profit contributed by the source firm to the target firm, the greater a target's dependence on the source.
2. The *role performance* approach suggests that a firm's performance reveals how well it carries out its role in relation with another company down or up the channel.
3. The *specific assets – offsetting investment* approach maintains that offsetting investments help to safeguard the target company against opportunism by the source.
4. The *trust* approach is the long-term relationship built on the extent to which companies trust one another.

Purpose

The emergence and arrangement of a wide variety of tourism intermediaries can be explained in terms of four logically related steps of an economic process:

● intermediaries can increase the efficiency of the process of exchange
● they adjust the quantities and assortments produced with the quantities and assortments consumed
● they make transactions routine
● they facilitate the searching process.

In essence, tour operators fill in time, space, quantity and variety gaps between production and consumption, and the communications information gap. Intermediaries close these gaps and reduce the number of transactional links between the sector of producers and consumers.

The decisions involved in the development of a channel strategy can be examined from two points of view: channel length and channel breadth. The concept of *channel length* is of importance in this tourism discussion as it is the extent to which intermediaries should be used or whether sales should be made directly to the consumer. This decision is not just a question of economics but should be governed by the extent to which the firm is prepared to trade off control of the marketing channel to intermediaries.

Today most tourism companies do not sell directly to ultimate clients, but use a variety of external intermediaries and this is a general rule for many industries. Intermediaries include distribution-orientated institutions and agencies, which stand between production and consumption. They usually represent independent businesses that assist producers and final users in the performance of the negotiatory functions and other distribution tasks. They operate usually at two levels: wholesale and retail.

The travel distribution system consists of travellers, travel product suppliers and three main types of intermediaries: tour operators, travel agents and so called 'speciality channelers', which include incentive travel firms, meeting and convention planners, hotel representatives, business travel offices, national tourist offices and tourism associations or organisations. 'Speciality channelers' play their role in the channels of distribution and they might be compared to an 'ancillary structure', the group of institutions that assist channel members in performing distribution tasks, but they are not the ultimate object of this chapter discussion. Additionally, it has been shown that the wholesale and retail levels are sometimes not easy to distinguish and often overlap.

There are different approaches defining the concepts of suppliers (principals) of tourism services, wholesalers and retailers in the tourism literature and there is no consistency within the tourism field. The EC Directive on Package Travel (1990) uses the terms 'organisers' and 'retailers' instead of travel agents and tour operators, a point which acknowledges the lack of EU-wide agreement on the meaning of these terms. 'Organiser' is defined as a company where packages are organised and offered for sale, whether directly or through a retailer. The 'retailer', an equivalent to a travel agent, is defined as a person who sells or offers for sale the package put together by the organiser. In the UK there is a clear distinction between tour operators and travel agents. That is not the case in many other European countries.

A tourism distribution chain begins with a principal, first in rank of importance. The principal is a supplier of a service in the travel and tourism industry and provides the basic travel products, the 'core' product, such as transport, accommodation and amenities. Without them there would be no further organisations down the chain of distribution; they are principals to tour operators and travel agents. Medlik (1997) advances the argument that by buying individual travel services (such as transport and accommodation) from providers (such as carriers and hotels) and combining them into a package of travel, a tour operator creates a new product. Thus, although sometimes described as a wholesaler, a tour operator is, in fact, a 'manufacturer' of travel products with a role which in some ways is similar to that of a bulk-breaker in wholesale goods distribution. A travel agent is usually described as a person or organisation selling travel and ancillary services on behalf of principals for a commission. The main functions of travel agents are those of a retailer – to provide access for a principal to the market and to provide a location for the customer to buy travel services.

Travel agents carry no stock and therefore bear limited financial risk, (although they argue that the stock of brochures is huge and it is costly to keep them all); travel agents never actually purchase the product but act on behalf of consumers. The process involves no financial purchase and usually there is no charge to the customer for using the travel agent's services. This could change in the future; some tourism associations advance the argument that agents should introduce fees for customers, because relying only on commission provided by tour operators renders travel agents vulnerable and weakens their negotiating position with the operator. So far, agents receive commission on sales and are therefore compared to insurance brokers or estate agents.

In tourism, various structures are employed, but – in general – tour operators and travel agents provide the services of a distribution channel linking the great variety of tourism companies which supply the tourist with the destination services of their ultimate clients.

Risks

Numerous risks can be identified in the operation of tour operators particularly in monitoring competitive threats, specifically with respect to price. Additionally new products may emerge from the potential for expansion based on the needs of, for instance, elderly travellers. Equally a threat may arise from experienced travellers who may prefer to make their own arrangements.

STRATEGIC RESPONSES

Channel Management: its Organisational Implications

The main strategic response from the tour operator has focused on organisational patterns within marketing channels and can be separated into two main groups:

1. conventional marketing channels
2. vertically integrated marketing channels.

Within these two main groups, three options in terms of channel control can be advanced:

1. A corporate system – the manufacturer owns and operates a vertically integrated channel system.
2. A contractual system – an agreement between the manufacturer and the intermediary exists on the basis of a written contract (for example franchise agreements).
3. A conventional channel system – employing independent intermediaries (agents, wholesalers, and retailers).

Organisational dimensions of conventional and vertical marketing systems are presented in Table 10.3.

Table 10.3   Organisational dimensions of conventional and vertical marketing systems

Dimension	Conventional	Administered	Contractual	Corporate
Relation of units to an inclusive goal	No inclusive goals	Units with disparate goals but informal collaboration for inclusive goals	Units with disparate goals but some organisations for inclusive goals	Units organised for achievement of inclusive goals
Locus of inclusive decision-making	Within units	In interaction of units without a formal inclusive	At top of inclusive structure, subject to unit ratification	At top of inclusive structure
Locus of authority	Exclusively at unit level	Exclusively at unit level	Primarily at unit level	At top of hierarchy of inclusive structure
Structural provision for division of labour	No formally structured division of labour within an inclusive context	Units structured autonomously, may agree to ad hoc division of labour, without restructuring	Units structured autonomously, may agree to a division of labour, which may affect their structure	Units structured for division of labour within inclusive organisation
Commitment to a leadership sub-system	Commitment only to units' leaders	Commitment only to units' leaders	Norms of moderate commitment	Norms of high commitment
Prescribed collectivity orientation of units	Little or none	Low to moderate	Moderate to high	High

Source: Stern *et al.*, 1993: 324.

A relationship thus evolves in the process of partner selection, which is affected by the organisational pattern utilised in the industry. For example – in a conventional, non-integrated pattern (which is not necessarily the most efficient one) channel members are committed only to themselves, therefore they can select whoever they wish as their channel partners. In vertically integrated systems (contractual or corporate) members are committed to relationships, existing within the system and thus usually they are not as free as members of conventional structure in choosing their channel partners. Sometimes they have no choice at all and have to deal with the integrated members of the same business entity.

Technology

The attention of technology vendors, initially the airlines, is now fixed on working closely with their major customers which includes both the tour operators and multiple agencies. It is important to draw a distinction between the role of the international distribution companies and the national distribution centres. The former's concern are the globalisation of the CRS business: on providing mega-agency groups with global passenger number records, access and management information systems, and agency specific requirements. The Rosenbluth Alliance (the third largest US travel agent), for example has established global access through a dedicated partition in Apollo (that is, Rosenbluth Alliance agents are able to access a closed area of the Apollo CRS to swap/transfer bookings data to produce world-wide bookings data.) It can consolidate corporate travel expenditure information from its headquarters in Philadelphia or from London.

Relating the matter of technology back to industry structure, in 1989 it was estimated that the top 10 travel agencies – most of whom specialise in corporate travel – accounted for 10 per cent of the total travel market. Structural changes in the marketplace as a result of mergers and acquisitions indicated that in 1995 the top 10 agency groups accounted for over 15 per cent of the corporate travel market booked through travel agents.

The rising share of the corporate travel market by the largest multiple agencies is being reinforced by the CRSs since their policy towards product and services development favours their largest customers and their technological advantages will slowly extend their dominance in both national and cross-border markets. An example of how this will work follows and is based on a major agency group's experience with global networking.

The travel agency group in question established global access through its CRS and promoted the capability to its US customers with European operating subsidiaries. Rather than encourage the European subsidiaries to appoint it on a pan-European basis, the agency waited for the benefits of global access to trickle down to them. Eventually the European division invited the agency group to handle their corporate travel arrangements. By 1990 global access and the associated benefit of compiling global management information in the US was regarded as a key selling point for the largest US agencies with global networks or partners. However, their attempts to persuade US agent/agency grouping were not successful. European division were unwilling to forsake control of travel management. What has actually happened has been that the European company division have gradually accepted the need for agency consolidation and perceived the benefits associated with global communications links. The current relationship between the CRS vendors and corporate travel agents and tour operators suggests that the technology gap between the largest multiples and the small to medium sized sector will increase in each of the major European business travel generating markets.

By the end of 1992 the CRS vendors achieved saturation in terms of penetrating business travel and started to develop products for the leisure travel market aimed at increasing access and system usage. The four CRSs in Europe have already signed the agencies/operators with the largest volume bookings with the market potential for technology penetration among European leisure firms enormous. Europe's largest agents/operators need to exploit their size to extend their share of the travel market. To do this they must develop CRS technology to create genuine difference in the costs of servicing their customer base and segment this base to reflect both the cost and the level of service provided. By clearly segmenting their business customer base and squeezing suppliers through better purchasing mechanisms, the largest pan-European and global firms will be able to put pressure on both the national chains and the less technologically advanced operations, thereby improving their margins while maintaining a competitive edge.

The power of today's CRS to control the international tourism industry's sales and distribution process presents tremendous opportunities as well as serious problems for both major airlines, travel tourism marketing intermediaries and government policy-makers. Government regulations have already been imposed regarding CRS operation in the US. These regulations have eliminated only the most blatant abuses of display bias. However, the more subtle of bias continue to exist. The response from the major travel firms will be to continually exploit the benefits of technology at the expense of the smaller operators. Reliance on airline controlled CRS technology will be regarded with suspicion both by travel intermediaries and increasingly the regulators.

SUMMARY

This chapter has shown that the whole purpose of intermediation is to connect the routes by which products are moved from producer to the consumer. There has however been in recent years the growing domination of the sector by a few multiple-agency chains, each owned by one of the major tour operators. This consolidation has impacted the low profit margins enjoyed by travel agents resulting from the smaller size and resources of travel agencies compared to tour operators. The smaller firms have the impossible task of stocking and selling the full range of overseas inclusive holidays, let alone domestic products.

The industry structure has led to both horizontal and vertical integration, the former being the merging between two companies offering competitive products, occuring between companies offering complementary rather than competing products. The latter takes place when an organisation at one level in the chain of distribution merges with another.

ACKNOWLEDGEMENT

The authors greatly thank the assistance of Dorota Ujima, University of Luton, in her initial help in the preparation of this chapter.

REFERENCES AND FURTHER READING

Cooper, C., Fletcher, J., Gilbert, D., Shepherd, R. and Wanhill, S. (1998) *Tourism Principles and Practices*, 2nd edn, Addison Wesley Longman: Harlow.

Garnham, R. (1996) 'Alliances and liaisons in tourism: concepts and implications', *Tourism Management*, **2**(1): 61–77.

Gilbert, D.C. (1990) 'Tourism product purchase systems', *The Service Industry Journal*, **10**(4): 664–79.

Laws, E. (1997) *Managing Packaged Tours*, International Thomson Business: London.

Medlik, S. (1996) *Dictionary of Travel, Tourism and Hospitality*, Butterworth-Heinemann: Oxford.

Medlik, S. (1997) *Understanding Tourism*, Butterworth Heinemann: UK>

Middleton, V.T.C. (1994) *Marketing in Travel and Tourism*, 2nd edn, Butterworth-Heinemann: Oxford.

Mintel Report Holiday Booking Via the Internet, 25 March 1998.

MMC Reports (1997) Foreign package holidays: a report on the supply in the UK of tour operators' services and travel agents' services in relation to foreign package holidays, 19 December, CM 3813, Stationery Office: London.

Sheldon, P.J. (1994) *Tour Wholesaling in Tourism Marketing and Management Handbook*, 2nd edn, in S. Witt and L. Moutinho (eds) Prentice-Hall: Hemel Hempstead, pp. 399–403.

Travel and Tourism Gazette Directory (1998) Miller Freeman: Tonbridge.

Yale, P. (1995) *The Business of Tour Operations*, Longman Scientific and Technical: Harlow.

CHAPTER 11 Strategic marketing in the travel agency sector

STRATEGIC MARKETING IN THE TRAVEL AGENCY SECTOR

J. E. BIGNÉ AND L. ANDREU

OBJECTIVES

By the end of this chapter the reader should:

- Understand the role of the travel agent.
- Be able to recognise the trends in the travel distribution system.
- Be able to recognise the impacts of information technology (IT) and new distribution channels such as the Internet in the travel agency sector.
- Be aware of the main factors affecting the strategic marketing process in the travel agency sector.
- Be aware of how global distribution systems play a part in the tourism distribution system.
- Be able to identify marketing strategies to be adopted by travel agencies in a changing environment.
- Understand how technology can be incorporated into strategic plans by travel agencies in order to achieve a competitive advantage.
- Understand how the perpetuity and need for travel agencies will depend on the effectiveness of their marketing strategies and responses.

INTRODUCTION

The travel and tourism industry is currently experiencing changes which are directly related to the impact of information technology. New distribution channels such as the Internet and multi-media kiosks are appearing which potentially represent both significant changes in the traditional distribution system, and improvements in the way that travel and tourism products and services can be marketed and sold. Figure 11.1 shows the tourism distribution system with the introduction of new technologies.

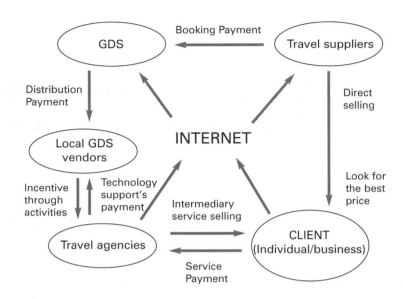

Figure 11.1   The tourism distribution system (WTO, 1998a)

The development of computerised networks and electronic distribution through the development of computer reservation systems (CRSs) and global distribution systems (GDSs) since the early 1970s has led dramatic structural changes within the tourism industry as they became central to the distribution mix and strategy (Buhalis, 1997). The travel agencies must, therefore, respond quickly to these changes and embrace them to consolidate the supply chain.

This chapter will focus on the strategic marketing process in the travel agency sector. First, an overview of the travel agency sector is presented, taking into account a global view. Second, emphasis is placed on the trends that are currently influencing the travel agencies, and specifically, how trends affecting both the consumer and the tourism distribution system are analysed. Technological innovations are supplemented by case studies (GDS, electronic trade, ticketless, Internet booking and virtual travel agency). Looking at the future, and given the fragile position of travel agencies, a range of marketing strategies and responses to be adopted are analysed. The chapter concludes by discussing the future role of the intermediary.

OVERVIEW OF THE TRAVEL AGENCY SECTOR

From an international perspective, it is important to highlight that although there are differences in travel agencies' classifications depending on countries, this chapter will be focused on *retail travel agents*. Within the travel distribution system, the retail travel agents' main role is to serve as *intermediaries* between travel product suppliers and consumers. They sell the products offered by travel suppliers such as package tours, airlines, cruise ships, railroads, bus companies, car rental firms, hotels and sightseeing operators to the general public, often adding special services and customising arrangements according to specific client needs. Travel agencies inter-relate with other elements of the tourist distribution system, and this means that their relationships may tend to change according to the environment development.

The travel agent is compensated in the form of a commission. Although travel agents sell many products, they remain heavily dependent upon *air travel* sales. Currently, 60 per cent of the travel agency industry's gross income is derived from the sale of airline tickets (see Table 11.1).

Table 11.1   Travel agency industry's gross incomes by travel suppliers

Travel suppliers	$(Millions)	Percentage (%)
Airlines	55,900	60
Cruise ships	14,000	15
Hotels	10,300	11
Car rental firms	6,600	7
Others	6,500	7

Source: *Travel Weekly* (14 August 1994).

Deregulation politics and globalisation in airlines have led to a competitive war. In order to save on costs, the companies are adopting different strategies, and this is affecting the travel agencies: decreasing or eliminating intermediaries' costs, direct selling (see Table 11.2), self-service ticket, on-line services and ticketless.

Table 11.2   Methods of distribution for the principal threats to travel agencies

	Advantages	Disadvantages
Using the travel agency network	● Many outlets to provide customer service.	● Getting the brochure racked by the travel agent.
	● Many agents to administer the actual booking.	● Servicing the agent, commission fee, overrides and incentives.
Selling direct	● Eliminates travel agent's commission.	● Increases in advertising and organisational costs.
	● Place control over sales.	● Costs of setting up and maintaining a sales team with the company.
	● Helps to introduce brand loyalty (advertising direct).	

Source: Adapted from Bennett (1996).

Cruise ship ticket sales represents the second largest source of income for travel agents and is the segment with the highest growth rate. The cruise ship industry is heavily dependent upon travel agents. Vladimir (1997: 18) pointed out:

> There are 74 million people 25 and older who have household incomes of $20,000 or more out there who are interested in buying a cruise, according to a new study by Cruise Lines International Association. Eighty per cent of those cruises will be sold by 20 per cent of all travel agencies.

Travel agents also make *hotel and resort* reservations for customers, which represent a stable component in travel agents' annual revenues stream, and rank third in importance for the production of agency revenue.

Car and other vehicle rentals represent the fourth major component of travel agency sales. Many agents find that selling car rentals can make a substantial contribution to their commissions with minimal additional effort.

Today these relationships between travel suppliers (principals) and travel agencies are supported by the computerised reservation systems (CRSs).

A CRS is basically a database which enables a tourism organisation to manage its inventory and make it accessible to its partners. Principals utilise CRSs to manage their inventory and distribute their capacity, as well as to manage the drastic expansion globally. Since the mid-1980s, airline CRS developed into global distribution systems (GDSs) by gradually expanding their geographical coverage as well as by integrating both horizontally, with other airline systems, and vertically by incorporating the entire range of principals, such as accommodation, car rentals, train and ferry ticketing, entertainment and other provisions. Using GDS, suppliers, intermediaries, and customers world-wide can now interlink to exchange information on a wide variety of tourist products including airfare, accommodations, ground transportation, and destination information.

In 1995, the leading GDS companies world-wide, were Amadeus, Galileo, Sabre and Worldspan. Their shareholders are shown in Figure 11.2.

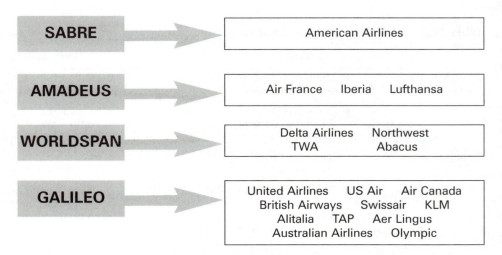

Figure 11.2   Main global distribution systems (GDSs) (WTO, 1995)

After describing the elements of the distribution system that are related to travel agencies, we will now focus in more detail on the retail travel agencies.

A retail agency may also arrange some of its own packages and in this way act as a *wholesaler or producer*. Furthermore, travel agencies act as *advisors* or *counsellors* in contact with the consumer and, can be particularly helpful to travellers organising their holiday.

Retail travel agencies can be also divided into *issuing* travel agencies and *receiving* travel agencies. Issuing travel agencies send the travellers to different destinations and receiving agencies take care of the reception of travellers in the place of destination.

While product knowledge and enthusiasm were enough to generate travel sales in the past, marketing skills are necessary ingredients for a travel agency's survival and growth today. A successful agency's purpose is to be a retail merchant as well as service professionals. They place much greater emphasis on finding new prospects and convincing them to use the agency's services to purchase travel products. Since travel agents are influential in the selection of holiday destinations, they are important marketing intermediaries for countries, states, cities, tourist businesses, and visitor attractions (Klenosky and Gitelson, 1998). Consequently, cities, states and countries actively compete to host the meetings of travel agents' associations. At the same time, travel agents are associated among themselves to be able to better protect their interests, such as ASTA (American Society of Travel Agents), ABTA (Association of British Travel Agents), AEDAVE (Spanish Association of Travel Agents), TAANZ (Travel Agents Association of New Zealand).

Unlike other retailers, travel agents do not sell a tangible product that can be seen, touched, packaged and carried home. Within an environment of information bombardment (advertising, travel writers, entertainment media, word of mouth), travel agents play an important role in creating and selling *anticipated travel experience.* Clients look to the travel agent as a professional to provide objective counselling and realistic expectations.

Consumers vary in their information needs. An essential division is between independent travellers and those who purchase a package holiday. Independent travel involving custom-made itineraries requires a tremendous amount of information. Without this information the growth of this segment of the market would be hampered. Perhaps what is most important for consumers in general is having access to information on travel. A principal source of information has always been the agent, but with developments in electronic media, the way in which consumers access such information is changing. On the other hand, people who usually purchase a package holiday are looking for better prices, ease of purchase, and the elimination of risk factors. The image presented in the tour operator catalogues is very important in the selection of the package holiday, and also the supplementary information provided by the travel agent.

Travel agents are a critical source of information about customers. Travel agents should recognise that a customer's evaluation of a service is often based on numerous impressions that include performance of supplementary services as well as the core service. Understanding and managing the *service encounters* that take place between customers and travel agents is central to creating satisfied customers who are willing to enter into long-term relationships with the service provider (see Box11.1).

BOX 11.1

AMERICAN SOCIETY OF TRAVEL AGENTS

ASTA's Mission Statement
'The American Society of Travel Agents' mission is to enhance the professionalism and profitability of member agents through effective representation in industry and government affairs, education and training, and by identifying and meeting the needs of the travelling public.'

Code of Ethics
'We live in a world in which travel has become both increasingly important and complex in its variety of modes and choices. Travellers are faced with myriad alternatives as to transportation, accommodations and other travel services. Travellers must depend on travel agencies and others in the industry to guide them honestly and competently. All ASTA members pledge themselves to conduct their business activities in a manner that promotes the ideal of integrity in travel and agree to act in accordance with the applicable sections of the following Principles of the ASTA.'

Code of Ethics. Complaints arising under this Code should be filed in writing with the ASTA Consumer Affairs Department.

ASTA has the following categories of membership: Active, Cruise-Only, International, Individual, Allied, Travel School, Associate, Associate Independent, Senior and Honorary.

Responsibilities of All Active, Cruise-Only, International Members (and Associate members of such firms) and Associate Independent and Individual Members:

1. *Accuracy*. ASTA members will be factual and accurate when providing information about their services and the services of any firm they represent. They will not use deceptive practices.
2. *Disclosure*. ASTA members will provide in writing, upon written request, complete details about the cost, restrictions, and other terms and conditions, of any travel service sold, including cancellation and service fee policies. Full details of the time, place, duration, and nature of any sales or promotional presentation the consumer will be required to attend in connection with his/her travel arrangements shall be disclosed in writing before any payment is accepted.

BOX 11.1 (cont'd)

3. *Responsiveness*. ASTA members will promptly respond to their clients' complaints.

4. *Refunds*. ASTA members will remit any undisputed funds under their control within the specified time limit. Reasons for delay in providing funds will be given to the claimant promptly.

5. *Co-operation*. ASTA members will co-operate with any inquiry conducted by ASTA to resolve any dispute involving consumers or another member.

6. *Confidences*. ASTA members will not use improperly obtained client lists or other confidential information obtained from an employee's former employer.

7. *Confidentiality*. ASTA members will treat every client transaction confidentially and not disclose any information without permission of the client, unless required by law.

8. *Affiliation*. ASTA members will not falsely represent a person's affiliation with their firm.

9. *Conflict of Interest*. ASTA members will not allow any preferred relationship with a supplier to interfere with the interests of their clients.

10. *Compliance*. ASTA members shall abide by all federal, state and local laws and regulations.

Source: www.asta.com (November, 1998).

TRENDS IN THE TRAVEL AGENCY SECTOR

In this part, we attempt to synthesise the trends that are currently influencing the travel agencies. First of all we will apply the SWOT analysis to understand the external (opportunities and threats) and internal factors (strengths and weaknesses), which are influencing the travel agency sector. Following this initial analysis, we will provide guidelines for the study of the market, product and consumer.

SWOT Analysis

The SWOT analysis deals with the way the organisation relates to the external environment and how well it is equipped to cope. It sums up and presents logically the information collected and processed in the analytical process.

Weaknesses

The competition between the large travel agencies and the small ones, the electronic ticket, Internet, the new distributors, the integration of the large groups and competitiveness, are aspects which are indicators of risk for the agencies. These risks are accentuated depending on the position of weakness of each agency. In a very general sense, we can mention the following aspects as weak points, but this will vary depending on the agency:

● The agency loses its central role and a part of the functions of agencies allows for alternative vias of realisation.

● The competition brought on by the new distributors, generally associated with technologies and businesses related to computers, brings to light a structural weakness of the travel agency, which normally does not have this capacity of organisation nor of movement of capital and interests.

● The breaking up of the sector, organised in large part in small agencies, places them in a difficult situation when negotiating for any type of material. They are also hindered in the development of their capacity for launching themselves into areas of new technology and in developing new services.

● Apart from proprietary information held by some individual agencies, relatively little is known about the clients who regularly patronise travel agencies. Many small travel agencies have little detailed knowledge of their clients' characteristics, past buying habits or even their travel preferences and aversions.

● Many people do not have confidence in the independence of their travel agents. They believe that travel agents are driven more by override compensation than by a desire to meet their clients' needs. This distrust, combined with a willingness and ability to undertake independent research, suggests that the power of experienced travellers relative to agencies is growing and will continue to grow as technology places more and better information at their disposal.

● There are disparities between the small agencies and the large ones. The process of integration of the large agencies has strengthened them, to the detriment of those that function independently. Specifically, these difference refer to:

1. *Objective of the agencies.* While the mission of the small or independent agencies is to serve the user, in those agencies that are associated with other activities or groups, their primary objective is to direct the demand towards the products of their group, transport, hotel and so on. If the former must show results of their own at the end of the year, the large agencies have to show group results and are not subject to the same individual demands and this allows them to operate in way that is not possible for the rest.

2. *Power of negotiation.* The large agencies have greater power to negotiate, not only in aspects such as commissions with the distributors, hotel chains and so on, but also these same aspects for their own clients, as is the case with business travel.

3. *Access to the technologies and innovation.* The large agencies have greater access to the technologies and fewer difficulties to innovate. For example, the technological associations that have been formed by the large groups, such as THISCO (The Hotel Industry Switch Company) or WIZCOM, are a way of eliminating the smaller agencies from the offering in many cases, and in others, from establishing dependent relations between large and small agencies.

Strengths

It is possible that the strength of the travel agencies is greater than the travel agents themselves believe. For example, the electronic ticket will take time to be generally accepted and widespread, because of the habits of the travellers as well as difficulties in implementing it, if we take into account that for this system to function, computer systems, airports and so on will have to be adapted. On the other hand, the complexity of the world of tourism or of the reservation systems requires the intervention of tourism specialists and professionals. The agencies presently are in a strong position that they can and must maintain. Strengths, therefore, can be summarised as follows:

- The proximity to the user is the major asset of the agencies, and no actor or producer seems willing to renounce this. The geographical dispersion of travel agencies has resulted in very easy access for most consumers of travel products.
- The present position of the travel agencies through which they distribute close to 90 per cent of some tourist products, such as transportation.
- The experience of the agencies, knowledgeable in the business and in the products they distribute and market. The large agency share of the existing market for most travel services; and the accumulated experience and 'know-how' that give them advantages against newcomers (that is, 'Viajes El Corte Inglés', see Box 11.2).
- Possession of means for search and consulting of those destinations and optimum services which are not within the reach of their challengers nor of the final user.
- Interlocutor and consultor function of the agency, and depository of trust of the user, who prefers to deal with people who can advise and also commit themselves to a good choice.
- Optimum position to look for those associations that are considered most expedient with a view to providing services.

The strength of the agencies can increase, therefore, through undertakings of association, federation of efforts and co-ordination of activities.

BOX 11.2

HOW 'VIAJES EL CORTE INGLES' DEALS WITH ITS CONSUMERS

Viajes El Corte Inglés (VCI) is a subsidiary company of the *El Corte Inglés* Group, one of the most important business groups in Spain. Today VCI is one of the foremost travel agencies in Spain, a leader in the sector with sales in excess of 535,013,672.6 Euros. The Corte Inglés is Spain's largest department store chain, with a very positive upscale image in the minds of the Spanish consumer. This firm invests heavily in advertising, and the travel agency is a logical complement to the services that this firm offers to its clients.

Mission statement

The philosophy of the company is *customer service and attention*. In other words, it is based on customer satisfaction through a wide offering of programmes (cruises, honeymoon trips, adventure tourism, Bonoplus tickets, health tourism, among other options), guarantee to the customer and formation of personnel for improvement in the quality of the service offered.

Business areas in which VCI is present

1. *Business travel*. The business of business travel is becoming more and more unprofitable for two main reasons. On the one hand, the policy of reducing airline company commissions and the tendency toward direct sales, and on the other, the practice that exists in this sector of ceding part of these commissions to the business companies. Even so, the Corte Inglés continues in this sector for the following reasons:

   ■ It generates a large volume of activity (and of sales).

   ■ It produces synergies in relation to other more profitable products, such as vacation, congresses and incentives.

   ■ Know-how of what the needs of business companies as clients are (service, information, and guarantee) through personnel which is highly qualified in this aspect of the business. The company has to transform itself into a consultant for trips, managing the account of these clients so that their travel expenses are as low as possible, and the relation between quality and the price paid is optimum.

   ■ They are waiting for changes in the Spanish market and support the present situation in some of the European countries, where the business companies pay a fee for these extra services a specialised travel agency can provide.

2. *Pleasure travel*. Holiday packs and travel products represent an important source of income in the present sales of the agency.

3. *Congresses and incentives*. Within the area of professional travel, 8 years ago VCI created a special department for congresses and incentives, which is further sub-divided into issuing and receiving areas, with very specialised

---

BOX 11.2 (cont'd)

personnel. This is a high performance segment. According to Hill (1997) 'Meeting planning can be a good money-maker and valuable client service for agencies, but it is a complex and demanding endeavour that requires years of experience and hard work for proficiency'.

Examples of VCI marketing strategies for confronting the problems

■ The *behaviour of the Spanish tourist* is such that he/she always tends to leave holiday reservations to the last moment. This produces, during certain periods of the year, an excessive influx of people, and the result is that the travel agencies are saturated and they are unable to attend to the clientele adequately. Second, the operators never know until the last minute what the demand is going to be like, so their services are not as good as they could be. What was the solution? VCI offers a certain percentage of discount for early reservation of their products. This is not a commercial discount, but is intended exclusively to motivate the customer to make his or her reservations early.

■ The *evolution of the technologies* seems to be putting the position of the travel agencies in danger. How does this affect their marketing strategies? VCI continually strives to keep themselves in the vanguard as far as the new technologies applied to the distribution of tourist products is concerned, as well as the new marketing strategies, to be able to open up new inroads in the area of tourist marketing and be able to offer more convenient services to their clients. For example, VCI offers sales via telephone, at full capacity. As far as Internet is concerned, VCI has had a web site for some time now ('Welcome to a world of services and advantages') for institutional purposes (www.viajeseci.es). For VCI, Internet is a tool at the service of the agencies, an instrument for marketing that they plan on making use of in the near future. If it proves to be as efficient and attractive as it promises to be, it will be a new and successful commercial channel that will force them to carry out new efforts to establish themselves within a vibrant source of continually up-dated information and offers.

Source: NEXOTUR (5 October 1998).

Threats

● The Internet presents the possibility of a truly computer-driven retail distribution function – a true 'substitute' for travel agencies. If the Internet lives up to its theoretical potential, it can drastically reduce distribution costs on several fronts. Suppliers will have the opportunity to eliminate one of the largest cost components in travel distribution: the cost of labour for interacting directly with clients. Internet users are able to see, in the times available windows, on which flights electronic issuing of tickets is possible. To date, seven airline companies are offering electronic ticket issue: Continental, Delta, America West, Northwest, TWA, United and US Airways.

● Development of new electronic communication: computerised reservation systems (CRSs) and global distribution systems (GDSs), virtual travel agencies[1] and ticketless travel (see Box 11.4). In late 1997, 615 of ABTA's member companies completed a survey on their current and likely future use of IT – 116 operators and almost 500 travel agents. Box 11.3 shows the headline results of the ABTA survey.

BOX 11.3

HEADLINE RESULTS OF ABTA IT SURVEY

Staff numbers. Companies employed over 22,000 staff in total. 73 per cent of agencies and 40 per cent of operators employed fewer than 10 staff.

Reliance on IT. 58 per cent of companies were totally reliant on IT – that is, 100 per cent of their staff relied on IT to carry out their job effectively.

Telephone lines. Between them the 615 companies used over 17,000 telephone lines. Of these 12,400 were used for speech and 2180 for viewdata.

Telephone suppliers. Well over 50 per cent of companies were using suppliers other than BT.

Viewdata.[2] 40 per cent of agents were using viewdata sets only (of these 40 per cent had no plans to upgrade). 60 per cent were using PCs for viewdata access, sometimes alongside viewdata sets.

Viewdata hardwires. Over half of agencies were hardwired. AT&T were the dominant supplier.

Airline reservations. Viewdata was the most popular route (Easylink/BA Link). Of the CRS/GDSs Galileo was the major supplier.

Agency systems. Most frequently used were TARSC, ICC Concord and Voyager systems.

Tour operator systems. Most frequently used were in-house developed systems, Anite and FSS.

Polling systems. One third of agencies subscribed to a polling system for late availability.

---

1. In the United States, the virtual agency Expedia has sold one million air tickets since it opened in October 1996 (EDI-TUR, October, 1998, no. 2.015–2.016, p. 12). Along the same line, Priceline on the Internet (www.priceline.com) is a service that finds the best price for the user, taking into account the factor price. Other examples are: www.travelocity.com and www.city.net.
2. Viewdata is information that is transmitted by telephone line on VDU or TV. It excludes teletext, which are communicated via TV transmitter. The trend is to link CRS and Viewdata systems together (Horner and Swarbrooke, 1996).

BOX 11.3 (cont'd)

Operating system. Windows'95 had overtaken 3.11, but among agents there was an even three way split with DOS.

Internet. One third of agencies and 70 per cent of operators had Internet access. 85 per cent were using it to seek information and over half planned to advertise their company.

IT Training. 73 per cent saw a need for specialist IT training for their staff.

Year 2000. 38 per cent foresaw the year 2000 as a problem for their software.

Other areas. The full survey covers many other areas including credit card authorisation, the SPS scheme, moving message systems, TV/video usage, fax modems, CDROM, on-line banking.

Source: www.abta.com (November 1998).

The underlying theme is one of offering customers more choices. Some people opt for face-to-face contact, others like telephone contact with a human being, and still others prefer the greater anonymity and control offered by more impersonal contacts. In each instance, although the core product may remain the same, the wide differences in delivery systems means that the nature of the overall service experience changes sharply as the encounter moves from high contact to low contact (Lovelock, 1996).

The growth of electronic channels is creating a fundamental change in the nature of marketing. Customers are moving from face-to-face contacts with suppliers in fixed locations that only operate during fixed hours to remote contacts 'anywhere, anytime'. Many service marketers now recognise the potential of the Internet as a communications medium and even as an alternative distribution channel for information-based services, but it must not be imposed without reference to customer needs and preferences.

● Other technological advancements have facilitated the distribution of travel while cutting costs and increasing responsiveness. Satellite ticket printers (STP) now allow travel intermediaries to issue tickets directly. The electronic ticket delivery network (ETDN) is another form of STP. The difference between them is that the supplier collects a commission for the usage of ETDN, while only a printing fee is received in the case of the STP. Electronic kiosks, which are stand-alone computer terminals found in hotel lobbies, airport terminal, and tourist information offices, now allow travellers to perform a series of different functions such as hotel check-in, purchase of airline tickets, or receipt of information about what a destination has to offer. Another development in facilitating the distribution of travel are electronic travel documents, simply referred to as ticketless travel, where the passenger's personal information exists in an electronic file with the airline (WTO, 1997).

BOX 11.4

TICKETLESS TRAVEL

Reasons for the success of ticketless travel

■ *Reduction in costs for the airline companies*. According to forecasts, the cost of the distribution circuit today accounts for 20 per cent to 25 per cent of the volume of business of the US airline companies taken as a group, and it is estimated that an elimination of the ticket (labour, printing and commission to agencies), would allow for a savings of between 12 per cent and 14 per cent of these costs.

■ *Better attention and quality of the features offered to the customer*. By eliminating the ticket, the customer no longer has to go to his/her agency to pick up the travel documents. This also avoids risks of loss and theft.

■ *Adapting to the new criteria of the consumer*. Customers who are tending to travel more and deciding to travel later are asking for greater flexibility on the part of their air transport companies.

Stages in the ticketless process

■ The customer goes to an airline company or travel agency for a flight reservation.

■ The customer receives a confirmation number or a reservation search number.

■ The customer pays giving his/her credit card number.

■ The customer is sent an itinerary and receipt by fax.

■ The customer goes to the boarding gate and gives his/her confirmation number or introduces his/her credit card into a terminal that identifies him/her.

■ The customer is assigned a seat and is given a boarding pass.

Consequences

■ *Savings for the airline companies*. The savings are based on the inventories of tickets, on their distribution, and so on, but also on the commissions paid out to the travel agencies. They also hope to create a habit of direct acquisition, especially since the customer will no longer have to go physically to his/her travel agency.

■ *More profitable sale of airline products*. This represents an opportunity for the travel agency to sell these products without the cost of printing a ticket.

■ *Risk of intermediary elimination*. The no-ticket system eliminates the link between the customer and the travel agency. This means that a greater number of customers are going to be dispensing with the services of their agency, beginning with those customers who make their own reservations and later have their tickets printed out by their travel agency.

BOX 11.4 (cont'd)

Implications for retail travel agencies
The establishment of a no ticket system is going to force the travel agencies to find *new forms of added value*, without which these intermediaries run the risk of disappearing from the distribution circuit of airline products.

Source: WTO (1995).

- Political unrest, wars and terrorism can destabilise tourism overnight as in the Lebanon during the 1970s and the former Yugoslavia during the late 1980s. Between 1983 and 1995, the air portion of agency business dipped briefly during the Gulf War, but rebounded and is now stronger than ever.

- Crisis in economies, such as Southern Asia. The airline companies operating in this market are seeing large losses, and to compensate for them, together with reducing personnel, they are also reducing commissions to travel agencies.

- Travel suppliers are going to be providing consumers with the means to abandon travel agents as their primary source of retail travel services.

- Competitive situation of the travel agency sector. According to Porter (1982), there are five competitive forces:

  1. *Intensity of the competition among existing travel agencies servicing the market.* This addresses the degree to which existing travel agencies are competing with each other, not only in terms of the products offered and clients sought, but also in terms of the overall competitive strategy used to seek business from those clients with those products.

  2. *The threat from substitutes using different technology.* Substitute services are not more or better versions of the same services being offered by existing firms; they are the true alternative to the service offered in the market now such as financial institutions, home computers, department stores, super-markets and direct selling by travel suppliers. Even teleconferencing competes to a degree with travel agencies in the business travellers market (Gee *et al.*, 1990). Developments in communications technologies affect the movement of people as they choose to use the new media rather than moving themselves to communicate over long distances. Consequently, the volume of travellers may fall, and instead business people could begin to hold teleconferences and potential holiday travellers may take 'instant trips' with audio-visual media.

  3. In the travel industry, the *threat of new entrants* deals with the possibility that new travel agencies, indistinguishable in concept from existing firms and offering similar competitive services, will easily enter the agent's market. Also, it can be argued that the travel agency industry is a classic

example of a fragmented industry, one in which no firm has a significant market share and, thus, no firm can strongly influence the industry's competitive outcome. The principal reasons for fragmentation, all applicable to the travel agency industry, include:

- Low overall entry barriers.
- No economies of scale or experience curve.
- Diseconomies of scale in some important aspects.
- Exit barriers.

Furthermore, there are no structural obstacles to entry:

- Travel agencies take no inventory risk in most of the products they sell.
- The cost of the central accreditation system for travel agents is relatively low compared to the cost they would face if individual accreditation and appointment were necessary with each airline.
- Non-airline travel suppliers do not have to maintain elaborate internal machinery for evaluating prospective agents.
- Government regulation has either been extremely limited or non-existent.

Threats could be grouped, as can be seen in Table 11.3, on the basis of their origins in: those that signify a decrease in income, those that provoke a decrease in the activity of the agency, and those related to loss of intermediary function (disintermediation) and other risks.

Table 11.3   Threats to travel agencies

Threats	Origin	Effects
Decrease in income	Policies of producers	Decrease in commissions
	Tourist market	Lower prices
Decrease in activity	New technologies	Globalisation of businesses
	Strategies of producers	Concentration
	Technification of agencies	Excess of productive capacity
	Increase in the number of agencies	Loss of competitiveness
Disintermediation	Function, size and management of business	New distributors
	Electronic ticketing	
	Services on the Internet	New sales channels
	Automatic dispensers	
	Direct sales	
Other risks	Costs crisis	Economic and latent crises
	Productivity crisis	
	Economic recessions	

Source: COTEC (1997).

4. *The bargaining power of customers.* Travellers are becoming more experienced and sophisticated, demanding more from the travel agent. The retailer's choice of buyers to whom to sell can thus be an important determinant of competitive position and profitability.

5. *The bargaining power of suppliers.* The bargaining power of suppliers and agents' resultant dependence on their suppliers is a key force in the agency competitive picture. Much of the leverage of suppliers over travel agents results from the fact that the suppliers pay the agents, while consumers are told that the services of the agents are free. Agents are taking few risks in the sense of acquiring inventory for which they must pay if the products are not sold. Travel agencies, for the most part, therefore, continue to be dependent upon suppliers' pricing practices, since commission income is tied directly to the price of the product sold.

The power of important suppliers as it relates to most travel agencies is overwhelming, and supplier policies are often set unitarily and without meaningful consultation with agents. There are, however, two major offsetting factors: (1) the large share of consumer business enjoyed by travel agents, and (2) travel agents' ability to influence consumers' selection of supplier.

Suppliers' leverage over agencies is particularly evident in pricing policies. Frequent price changes combined with yield management create uncertainty. This uncertainty helps create the demand for the services of travel agents. In that sense, the power of suppliers to control prices rebounds to the benefit of their agents. This power also exacts a price from agents. If airline pricing decisions result in travel agency revenues falling below costs, there is little the agency can do in the short term to adjust, as long as agency income is determined by commissions tied to the price of the ticket sold.

Opportunities

- If travel agencies adapt to the new technologies, and current evidence indicates that most clients will do so, the Internet will become not a substitute for travel agencies, but merely a tool to be used by all the existing competitors to reach the consumers and their business. Thus far, the public has shown a marked preference for dealing with firms that can provide a full array of travel procurement services for all types of travel products, using human beings to interact directly with the consumer (see Boxes 11.5 and 11.6).

- Europe integration means an area without internal frontiers within which free movement of goods, persons and services is ensured. The abolition of border controls, the harmonisation of taxes and the deregulation of transport in the European Community can encourage tourism.

- The emergence of market economies in eastern Europe, and the opening of the borders symbolised by the demolition of the Berlin Wall, are paving the way for eastern European countries to participate more fully in travel movements, particularly to western countries. In addition, eastern Europe is becoming a leading international destination.

- Government and country blocs pass laws affecting the provision of tourism. For example, EU regulations on package companies and travel agents, that is, British Airways can no longer sell packages/organised trips in Madrid, as a result of the formal complaint lodged by AEDAVE (Spanish Association of Travel Agents), unless BA formally establishes itself as a travel agency .

- Governments may support certain kinds of tourism through grant aids for development, or restrict it through entry quotas. After years of isolation, for example, the Islamic Republic of Iran is beginning to welcome increasing numbers of visitors.

- Fluctuations in exchange rates which can make some countries cheaper or more expensive in relation to competitors.

- Introduction of the European currency (Euro). The Euro is expected to become as widely accepted in tourism as the US dollar, benefiting tourists with more competitive prices and stimulating the European tourism industry with higher quality and more innovative products (WTO, 1998b).

- Emergence of multi-national corporations that provide tourism services in various countries.

- Growth of vertical integration strategies, that is, in the UK, Thomson Travel Group (Thomson Holidays, Lunn Poly, Britannia), Airtours (Airtours, Going-Places and Airtours International Airways), First Choice Holidays (First Choice and Air 2000).

- The tourist business is increasing, with new consumers as well as with higher levels of spending. The Travel Industry Association of America seems to confirm this point: in 1997 the tourist industry in the United States moved $502,000 million, compared to $489,000 million in 1996.

- Fuel costs (which affect travel and transport costs).

- Changing consumer patterns of expenditure, leisure and tourism are now more important.

- Changing patterns of life cycle and lifestyles such as later marriage, an increase in the female workforce, couples having children later in life and increased numbers of single and childless couple households. Senior citizens and empty nest families are becoming increasingly more important, with above-average financial resources and the consequent possibility to travel frequently. Environment is becoming one of the main concerns of our society. From the tourist's point of view, the attraction of the landscape consists in its diversity and the contrast it offers with regard to his or her daily environment. It is the degree of contrast that will determine the attraction for tourists.

- Convergence in world tastes and product preferences to produce globally standardised products.

- Population growth in developing countries.

- Transport innovations, that is, high speed trains and the Channel Tunnel between Britain and France.

BOX 11.5

HOW NEW TECHNOLOGIES CAN IMPROVE CUSTOMER SERVICE IN THE TRAVEL AGENCY SECTOR

In the travel agency sector, we can distinguish three possible areas: the office itself ('back office'), the office that attends the public ('front office') and the co-production on the part of the client.

The *back office* is the part of the service which is invisible to the client, but in no way less important or necessary for performance. In a travel agency, this area deals with, for example, confirmations, elaboration of files on clients, mailing out of documents and so on.

The *front office* accommodates the activity in contact with the client. This is the area of direct physical or telephonic relation of the agent with the client.

The *co-production* on the part of the client corresponds to the part of the service that the client does for him/herself, for example filling out a form or card describing exactly what kind of trip he/she wants.

Automatisation of the back office
- Reduces the time expended in taking care of an order (that is, the ticketless).
- Records preferences, special prices according to segments. For example, by means of files on clients.

Instruments for the front office
- Facilitate the marketing activity of the distributor, by means of computer programs that are able to offer contextual information or multi-media documents (that is, catalogues of hotels that allow the distributor to show the client the room he/she has reserved).
- Accelerate the reservations process through immediate access systems, such as the GDS.
- Look for the best prices thanks to tariffs analysis programmes ('Fare auditing').
- Issue the different transport titles.

Co-production with the client
- Allows the client who acquires and prints out a ticket to fill out the administrative formalities to obtain a vehicle or conveniently consult the desired data, through interactive terminals.
- Allows the client to obtain information and even place an order without leaving his/her home. For example, the possibility to place orders on line through World Wide Web.
- Allows the client to obtain information in multi-media catalogues (for example CD-ROM).

Source: WTO (1995).

BOX 11.6

THE CASE OF LEISURE PLAN

Created in 1995 by grouping the potential of three companies, Thomas Cook Ltd, Philips Media Service and TWINE Media, all of them leaders in their respective sectors. Their activity is being carried out for now in the United Kingdom, Belgium and South Africa. It consists of a database of more than 30,000 tourist products from all over the world. Leisure Plan provides multi-media information to travel agencies and tour promoters in such as way so as to make it possible for clients to plan their holidays. Leisure Plan is available in two formats, one of them LeisurePlan Pro in CD-ROM multi-media for promotion tasks, and the other LeisurePlan LIVE, which is available through the Internet and also has computerised mechanisms which make it possible to consult availability, prices, and to make reservations when desired. The company plans to introduce interactive TV when it is available.

Source: COTEC (1997).

Other Analyses

Market Analysis

Trends in the market should be analysed through an analysis of the market, focusing on the agency's market share and the market potential for the specific area. *Market potential* refers to the total market available for travel agency services within a selected geographical area. The portion held by an individual agency is referred to as *market share*.

Market potential can be determined by:

1. Total sales volume of all agencies in an area (a percentage for available business that is not obtained by any agency but could be through aggressive marketing should be added to this).
2. Deriving a ratio of market potential through demographic segmentation, buying power index, economic activity, or other variables.
3. Using industry statistics when available.

The market potential available to an agency in any geographic area is a composite of several different market segments. An agency must decide which segments offer the greatest opportunity and which segments cannot realistically or profitably be serviced. Once these segments are identified and the best options selected, they become target markets and products and services are then specifically designed to serve them.

Product Analysis

From the product analysis, the travel agencies' products and services are evaluated with respect to the market and competition. While some of them produce considerable amounts of cash, others do not. Where considerable cash is generated, it is often more than necessary for operational expenditure and for additional investment in facilities and staff. In other cases, however, the cash generated may be insufficient to cover operational expenditure. As we shall see, products that are not satisfactorily contributing to profits and overheads of the firm may well be dropped from the product mix. However, there may well be particular reasons why some products are such poor cash generators at a particular moment in time. Indeed, it may well be that such products go on to become the big cash earners for a company in the future. Product portfolio models provide a means of rating products and/or services in order to assess the future probable cash contributions and future cash demands of each product or service.

Portfolio analyses start by examining the positions of products. They consider two dimensions: the *attractiveness of the market* and the *ability of the business to operate competitively* within the market. One of the best-known portfolio models is the Boston Consulting Group (BCG) model. In the BCG model, market growth rate was employed as an indicator for market attractiveness and relative market share was used to indicate competitive position.

Specifically, the market growth rate on the vertical axis indicates the annual growth rate of the market in which the business operates. The horizontal axis, relative market share, refers to the share of the market that the product has relative to its largest competitor. It serves as a measure of the company's strength in the relevant market. Relative market share is divided into high and low share.

The growth/share matrix is divided into four quadrants, each indicating different type of products:

- Products falling into the high growth, high market share quadrant, are termed 'stars'. They are tomorrow's cash earners. Being high market share businesses, they will be highly profitable and generate a lot of cash, but at the same time their high growth will also mean that they will require a lot of cash.

- Products positioned in the low growth, high market share quadrant, are designed 'cash cows'. These are the real cash generators, being profitable as a result of their high relative market share.

- Products falling into low growth, low relative market share quadrant, are designated 'dogs'. These are inherently unprofitable and seem to possess no future, although their cash requirements are low.

- Products in the high growth, low market share segment have been referred to 'question marks'. They are unprofitable as a result of their low market share, and they consume a lot of cash merely to maintain their market position because of the high growth rate of the market.

Consumer Analysis

Through consumer analysis the travel agency will know who its customers are, where to find them, what they want, how and why they purchase, which ones are profitable, which are unprofitable and which markets are untapped. In the final analysis, a successful marketing effort will be the result of an agency's efforts to understand customers or potential customers, how they fit into the marketplace, and how the specific travel services that are sold match and fulfil the needs of customers.

Research and a thorough analysis of the agency's existing client mix are, therefore, required. The client analysis should consist of the following:

1. *Classifications of clients by purpose of travel – commercial, pleasure, incentive and so on.* Agencies should develop an information file for each client. A computer can be invaluable in this task as it permits information to be updated, retrieved using different specifications and further analysed. Agencies can obtain information from new clients through the use of a questionnaire.

2. *Determination of key clients.* Most businesses have discovered that a majority of their sales and profits are derived from a minority of their customers. This is often referred to as the 80/20 rule, meaning that 80 per cent of the business is generated by 20 per cent of the clients. An analysis of client sales will reveal which clients provide the majority of sales and profits for an agency. Once identified, these key clients should receive special consideration as appropriate.

   The determination of key clients will also reveal unprofitable customers, clients who demand a great deal of service, absorb large tracts of time, and yet purchase very little. Travel agencies lend themselves to this type of customer since they historically have provided free information. Today, travel agencies may eventually be forced to alter their long-held policies and begin charging per transaction as some agencies have already done (Gee *et al.*, 1990).

3. *Determination of demographic and psychographic characteristics.* Demographics refer to easily quantified statistics or facts concerning the local population and/or the agency's clientele. The travel agency manager must decide what types of demographic data are needed to describe pleasure and commercial clients. A system of gathering, tabulating, updating, and using this information can then be implemented. The following is an example of potentially useful demographic information:

   ● Pleasure travellers: name, address, business phone, home phone, occupation, post code, income, education, marital status, sex, number and ages of children.
   ● Commercial travellers: company name, address, post code, division, type of company, number of employees, number of branches in market area, location, names of commercial travellers.

The most common uses of demographic data are to determine the degree of penetration that an agency has made in a particular market segment and to target new prospects.

Psychographics refer to the role of attitudes, opinions, interests, values, personality and lifestyle in consumer consumptive behaviour. These attributes affect travel habits, preferences and purchasing behaviour, which can be of substantial value to travel agencies. Psychographic data permits the agent to custom design a travel package that meets with the client's lifestyle. Generally, clients are quite willing to provide this information since they can immediately see its usefulness.

One of the most important marketing objectives is the selection of target markets (Cravens, 1994). Because of the fact that it is difficult to be everything for everybody, agencies are finding that some form of specialisation is needed.

Segmentation analysis plays a key role in the creation of an effective positioning strategy,[3] helping marketers to resolve such questions as:

- In what ways can the market for travel agencies be segmented?
- What are the needs of the specific segments that they have identified?
- What do customers in each segment see as their competitive advantages and disadvantages? Are the latter correctable?

STRATEGIC RESPONSE TO THE TRENDS: STRATEGIC CHOICES AND ALTERNATIVES

Technological change directly affects both *price competition* and *non-price competition*. The former is achieved through cost savings; that is, the communications costs between, on the one hand, principals and, on the other, travel agencies. At the same time, information technology enables an increased volume of transactions to be handled rapidly and effectively. The non-price competition means that travel offerings can be differentiated from one another in terms of their presentation, such as the use of videos to advertise holidays and in terms of their distribution and, here, the development of electronic direct sell is one variant.

In the previous section we analysed the internal and external environment, and the information that has highlighted the industry is characterised by intense rivalries and an expanding market, but low profit margins. Therefore, it is clear that companies operating in the travel industry cannot strategically afford to neglect the opportunities and threats posed by new technologies. The next stage of the strategic process is to consider the following issues.

---

3. Of particular interest for *segmentation strategy* are those services which are not only delivered to the customer in person but also require each user to share the same facility with many others. Examples of these high-contact, shared services include theatres, restaurants, hotels, airlines and retail stores such as travel agencies. The composition of the customer base has important implications for both the image of the service organisation and the nature of the service experienced (Lovelock, 1996).

Forecasting the Future and Making Assumptions

- Overall demand for travel is projected to grow for the long-term future.
- The Internet information glut will create opportunities for agents as synthesisers and analysts and small firms with few employees and little dedicated capital have considerable flexibility to adapt to changing circumstances.
- If retailers can influence consumer's purchasing decisions, they can gain bargaining power over suppliers.
- Buyer group power can be reduced if the agent focuses on buyers with the least power to influence them adversely.
- Buyer selection and differentiation may be key strategies for improving competitive prospects.
- Commercial alignments with other agencies, short of merger, through consortia and franchise arrangements, can also increase the bargaining power of smaller agencies.
- As the Internet becomes more accessible and as airlines and other suppliers find more ways to reduce their cost of providing internal customer booking and ticketing services (for example, EasyJet), travel agencies will have limited ways of resisting the loss of their best customers. They can only be successful if they understand intimately the needs and wants of those customers and are prepared to provide some new services for them.

Setting Objectives and Strategies

The core elements of a travel agency 'value chain' is the sequence of services, functions and steps by which travel agencies deliver their value to their clients. They are the crucial competitive ones that must either stand up to the changes predicted for the marketplace or be changed themselves to shore up the agency's position. The seven leisure segment value functions are:

1. To collect and distribute information on travel products.
2. To provide advice regarding product selection.
3. To operate booking services.
4. To distribute documents.
5. To package travel components.
6. To set prices.
7. To negotiate terms (including prices) with suppliers.

It is extremely important that agents who are considering changing their agency's position in the marketplace do so as a long-term strategic plan. At the outset (beginning) of the contest (competition), today, travel agencies have very important advantages:

1. *The customers.* The core of strategic process is not the suppliers, but the *customers*. The key is to know the customer and deliver what he or she wants.

That is the best and, ultimately, the only defence against displacement by technology or other moves by competitors. Smaller agencies doing battle with larger agencies with no discernible advantage in service can use this knowledge to their advantage.

2. *Relationship marketing in the travel agency sector.* The strength of travel agencies' relations with their clients has been repeatedly demonstrated and is an important countervailing force in the consumer's choices. In the end, consumers will decide the shape of retail distribution by the choices they make.

The essence of relational marketing consists in attracting, maintaining and intensifying the relations with the client. This implies that the traditional marketing activities, which are based on attracting clients, make up only one part of the activities of relational marketing. Relational marketing also includes all activities aimed at maintaining and consolidating the interchange with the other party over an extended period of time. The underlying idea is, therefore, that these interchanges should not be seen in an isolated way as a series of acts of a discreet nature, but rather as a means for establishing and increasing a relationship. The study of the interchange must therefore be broadened from the transactional focus to the relational (see Table 11.4).

Table 11.4   Differences between transactional marketing and relational marketing centred on the consumer

Transactional marketing	Relational marketing
● Centred on a simple sale	● Centred on retention of the client
● Orientation on the characteristic of the product	● Orientation on the benefits of the product
● Short-term scale	● Long-term scale
● Little emphasis on service to the client	● High emphasis on service to the client
● Limited commitment with the client	● High commitment with the client
● Moderate level of contact with the client	● High level of contact with the client
● Quality is the responsibility of the producer	● Quality is the principal responsibility of everyone

Source: Adapted from Christopher *et al.*, 1991.

3. *The know-how or travel expertise.* Fundamental strategic thinking does not mean simply moving toward the highest priced products or those that seem to pay the highest commissions. A much more thorough analysis of the market and the firm is required if a strategic positioning is to be reasonably assured of success over the long run.

Positioning Strategy

Positioning is the process of establishing and maintaining a distinctive place in the market for an organisation and/or its individual product offerings (Lovelock, 1996). This concept offers valuable insights by forcing managers to analyse their travel agencies' existing offerings and to provide specific answers to the following questions:

1. What does our travel agency currently stand for in the minds of current and prospective customers? What services that consumers value are the core of this agency's current business?
2. What customers do we now serve and which ones would we like to target for the future (that is, pleasure, business, holiday travellers and conventioneers delegates)?
3. What are the characteristics of our current service offerings (core product and their accompanying supplementary service elements)?
4. In each instance, how do our service offerings differ from those of the competition?
5. How well do customers in different market segments perceive each of our service offerings as meeting their needs?
6. What changes do we need to make to our offerings in order to strengthen our competitive position within the market segment(s) of interest to our firm?

Considerations

- The most volatile situation is one in which several equally balanced strategic groups, each following markedly different strategies, are competing for the same customer.

- Options to consider include: combining with compatible agencies to gain bargaining leverage by joining or starting a consortium, co-operative or franchise, merging with other agencies or buying their assets to increase critical mass.

- Dependency on domestic air sales leaves the agency vulnerable to reduced commissions, as well as declining ticket prices. The agency will want to re-evaluate its customer base and perhaps choose to focus on a portion of it, specialising by product type, product segment, customer type or geographic area.

- To avoid unwanted focus on prices, an agency must seek some form of brand identification with the customer. Differentiation may be accomplished by increasing the firm's value added by expanding the scope of services provided there.

- In mature industries such as travel agencies, the *core product* often becomes a commodity. The search for competitive advantage – and escape from price-based competition – often centres on the value-creating *supplementary services* that surround this core and add differentiation. Supplementary services are:

consultation,[4] information (confirmation of reservations, warnings, reminders, documentation), order taking (reservations, applications), exceptions (special requests, problem-solving, handling of complaints and restitution), payment (self-service, direct to payee or intermediary).

- Differentiation by specialisation places inherent limits on the firm's ability to grow in the target market, unless the target market is itself growing at an unusually high rate. A core competitive decision here is the agency's selection of customers to target. To determine the quality of customers, agencies should consider client needs, growth potential, buyer bargaining power and the cost of servicing the buyer.

- In response to the changing environment and increased competition, some agencies may charge a fee to customers for the services they provide, or share commissions with clients. With or without service charges, travel agents must make a decision about strategic positioning. Agents must be careful not to let technology direct them unwittingly into a strategic position under which they try to be all things to all customers. This position may be among the hardest for agencies to defend.

Growth Strategies

Applied to the tourist sector, the firms which intervene in the tourist distribution channel cannot choose their strategies nor plan their activities without taking into account the competitive position and the behaviour of the rest of the members of the channel (tour operators, retail travel agencies, booking centres, clients and so on). The elements of the tourist distribution channel have available to them policies which are capable of generating power, a power which will see its reflection in the greater amount of control that can be exercised on the rest of the members of the channel (see Box 11.7).

BOX 11.7

HALCON VIAJES' MARKETING STRATEGIES

Halcón Viajes, member of the *Globalia* holding, which is also part of Air Europa airlines and the tour operator Travelplan, has embarked upon a strategy for growth in Spain and Portugal. In 1997, Globalia Group reached 1,004,636,785 Euros in sales. Specifically, the figures for sales to business firms were as follows:

---

4. Providing information suggests a simple response to customers' questions (or pre-prepared information that anticipates their needs). Consultation, by contrast, involves a dialogue to probe customer requirements and then develop a tailored solution. Effective consultation requires an understanding of each customer' s current situation, before suggesting a suitable course of action (Lovelock, 1996, p. 344).

BOX 11.7 (cont'd)

- ■ Retail Travel Agency *'Halcón Viajes'*: 463,678,516.2 Euros
- ■ Airline company *'Air Europa'*: 386,398,763.5 Euros
- ■ Touroperator *'Travel Plan'*: 154,559,505.4 Euros

Halcón Viajes intends to open 100 new travel agencies in Spain and to situate themselves with 600 by the end of 1999, while in Portugal they are planning to establish themselves with a network of 30 offices in 1999 and have 50 in the year 2000.

One of the novelties of the new strategy of Halcón Viajes is its emphasis on business travel. We should also mention that Globalia is planning on entering into the hotel business with the acquisition of three hotels.

Source: EDITUR (1998).

The dynamic competitiveness that controls the distribution of tourist products has made growth *strategies* popular, either from the producers of the basic units (that is, tour operator or airline company) to the firms closest to the consumer (travel agency) or from these firms to the producers. Their attempts to position themselves and develop within those markets are also aimed at the possibility of controlling as much as possible the state or level of a channel, which is the case of the merging of tour operators or travel agencies. This can be achieved through their own means, or when this is not possible, by mergers or agreements of different types through which they try to obtain the concentration of means and efforts with the goal of reaching objectives than can serve as a common base for their relationships.

The idea of *concentration* as a system of protection and self-defence is brought out in the expectations that attempt to cover the associations that exist at each level of the channel. But even though these entities may be able to provide many special services to each of their members, there is still an infinity of areas within the tourism firms in which their objectives can only be perfected if they have much greater financial and economic backing, the level of backing that can be provided by the integration of firms.

Integration is a strategy of grouping firms so as to be able to develop more profitable businesses by means of mergers, acquisitions or co-operative agreements established on a long-term basis between the firms.

To bring about an increase in their size or importance following this strategy, firms can integrate or group by means of the following formulas.

Horizontal Integration

This is what is brought about between firms engaged in the same type of activity, that is, retail agencies among themselves, or wholesaler agencies among themselves. The principal objectives of this strategy are: higher market shares; elimination of competitors; reduction of costs by taking advantage of common resources; strengthening of brand name image; and improving the capacity for negotiation with suppliers and clients to be able to enjoy a stronger position in the market.

For the tour operators it is particularly important to strengthen their capacity for supply and contracting with consolidated purchase volumes, together with the capacity of assuming higher risks, which allows them to position their products in the market at more competitive prices. These integrations can be done in different ways: through absorption, merger, joint ventures or simple association which does not involve any changes as far as shareholding is concerned. The most recent international integrations of travel agencies have occurred horizontally in the area of distribution. In this way the two principal world-wide groups have emerged through the integration of the North American Carlson agency and the European Wagonlits. Today they are the most important world-wide network as far as sales outlets are concerned, and their annual sales places them in second place after the group that has emerged as a result of the acquisition of the accounts division of the Thomas Cook firm by American Express.

There is another formula for integration which maintains the independence of the firms. They can look to associate themselves with specific commercial ventures whose unity facilitates and transmits greater power for negotiation. For example, the Guild of European Business Travel Agents (GEBTA) is one of the most exclusive and professional groups in the world and its aim is to safeguard business travellers' interests. Founded in December 1990 GEBTA Spain is a non-profit association with 24 members. Since its foundation, GEBTA Spain has become a point of reference for all those questions affecting travel and business travellers.

The Spanish retail agencies are initiating a process of horizontal integration by means of agreements within a specific geographical area or through franchises such as Hippo Viajes, Viajes Ecuador or Alpina Tour. This type of integration is still incipient in retail agencies where the independents are predominant. Only a small group of agencies such as Marsans, Barceló, Halcón, El Corte Inglés, Carlson Wagonlits, among others, have a high degree of penetration with a large number of branch offices.

Vertical Integration

Vertical integrations are produced between firms with different activities, but which can complement each other in some way. The process of integration of different links in the distribution chain come about through agreements and shares in the capital of different firms (see Box 11.8).

BOX 11.8

THOMAS COOK AND CARLSON JOIN FORCES

Carlson Companies Inc., the giant group with its headquarters in the United States and multiple businesses in the travel, hotel and restaurant sectors, are going to merge their travel division in the United Kingdom with the Thomas Cook travel division. This merger will represent the creation of one of the largest groups of vertically integrated travel agencies in the UK.

As far as the United Kingdom is concerned, Thomas Cook has the fourth most extensive marketing network, made up of 385 agencies of their own plus Thomas Cook Direct; the sixth most important British charter company, Flying Colours, with 14 aeroplanes and the fourth position in the tour operator business, with the trade names Sunworld, Neilson Ski, Flying Colour, Club 18–30, and Thomas Cook Holidays, Time Off. They also market through teletext and the Internet.

Carlson, for their part, brings in their own 412 travel agencies, the fleets (18 planes, 12 of them very old) of Caledonian and Peach Airways, and the tour operators Inspirations, Orchild Travel and Skiers World, which gives them the fifth place in the ranking of wholesalers, as well as the consolidator Air Savers and the seats-only sales operation Flights By Inspirations.

Another element that Carlson can integrate as a synergy in the merger is the affiliation relationship they maintain with the 650 independently owned travel agencies, Artac (Association of Retail Travel Agents Consortia), that co-operate with Carlson under the name Worldchoice.

With this merger, Thomas Cook will become a serious competitor with the wholesaler First Choice in the battle for third place in the ranking of the British tour operators, after the leaders Thomson and Airtours.

Source: EDITUR (1998).

The objectives pursued by means of vertical integrations will be to: take advantage of the synergies between the different firms; guarantee the supply of necessary products; enter into contracts under better conditions; have a better knowledge of the market through presence in different areas of activity; eliminate dependency on other firms.

In the case of vertical integration, firms are looking for a greater control over the offerings as well as over the markets, depending on whether we are dealing with ascending or descending vertical integration. This is especially characteristic in the case of the tour operators integrating with the airline companies, in most cases charters, or with hotels. This is the case of the principal German tour operators (TUI, Neckermann) or the British (Thomson).

A new form of integration is the Lufthansa 'City Centers' system, recently introduced and through which the German airline company supports mid-size travel agencies by granting them a franchise under the name LCC (Lufthansa City Center). This establishes the image of a common trade name which is linked to logistic and formation support, which allows the agencies to enjoy certain commercial advantages, and the airline company is assured of its presence in the centre of the cities without the need to support the ever higher cost of maintaining its own office structures.

Together with the integration strategies in the area of tourism intermediaries, and in relation to the power and control over the distributors, it is important to mention the struggle between the GDS to capture the higher market share of the travel agencies using the system. It can be noted that this depends in large measure on the share that the airline companies that are the owners of each system themselves have. The competition between the GDSs has moved the European Union to establish a code of conduct to regulate the activity, and principally the way in which the information should be displayed so as not to favour the companies that are owners of the systems in detriment to the others. There is no doubt that the way in which the information is displayed on the different screens of the systems can condition choice, so this information should be displayed in accord with the interests of the passenger on the basis of an objective order (first direct flights, then flights with short stop-overs without change of plane, then flights with a change of plane and so on). It also covers the treatment and confidentiality of information on clients, which the CRSs store.

According to Gee *et al.* (1990), in terms of a growth strategy, the manager and/or owner of a travel agency is faced with three growth alternatives: status quo, retrenchment and planned growth.

1. *Status quo.* This strategy is used by the many agencies that operate without the benefit of a marketing plan and drift along with a status quo attitude (do nothing). Due to the many changes affecting the travel agency environment, however, it is becoming increasingly difficult to survive with a status quo mentality.

2. *Retrenchment.* A strategy of retrenchment (cut product offering, cut numbers of clients, cut locations, cut costs, cut employees) may be appropriate for a small or mid-size agency with an elderly owner or manager or one suffering from poor health. These individuals often lack family members who want to take on the agency's operations and consequently decide that they wish to remain active but prefer to operate on a reduced scale.

3. *Planned growth.* Growth can occur in many forms, including an increase in sales, profits or number of locations. It may entail selling existing products to new market segments, expanding the product line for existing markets, or even vertical integration – for example, a decision to package tours. The type of growth will determine the direction of the marketing plan.

THE FUTURE ROLE OF THE TRAVEL AGENCY

The central role of the agencies will be maintained or will decrease depending on a number of variables, among which are included the interests of the large firms and the way these large firms choose to implement or make use of the travel agencies. The relations between firms, consumer habits, laws that protect the consumer, the relation between the different tourist services and so on are all factors that will influence in the future of the agencies.

Faced with the prospect of an increase in direct sales due to technological innovation, the intermediaries need to adjust their marketing strategies and harness the new technologies. Specifically, to ensure survival in the longer term, it is vital that the travel agent focuses on the service it provides to the consumer. So long as consumers feel they are receiving good advice, they will continue to use the travel agent.

The new travel agency – or, in other words, the agency of the future – will be the one that manages to 'make the change', adapting to a market that is as dynamic as it is demanding. Some of the keys will be:

1. The new travel agent must be business orientated and enjoy selling tourist products and services.

2. Each agency must focus on defined lines of products, in accord with the demand and the strategy set forth by the firm.

3. The agencies are the ones who must select those suppliers that fit in with their interests and needs (and not the reverse).

4. The agencies have to decide what it is that they should (and want to) be selling, forgetting about the rest of the product, except under express petition of the client. Potentially more travel agencies may become specialists in different types of travel products such as activity holidays and destinations (Bennett, 1996).

5. Active participation in the management groups is essential to be able to negotiate more advantageously with the travel suppliers.

6. The new agency will have to establish commercial alliances (form consortia) – with the suppliers as well as with the retail groups – that allow them to earn more and differentiate themselves from the competition. This would enable independents to speak with one voice or at least a limited number of voices to gain preferential rates with principals and to market themselves more effectively to the all-important consumer.

7. The new technologies are also an ally. They must be placed at the service of the client, adding value to the service that is provided. Focusing on technological change can mean that human problems are not dealt with which are crucial in affecting consumer purchase behaviour and therefore, this represents a neglect of a customer orientation. A balance has to be made between the improvements technology can bring and other changes, such

as a greater investment in marketing. Effort at the retail end of the industry to make the selling experience more professional and pleasurable, the introduction of marketing ideas, such as market segmentation and catering to the total needs of the travel consumer, would provide commercial benefits (Witt and Moutinho, 1989).

8. Travel agencies' growth strategies can be based on horizontal or vertical integration. In the former, the travel agencies grow at the same level and in the latter, they are able to integrate with other elements of the distribution chain. Both strategies are important in this new environment, as we have mentioned throughout this chapter.

9. One of the strengths of the travel agencies, is the opportunity to forge a close relationship with the client; therefore, relationship marketing orientation is an excellent strategy to compete with in the new millennium. Relationship marketing consists in attracting, maintaining and intensifying the relations with the client.

10. Service quality is a key factor in the development of tourism and of travel agencies in particular. Although the usual income of the agencies is a commission of the price, the structure and characteristics of the sector, highly dispersed at the retail level and with little room for manoeuvre due to the high concentration of the wholesalers, lead to the identification of quality as a key factor in competitiveness and a basic element in differentiation and customer loyalty (Bigné *et al.*, 1997).

REFERENCES AND FURTHER READING

Bennett, M.M. (1996) 'The marketing mix: tourism distribution'. in A.V. Seaton and M.M. Bennett (eds) Marketing Tourism Products, ITBP: London, pp. 152–74.

Bigné, J.E., Martínez, C. and Miquel, M.J. (1997) 'The influence of motivation, experience and satisfaction on the quality of service of travel agencies', in P. Hunst and J. Lemmink (eds) *Managing Service Quality*, **3**: 53–70.

Buhalis, D. (1997). The Virtual Tourism Enterprise. Concepts, Practices and Lessons. III International Forum on Tourism in Benidorm, November.

Christopher, M., Payne, A. and Ballantyne, D. (1991) *Relationship Marketing,* Butterworth-Heinemann: Oxford.

COTEC (1997) Las Agencias de viajes frente a las nuevas tecnologias de distribución turistica, Tamayo, B. (ed.) *Fundación Cotec para la Innovación Tecnológica*, Madrid

Cravens, D.W. (1994) *Strategic Marketing,* 4th edn, Irwin, Homewood, IL.

Editur (1998) 'Halcón: a por viajes de empresa'. n. 2015–16, October, p. 13.

Editur (1998) 'Thomas Cook y Carlson unen fuerzas', n. 2014, October, p. 3.

Editur (1998) 'EE.UU.: perfiles del nuevo escenario', n. 2015–16, October, p. 12.

Gee, C.Y., Boberg, K.B., Choy, D.J.L. and Makens, J.C. (1990) *Professional Travel Agency Management,* Prentice Hall: New Jersey.

Hill, R.A. (1997) 'Marketing meetings for profit', *ASTA Agency Management*, February, **66**(2): 32–6.

Horner, S. and Swarbrooke, J. (1996) *Marketing Tourism Hospitality and Leisure in Europe*, International Thomson Business: London.

Klenosky, D.B. and Gitelson, R.E. (1998). 'Travel agents' destination recommendations', *Annals of Tourism Research*, **25**(3): 661–74.

Kotler, P., Bowen, J. and Makens, J. (1996) *Marketing For Hospitality and Tourism*, Prentice Hall: New Jersey.

Laws, E. (1997) *Managing Packaged Tourism. Relationships, Responsibilities and Service Quality in the Inclusive Holiday Industry*, International Thomson Business: London.

Linton, I. (1994) *Creating a Customer Focused Company*, Pitman Publishing: London.

Lovelock, C.H. (1996) *Services Marketing*, Prentice Hall International.

Nexotour (1998) 'Viajes El Corte Inglés reorienta su estrategia comercial de cara al 2000', Suplemento del n. 120, 5–11 October: 13–20.

Poon, A. (1993) *Tourism, Technology and Competitive Strategies*, CAB International: Oxford.

Porter, M.E. (1982) *Estrategia Competitiva. Técnicas para el Análisis de los Sectores Industriales y de la Competencia*, Mexico: CECSA.

Proctor, T. (1996) *Marketing Management. Integrating Theory and Practice*, International Thomson Business: London.

Ruden, P. (1997) 'Competitive forces in the agency industry', *ASTA Agency Management*, February, **66** (2): 26–31.

Ruden, P. (1997) 'Strategies for survival & prosperity', *ASTA Agency Management*, March, **66** (3): 30–2.

Seaton, A.V. and Bennet, M.M. (1996) *Marketing Tourism Products*, ITBP: London.

Tamayo, B. (ed.)(1997) *Las Agencias de Viajes Frente a las nuevas Tecnologías de Distribución Turística*, COTEC: Madrid.

Travel Weekly (1994) 'Travel agency industry's gross incomes by travel suppliers', 14 August.

Vanhove, N. (1997) Globalisation of Tourism Demand and the Impact on Marketing Strateg. III International Forum on Tourism, Benidorm, November.

Vladimir, A. (1997) 'Revealing the secrets of selling cruises', *ASTA Agency Management*, February, **66** (2): 18–19.

Witt, S.F. and Moutinho, L. (1989) *Tourism Marketing and Management Handbook*, Prentice Hall: Cambridge.

WTO (1995) *Global Distribution Systems in the Tourism Industry*, World Tourism Organisation: Madrid.

WTO (1997) *International Tourism: A Global Perspective*, World Tourism Organisation: Madrid.

WTO (1998a) 'Euro to challenge US dollar', WTO *Newsletter*, July/August.

WTO (1998b) *Introducción al Turismo*, World Tourism Organisation: Madrid.

CHAPTER 12   A word of conclusion

CONTENTS

A WORD OF CONCLUSION

L. BÉCHEREL AND F. VELLAS, WITH CONTRIBUTIONS FROM
FEATURED AUTHORS

In this chapter we look at the factors that will shape tourism in the future. The
first sections draw on predictions made by different organisations such as the
WTO and the Space Transportation Association as well as by noted academics
and futurologists. The rest of the chapter is devoted to the future of the tourism
sub-sectors.

TOURISM: AN INDUSTRY STILL IN ITS INFANCY

WTO's Vision 2020

In 1997, the World Tourism Organisation (WTO) published a forecast of tourism
in the year 2020 based on a survey conducted with national tourist authorities
from 85 countries and a Delphi survey of 50 experts. The report, Tourism 2020
Vision – which was updated in 1998 to include the economic crisis in Asia –
presented predictions about the development of the sector and the market,
arrivals and receipt trends world-wide and discussed factors shaping tourism in
the twenty-first century. The WTO estimates that by 2020 there will be 1.6 billion
international arrivals in the world spending in excess of US$2 trillion. Tourism as
a sector will grow at a faster rate than the global economy, which is forecasted to
expand at 3 per cent per annum. Indeed, international arrivals are predicted to
increase by 4.3 per cent a year and international tourism expenditure by 6.7 per
cent. The report points out that the potential for tourism growth is enormous. In
2020 just 7 per cent of the total potential travelling population will travel internationally. Currently the travelling population is 3.5 per cent of the total population. The report observes that tourism is 'an industry truly still in its infancy'.

A CHANGING MARKET

In 2020 Europe will still be the largest international tourism region both as a
receiver of international tourists and as a generator of tourists. However, its

market share will be greatly eroded. In 1960, nearly three-quarters of all tourists who travelled internationally, travelled to a European country. By the year 2000, Europe's share of world arrivals will have fallen to 50 per cent and by 2020 to 45 per cent. With an annual growth rate of 3.1 per cent, tourism to Europe will grow more slowly than to other regions of the world.

There are variations within the European region. With the fall of communism, central and eastern European countries now feature on the world tourism stage. For certain countries, such as the Czech Republic, tourism is considered as one of the main pillars of economic growth. By 2020, the Czech Republic will be the tenth most visited country in the world, with 44 million international tourists a year, equivalent to 2.7 per cent of world share of arrivals. Central and eastern Europe will be the fastest growing sub-region of Europe in terms of arrivals, recording an annual growth rate of 4.9 per cent between 1995 and 2020. On the other hand, the traditional tourist destinations of western and southern Europe, although still increasing, will grow at a slower rate than the world average of 4.3 per cent, registering 1.8 per cent and 2 per cent respectively.

This shows that the dominance of the traditional destinations is gradually being weakened and that new destinations are emerging. Despite the economic crisis at the end of the 1990s, the WTO estimates that by 2020 the East Asia and Pacific region will be the second largest of the world's regions, overtaking the Americas region, both in terms of arrivals and receipts. China is projected to be the rising star of world tourism. By 2020, it will the greatest receptor of international tourists of all countries in the world. It will host 137.1 million international visitors, accounting for 8.6 per cent of total world arrivals. China will also be the fourth greatest generating country after Germany, Japan and the United States, with 100 million Chinese trips abroad annually. Trends show that travel within a region (intra-regional travel) will increase in the future, particularly in the East Asia and Pacific region. There will be a large volume of first-time Asian travellers.

With advances in transport technology, long-haul destinations are becoming more accessible. According to the 2020 Vision report (WTO, 1998a), long-haul trips will account for nearly a quarter of all trips (24 per cent) by 2020 – a rise from 18 per cent in 1995.

The smaller tourism regions such as Africa, South Asia and the Middle East will also show impressive growth rates in terms of arrivals, albeit from a very low base. Indeed, inbound tourism to Africa will increase by 5.5 per cent annually (1995 to 2020), to the Middle East by 6.7 per cent and to South Asia by 6.2 per cent. However, together, these three regions accounted for just 7 per cent of world arrivals in 1995; this will increase to 10 per cent of world arrivals by 2020.

The most conclusive evidence that new destinations are successfully developing their tourism industries is provided by the following statistics. In 1950 the top five destinations in the world received 71 per cent of all tourists and the top fifteen together accounted for 97 per cent. The rest of the world received just 3 per cent of world tourists.

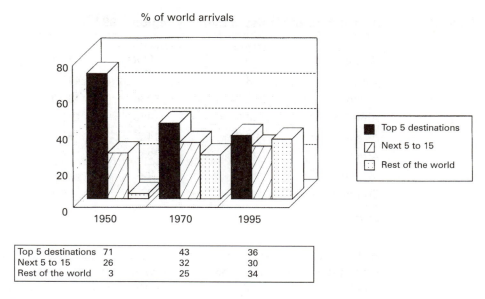

% of world arrivals

	1950	1970	1995
Top 5 destinations	71	43	36
Next 5 to 15	26	32	30
Rest of the world	3	25	34

Figure 12.1   The emergence of new destinations (adapted from WTO, 1998a)

By 1995 the top five destinations' share of total international arrivals had fallen to 36 per cent and the top fifteen to 30 per cent while the rest of the world's share increased to 34 per cent. The emergence of new destinations is set to continue as tourism development know-how increases allowing new tourism countries to build their industry and compete on the world stage, introducing proper operating methods and controls to ensure its success and sustainability. Tourism is seen as a desirable industry to develop as it provides much needed foreign exchange and employment, particularly at the semi-skilled level. Tourism development for developing countries is often funded by large international organisations such as the United Nations Development Programme and the European Union.

The Importance of Developing Countries in International Tourism

Most developing countries are remote from the mainstream of international tourism except from the newly industrialised countries, which are also new tourism markets.

International tourism is concentrated both in terms of visitors and receipts on three main regions – Europe, North America (USA and Canada) and the Far East and Pacific countries. In 1997 these three regions accounted for 84.3 per cent of international visitors and 87.3 per cent of income. It follows that international tourism accounts for only 15.7 per cent of visitors and 12.7 per cent of income in all African countries, Latin America, the Caribbean, the Middle East and South Asia (see Table 12.1).

Table 12.1   **Distribution of tourist activity by region, 1997**

Region	Arrivals (millions)	Arrivals (% of total)	Income ($ billions)	Income (% of total)
World	613.1	100	447.7	100
Europe	361.6	58.9	123.3	50.0
Americas	118.9	19.5	119.8	26.8
Asia and Pacific	90.2	14.7	83.2	18.5
Africa	23.2	3.8	8.7	1.9
Middle East	14.7	2.4	8.6	1.9
Southern Asia	4.6	0.7	4.1	0.9

Source: WTO.

In terms of international visitors, developing countries represent only 30 per cent of the world total – 183.9 million visitors in 1997. Of these, the 48 countries identified by the United Nations as the Least Developed Countries (LDC) occupy a very weak position.

On the other hand, the newly industrialised countries are in a particularly strong position. The eight newly industrialised Asian countries – Hong Kong, Singapore, Taiwan, Korea, Indonesia, Malaysia, the Philippines and Thailand – together represent 7.3 per cent (see Table 12.2).

Table 12.2   **Position of developing countries in international tourism**

Region	Arrivals (000)	Receipts ($ millions)
Developing countries	183,936	131,247
Least Developed Countries	4,684	1,854
China	23,770	12,074
NI Asian countries*	44,978	48,065
European Union	246,982	168,757
USA/Canada	66,533	83,881
Australia/New Zealand	5,901	11,834
Japan	4,226	4,425
World total	603,078	447,710

Note: NI Asian countries = Hong Kong, Singapore, Taiwan, Korea, Indonesia, Malaysia, the Philippines, Thailand
Source: Adapted from WTO, 1998a.

Receipts and international arrivals figures in Table 12.2 show that the level of economic development is a major factor for developing a successful tourism industry. The share of receipts for international tourism in developing countries is slightly lower than their share of arrivals (29.3 per cent and 30 per cent).

However, the proportions of arrivals and receipts in the newly industrialised countries stand out. The share of the world's receipts in these countries account for 10.7 per cent whereas their share of arrivals is 7.3 per cent.

The position is very weak for the least developed countries at just 0.4 per cent for both arrivals and receipts.

International tourists are attracted to new destinations by promotional campaigns stressing exotic images. However, the development of tourism in these destinations is also dependent on investment opportunities. Many countries have difficulty in attracting enough funds to develop their tourist industry. This is one of the reasons why newly industrialised countries progress at a faster rate than the other developing countries. This is also why countries with very weak economies are lagging behind in developing their tourism industry.

In some countries, tourism is in decline. Mostly, these suffer from political instability and the risks of insecurity. Obviously, international tourism demand is seriously affected even when they try to market their countries aggressively. In other countries such as in certain African countries the weakness of the economy impedes the development of the tourism industry resulting in a fall in the number of arrivals.

Factors that are Contributing to the Growth Tourism in Developing Countries

Both demand and supply factors play important roles in the growth of tourism in developing countries.

- *The need for tour operators to offer new destinations – geographical diversificaion*: Developing countries respond to the needs of the main generating countries by offering alternative destinations.

- *The need for tour operators to offer new products – product diversification*: Tourism demand is increasingly orientated towards new types of experiences, particularly cultural and environmental. New markets in developing countries often have a rich natural, cultural and historical heritage, which tour operators are promoting to cater to changing demand.

- *Opportunities offered by new distribution channels*: Developing countries and new markets can be represented on an equal footing on the global market, using electronic distribution channels such as the Internet. Indeed, it is cheap to set up a web site that can be accessed by any computer linked to the global network.

DESTINATIONS

The most successful destinations differentiate themselves from other destinations and adapt to demand to provide a range of products suitable for different market segments. Consumers now expect quality when they travel abroad and countries must invest in their infrastructure, superstructure, attractions and human resources to ensure that this is provided. Popular sites – described by the WTO as *honeypots* – need to be managed to protect the product. Visitor management techniques are already being introduced and will become more widespread in the future, such as no-go areas at the attraction (that is, Stonehenge in the UK), time-controlled ticketing and viewing by appointment to spread the number of visitors and avoid damage caused by crowding at peak times.

Destinations must adapt to socio-demographic changes in their generating markets. In the short to medium term, the major tourist generating countries of Europe and the United States will have an ageing but active population, used to travelling and expecting a certain level of quality. Fragmented leisure time will also be a major factor affecting the way destinations develop products and market themselves. Increasingly, tourists from industrialised countries have limited holiday time although they may take several holidays a year. As business becomes global, business travel will continue to provide high returns.

According to the WTO, future consumers of leisure tourism will want to participate in the production of the product – the focus will switch from service 'to delivering unique experiences that personally engage the consumer' (WTO, 1998a). This is already resulting in the development of holidays conceived around themes of interest to defined market segments such as special interest holidays in purpose-built theme parks.

Successful destination management combats seasonality by developing products for different market segments. Therefore tourism at a destination may occur year around at different levels – business, conferences, leisure, special interest.

As we have seen in Chapters 1 and 2, destinations are increasingly co-operating to attract tourists to their region. They pool their marketing efforts to create a regional identity or to build a joint product around a theme (see Box 1.5 for an example from Scandinavia).

For instance, the Black Sea Tourism Group has been created to promote tourism to the region. To quote Henryk Handszuh, the Chief of Quality of Tourism Development at the WTO, speaking at a conference in Sweden in 1998 (WTO, 1998b):

> The Black Sea region as a whole needs a more specific image to be regarded as a tourism destination. In order to progress, the content of the Baltic Sea tourism image must be strengthened, enhanced and, to the extent possible, co-ordinated. Co-ordination here does not mean any formal intervention, but identifying and working towards common objectives by tourism enterprises in the region and by their support bodies in the public and private sectors.

Countries will increasingly join together to develop and promote specific tourism products. Successful ventures already include the 12,000 kilometre-long Silk Road and the Slave Route in Africa.

- *The Silk Road:* Sixteen countries are participating in the WTO/UNESCO Silk Road project. A Silk Road logo has been designed and adopted by both the public and the private sectors, a brochure featuring sixteen countries as well as a promotional video have been produced and a 26-part television series has been filmed by a New Zealand media group. Incoming tour operators in the different countries along the route are co-operating to provide seamless products. A number of products are being developed to accommodate various market segments such as cultural tourism, eco-tourism, agro-tourism and adventure tourism, using different hotel standards and different modes of transport. Events and meeting are regularly held to discuss such issues as easing travel restrictions, improving transport and preserving cultural heritage and developing handicraft revitalisation centres along the route. In February 1999, Silk Road countries exhibited together for the first time in a joint pavilion at the Eastern Mediterranean International Travel and Tourism Exhibition (EMITT 99).

- *The Slave Route:* In 1994, UNESCO initiated the Slave Route project in Africa to develop intercultural co-operation, re-enforce human rights, provide education, establish historical and cultural awareness studies and research. A Cultural Tourism Project was launched with the WTO. The aims of the tourism project are to restore and conserve monuments, sites and places of remembrance of the slave trade. Sites linked with the slave trade in Africa, the Americas and the Caribbean are being rehabilitated and the living culture is being promoted by setting up cultural tourism itineraries for the Slave Route in Africa, the Americas and the Caribbean. A database has been compiled on the location and assets of different museums on the theme of slavery; a network of museums on slavery and travelling exhibitions on the slave trade are being set up (WTO, 1998c).

TOURISM PRODUCTS IN THE FUTURE

WTO identifies five market segments that are growing in importance:

- *Eco-tourism*: In 1997, it was established at the World Ecotour 97 conference that eco-tourism was worth US$2 billion a year and that nature-based tourism accounted for approximately 20 per cent of total international travel. Destinations are selecting and conserving areas for eco-tourism such as national parks and protected areas.

  However, the WTO warns that the term *'eco-tourism'* now encompasses a large range of products depending on how it is defined and some tourism organisations and businesses are avoiding use of the word feeling that the concept has become devalued.

- *Cultural tourism*: One of the consequences of globalisation is the homogenisation of products, to a certain extent tastes (food, popular culture) and behavioural norms. The WTO points out that in the future, there will be a conflict in developing countries between identity and modernity. One of the draws of travelling is to experience different cultures and way of life. Tourism is helping to preserve cultural identity, as tourism demand is increasingly orientated towards understanding about ethnicity, religion and ways of life of other cultures. WTO predicts 'a strong growth in cultural themed tourism to Europe, the Middle East and Asia from virtually all source regions'.

  The search for knowledge and culture is an important motive for travel and tourists increasingly want to combine learning and leisure.

- *Themes*: Products are being developed around particular themes and special interest by tour operators who package the appropriate components for target groups but also by destinations which house theme parks. The city of Orlando, Florida, has one of the largest tourism centres in the United States, including Walt Disney World, Universal Studios and Sea World. In a recent economic impact study, Orlando received an economic impact of $13.1 billion in 1995 from theme parks, hotels, restaurants and shopping centres (Coniglio, 1997).

  Themes may be based on popular culture (Disney World, Disneyland Europe, Legoland and so on), industrial heritage, historical themes or within a particular environment. The OASIS Lakeland Forest Village is set on a 400-acre site in the Lake District in the UK. The resort provides a variety of indoor and outdoor activities and therefore can operate year-round. Holidaymakers can enjoy walks and cycling in the forest, sailing and windsurfing on the lake as well as golf, rock climbing, tennis and fishing outdoors. With especially built indoor facilities such as a sub-tropical *World of Water*, they can also enjoy pools, spas, fountains, water slides and wild water rapids as well as tennis, squash, basketball and so on, whatever the weather outside.

- *The cruise market*: According to the WTO, 7 million people took cruises in 1997 and this is expected to increase to 9 million by the year 2000. The cruise product has lost its elite status and is now being offered by mainstream tour operators. Cruising around the Mediterranean is becoming very popular. There is such demand for cruising that in 1998 42 new ships were being built.

- *Adventure tourism*: Adventure tourism is becoming big business. Trekking is now a well-established product but also more extreme forms of adventure tourism is taking off. WTO notes the trend to travel to high places (mountain climbing), underwater (2 million people took a submarine ride in 1996 and an underwater hotel – the Jules Undersea Lodge off the coast of Key Largo, Florida – has been in existence since 1986), to the ends of the earth (10,000 people travelled to Antarctica in 1997) and, while not possible now but will be in the near future, into space.

SPACE TOURISM

One adventure product of the future is *space tourism*. By the early twenty-first century, it is expected that space tourism will have taken off. According to Coniglio, 'the demand for space tourism exists, and the first company to develop the market will reap millions of dollars in profit'. This has been supported by a number of surveys including one by the Japanese Rocket Society, which showed that space tourism could be worth US$12 billion by 2010 (Coniglio, 1997; WTO, 1998a).

Coniglio summarising a presentation by Makoto Nagamoto of the Japanese Rocket Society suggests that there are several phases before space tourism becomes established:

1. First, a reusable space vehicle must be developed. Several prototypes have been built, mostly government funded. An international competition has been launched – the X Prize – to award US$10 million to the first non-governmental organisation to develop 'a vehicle that can carries three passengers to an altitude of 100 kilometres and back, twice'. However, sponsors are still being sought to cover the prize money.

2. Then, a campaign must be launched to educate the general public. Theme parks and exhibits on space such as Disney's Space Mountain are already popular. FuturePort, a theme park completely devoted to space, will open in California in 1999.

3. Next, space cruise ships will offer trips to low earth orbit. Several companies have already proposed designs for a space cruise ship and according to WTO 'two American operators are hoping to offer low-orbit flights in 2001 for US$100,000 a ticket'.

4. Finally, the WTO estimates that the first space hotel will be built probably by 2020. Coniglio explains that the Shimizu Corporation, a construction company in Japan, already opened a space project office in 1987. 'Shimizu has been doing advanced research on space stations, space factories, lunar bases and rocket launch facilities.' They would therefore be in a position to build a space hotel.

According to Coniglio, for space tourism really to develop a major tourism or entertainment company such as Walt Disney World, MCA/Universal, Paramount or Time/Warner must become involved to legitimise the industry. Several smaller companies have already been formed to operate in niche markets but they do not have the financial resources to develop the commercial space industry.

TECHNOLOGY

It has been discussed throughout this book that technology has transformed the way tourism products are developed and distributed and more changes are expected in the future with further advances in technology.

The World Future Society identified ten technologies as most important for the next ten years: genetic mapping, super-materials, high-density energy sources, digital high-definition television, miniaturisation, smart manufacturing, anti-ageing products and services, medical treatments, hybrid fuel vehicles, and 'edutainment' (Cetron, 1998).

The WTO explains that within the next decade, tourists will be able to use smart cards at destinations for discounts and for travellers' cheques. Before travelling, they will be able to look via the Internet at different rooms and facilities at a hotel in real time through strategically placed cameras. CD-ROM brochures will eventually replace paper brochures. On-line booking via the Internet and e-ticketing will become established and grow at a very strong rate in the next few years. And traveller information about preferences and lifestyle kept on databases will be sold on a commercial basis.

According to futurologists William Zuk and Douglas Olesen hotel and resort design will be revolutionised with smart building materials, super-structural systems and environmental and energy advances (Wolff, 1998).

Smart building materials include architectural glass that can change properties, such as transparency and colour, super-strength steel, wood, and concrete to protect against the elements and natural disasters and strong plastics that can change molecularly to resist stress.

We may see super-structures with high-rise buildings up to 500 stories high, whole areas could be covered using geodesic domes to protect against the elements and extreme climates and resorts may be built on platforms above the water.

Solar panels used for both cooling and heating, smart walls which keep rooms at constant temperatures and portable inexpensive fuel sources will help save energy (Wolff, 1998).

GREEN ISSUES IN THE FUTURE

Green issues are expected to dominate the future strategies of the companies and destinations. Companies will incorporate environmental policies into their strategies in order to attract more business either by making the environment the focus of their product to target specific consumers and/or by using their environmental-awareness credentials to enhance their image.

Destinations will continue to promote and develop sustainable tourism and eco-tourism to enhance their appeal to a wider tourism audience.

However, these strategies may not represent genuine consideration by the companies and organisations towards green and sustainable issues. There is alarm that environmental concerns are increasingly used as a marketing ploy to tout for more business.

INTERNATIONAL AND NATIONAL TOURISM MARKETING POLICIES

Public–private sector partnerships in tourism management and promotion will continue to grow in the future. In countries developing their tourism industry or where the private sector is weak, the public sector will take the forefront in marketing destinations as it does today, however, where tourism is well established, the public sector will provide a supporting role. For instance, Turkey, which registered a spectacular growth in arrivals of 18 per cent in 1997, announced that it has changed its strategy. According to the Under-secretary of State for Tourism, Fermani Uygun: 'We believe the State should not act as an entrepreneur, but should create the best possible environment for development of the tourism sector.'

Partnerships will increasingly develop at local levels. One such initiative exists in California in the USA, where the California Travel and Tourism Commission (CTTC) receives funds of US$7.3 million from the state government and US$7.5 million from all tourism companies, organisations and related industries in the state which benefits in some way from tourism. The budget is used to help improve visitor information and facilities and increase promotional and marketing effort.

The General Agreement on Trade in Services (GATS)

The General Agreement on Trade in Services (GATS) establishes rules and disciplines for policies affecting access to service markets to extend the coverage of the multilateral trading system.

GATS consists of four main elements:

- general concepts, principles and rules that apply across the board to measures affecting trade in services
- specific commitments on national treatment and market access that apply to a number of service sectors and sub-sectors
- an understanding that periodic negotiations will be undertaken to progressively liberalise trade in services
- criteria that take sectoral specificities and ministerial decision into account.

Inevitably, GATS will have an influence on tourism strategies. It will help tourism enterprises to set up business in other continents with franchises, management contracts and technical service agreements.

DEVELOPING TRENDS IN HOSPITALITY

Key trends in hospitality are no different from those in other industries. The dynamics of business have been driven for years by consolidation, as companies seek to maximise market share and enhance shareholder value. Over the past decades, it was the railroads, then the automobile industry, airlines, the electronics industry, and in today's world we see so-called 'mega-mergers' in such industries as technology and entertainment. Just as this has happened in these industries, it will also occur in hospitality. This trend commenced in the 1990s and will continue into the next millennium. The drivers for this development will be the availability of capital; the ability to effect cost savings and operational efficiencies; the increasing importance of branding, and the growing trend towards world-wide travel – building even further tourism's current status as the world's largest industry – will bring even more consolidation in hospitality.

With this consolidation, the importance of a good brand – or collection of brands – is a key criterion for success. However, during the 1990s branding is largely an American phenomenon. About 70 per cent of the hotels in the United States are branded, while the rest of the world averages below 20 per cent. In Europe about 20 per cent of the hotels in the UK are branded, while the remainder of western Europe averages only around 10 per cent. In these statistics lie opportunities which will be exploited over the coming years by hospitality firms. The fact that relatively few hotel properties in Europe, Asia, the Middle East and Latin America carry brand names provides significant potential for the major hotel brands to expand from regional bases. It is interesting in this specific issue to contrast the subject of hotel branding with casino businesses (many hospitality firms are involved in both). In hotels, branding is extremely important. In the gaming business, however, the industry is probably some years away from seeing any kind of true branding advantage. Customers go to particular casino properties drawn by the experience, the entertainment and the value, not by the brand. In Las Vegas it would be difficult to find customers who know that the Mirage and Treasure Island are both owned by Mirage Resorts Incorporated, or that the Flamingo and Bally's are both owned by Hilton Hotels Corporation. A customer at a Harrah's casino in Mississippi does not immediately seek out the Harrah's property when arriving in Las Vegas. To gaming customers branding does not much matter.

The third trend within hospitality which will develop apace over the coming years will be technology. With it comes the ability to communicate more effectively with both present and potential new customers, with the central objective of enhancing the customer experience. It is through this issue of communication that brand loyalty will be enhanced. Additionally, these benefits of technology will assist in co-operation on franchise and management agreements around the world (key growth strategies), with the benefit of further enhancing the brand.

Globalisation, consolidation, world-wide branding, the shrinking globe, developing technology, increasing levels of disposable income, a truly international economy – all of these will contribute to further expansion of the hospitality industry.

WHAT DOES THE FUTURE HOLD FOR TRAVEL AGENCIES?

The travel agency sector is characterised by intense rivalries and an expanding market, but with low profit margins. Within the distribution system, the retail travel agents' main role is to serve as intermediaries between travel product suppliers and consumers. This role will be maintained or will decrease depending on a number of factors, among which we should mention the relationships between travel suppliers, consumers and the evolution of new technologies.

The travel agency of the future will be the one that manages to 'make the change', adapting to a dynamic environment. The new agency will have to establish commercial alliances with suppliers as well as with retail groups that allow them to earn more and differentiate themselves from the competition. The new technologies are also supporters as they must be placed at the service of the client, adding value to the service that is provided. If the Internet proves to be as efficient and attractive as it promises to be, this will be a new and successful commercial channel that will force travel agencies to make new efforts to establish themselves within a vibrant source of continually up-dated information and offers. If travel agencies are able to adapt to the new technologies, understand intimately the needs and wants of their customers, and are prepared to provide some new services for them, the Internet will not become a substitute for travel agencies, but merely a tool at the service of the agencies.

As argued throughout Chapter 11, it is possible that the strengths of the travel agencies are greater than the travel agents themselves believe. Strengths can be based on the proximity to the user, and on the know-how of the agencies in the business and products they distribute and market. The key here is to research the agency's existing customer and deliver what he/she wants, come to a clear understanding of how and why they purchase, which ones are profitable, which are unprofitable, and which markets are untapped (customer analysis). This should be considered as an opportunity to forge a close relationship with the client, under the view that relationship marketing orientation is an excellent strategy to be able to compete effectively in the new millennium.

FUTURE DEVELOPMENTS IN THE AIRLINE INDUSTRY

Deregulation and privatisation have transformed the airline industry. These have led to the strategic alliances discussed in Chapter 9.

An indicator that gives an insight on future expectations in the airline industry is the number of aircraft ordered by airline companies.

Activity in the aeronautic industry is inextricably linked to domestic and international air transport. In 1998 aircraft manufacturers enjoyed their best year yet. In 1996 1003 new aircraft were ordered and in 1997 a record of 1309 orders were place. In 1998 this record was bettered, with, for the first time, Airbus equalling Boeing for the number of orders.

With the exception of the Asia region, airline companies also registered a strong growth in traffic in 1998. Profits were exceptional – for instance 25 to 30 per cent increase for American Airline and British Airways.

However, despite these successes, 1999 started in an uncertain, even pessimistic, climate. The forecasted economic slowdown in the United States and especially in Europe led to fears that there would be over-capacity in the future, particularly since many companies have increased and renewed their fleets in the last few years.

The Pessimism of Airline Companies

The predicted economic slowdown is taken very seriously by the airlines, with the 1990–1994 economic crisis still fresh in the memory. Many suffered negative financial results because they did not anticipate the slackening in the growth rate of demand and even its fall in 1991.

For this reason, airline companies will be nervous about ordering new aircraft despite the positive results in 1997 and 1998 as shown in Table 12.3.

Table 12.3   **Main air transport indicators (ICAO)**

Indicators	1995	1996	1997
Aircraft ordered	678	1,003	1,309
Receipts *	267	282.5	291
Profits (%)**	5.1	4.4	5.7
Passengers (%)***	8.1	9.6	6.8
Passengers/km (%)***	9.3	10.2	7.3
Freight Tk (%)***	8.7	7.3	12.6
Mail Tk (%)***	7.1	2.1	2.4

Key: * in billions of US Dollars, **operating profits in percentage operating receipts, *** International Services, Tk Tonnes/kilometre carried.
Source: ICAO, 1998.

Faced with a slowdown in demand in the first three months of 1999, the airline companies (particularly American Airlines and United Airlines) put in place measures aimed at reducing or deferring capacity. They revised the increase of supply for the year from 3.5 per cent to 2.5 per cent, to allow them to keep load factors up to over 70 per cent, despite the reduction in the growth of traffic.

Furthermore, the international crises in Asia, Latin America and Eastern Europe, added to the expected economic slowdown in Europe and the USA will mean that the positive cycle that the aircraft manufacturers have enjoyed in recent years may be coming to an end.

The End of the Cycle for Aircraft Manufacturers

Although the aircraft manufacturers have orders that will provide work for four to five years, fewer orders will be taken in 1999. Asian airline companies have already cancelled orders. In the short term, it is unclear what the European and American airline companies will do. However, the medium- and long-term forecast of aircraft manufacturing until 2012 is good, as shown in Table 12.4

Table 12.4   **Forecast for aircraft manufacturing, 1998 to 2012**

Type of aircraft	Predicted orders		
	1998–2002	*2002–2007*	*2007–2012*
Aircraft with a central aisle			
50 –90 seats	418	279	439
91–120 seats	571	550	608
121–170 seats	1374	914	1418
170–240 seats	512	659	895
Aircraft with two aisles			
180–249 seats	449	413	459
250–399 seats	400	550	577
400 seats and over	174	163	249

Source: Boeing, 1998.

With higher productivity, more efficient maintenance programmes and technological advances, air travel will continue to fall in price, and speed, levels of comfort and safety will continue to increase. With the globalisation of business and the growth of both long-haul and short-haul travel, travellers rely on air transport to reach their destinations. Airline companies are responding by developing their fleets with different types and sizes of aircraft and are structuring their timetables to provide a more efficient service.

The marketing strategies of the twenty-first century will ensure that travel and tourism remains the world's largest industry as we move towards a more integrated global market. The winners will be the organisations that adapt their development, operations and marketing methods to contend with advances in technology and lifestyle trends, and that think and act strategically.

REFERENCES AND FURTHER READING

Boeing (1998) *Current Market Outlook,* Boeing Company: Seattle.
Cetron M. J. (1998) 'Ten hospitable trends for the tourism and hospitality industry', *Travel Impact Newswire*, editions 17, 18, November.

Coniglio, S. (1997) Practical Space Tourism. Paper presented at the 1st International Symposium on Space Tourism, Bremen, 20 March.

ICAO (1998) Annual Report, 1996–97, Chapter 1 and Annexes, ICAO: Montreal.

Wolff, H. J. (1998) *A Tour of the Future*, Wimberly Allison Tong & Goo; Web page 1998 Finan Publishing.

WTO (1998a) *Tourism 2020 Vision – Revised and Updated 1998*, World Tourism Organisation: Madrid.

WTO (1998b) WTO *News*, May–June, World Tourism Organisation: Madrid.

WTO (1998c) WTO *News*, January–February, World Tourism Organisation: Madrid.

INDEX